THROUGH THE RAPIDS

The History of

Princess

Louisa Inlet

 CHARLES WILLIAM HITZ

Sitka 2 Publishing
Kirkland, Washington

ISBN# 0-9720255-0-2

Library of Congress Control Number: 2003092782

Front Cover photo by Peter Talbot (used with permission) – Aerial photo of the Malibu Club, Malibu Rapids, and Princess Louisa Inlet.

Back Cover photo(s) by C.W.Hitz of One Eye Images and Sound.

Cover and Interior Design © TLC Graphics, www.TLCGraphics.com.

Photographs from this book, taken by C.W. Hitz of One Eye Images and Sound, are available for purchase at www.hitzcomm.tv under the One Eye Images and Sound Division category.

Chapter 3's chapter heading page quote is from "Three's a Crew" by Kathrene Pinkerton and is used with permission.

Chapter 5's chapter heading page quote of 1 Corinthians 3:10 is Scripture taken from the HOLY BIBLE, NEW INTERNATIONAL VERSION. Copyright © 1973, 1978, 1984 International Bible Society. Used by permission of Zondervan Bible Publishers from New International Version Bible.

Chapter 5's Young Life quote on page 142 from www.younglife.org used with permission.

Young Life's Malibu Club 50th Anniversary Edition
Printed in Canada

Table
of Contents

Dedication

This book is dedicated to Len Andis,
John Teiman, and Kathy Murphy.

Gone is your sprit, no more do you work.
Your light has departed, vanished is your presence.
But your memory lives on in those who continue
by a ministry of youth, a camp of excitement,
and an Inlet of beauty.

C.W. HITZ (2003)

The Light of Malibu (2001)

Acknowledgements

EDITORS

Suzanne K. Hitz and Maureen Hitz

COVER DESIGN & INTERIOR BOOK LAYOUT

TLC Graphics at www.tlcgraphics.com

FRONT COVER PHOTOGRAPH

Peter Talbot

BACK COVER PHOTOGRAPH(S)

C.W.Hitz of One Eye Images and Sound

PHOTOGRAPHERS

Chaz Hitz of One Eye Images and Sound,
Peter Talbot, Jason Koenig, John Leaf, Elizabeth Hamilton
Sunde, John A. Wilson, and Bob Pritchard.

*The author would also like to acknowledge the number of
people involved and their support and assistance in making
this book happen. It is much appreciated!*

Abby and Ruth Chan plus family, Add & Loveta Sewell,
Andy Buhler of the BC Health and Human Services Library in
Victoria, BC, Elizabeth Hamilton Sunde, Bob & Maureen Hitz,
Bob 'Kim' Hussein, Bob Goff, Brent McBride of the
BC Archives, Carolyn Mortensen of the Malibu Club,
Don and Janice Pritti, Dr Barry Gough, Eddy Schroeder,
Francois Houle, Frank Muncy, Gail Grimston,

Harold and Teri Richert of the Malibu Club,
Ian & Trish Millar, John A. Wilson,
Mike & Jacqueline Lewis of the Malibu Club,
James "Jim" Rayburn III, Jan Morton of Young Life's
Legal Dept, Jason Koenig, Jerry Vernon, Jim Eney,
Joe & Cherry Kempston, John & Merilyn Cooke,
John H. Long, John Leaf, Judy Strelioff of the BC Lands
and Park Dept. in Victoria, BC, Karen Stemwell,
Kathy Cook, Kristin Fraser of the National Archives
of Canada, The Langley BC Air Museum, Larry Hamilton,
Marc-Andre Morin, Marge Anderson, Michelle Clark of the
Malibu Club, Neal Schroeder, Noel Allard,
Paul Sherrill of Young Life's Legal Dept,
Peter B. Smith, Peter Talbot, Richard Kaiser,
Rob Dyker of Beyond Malibu, Robin Millar of the Malibu Club,
Sara Knott of the Young Life Communication Dept,
Steve & Pam Guyer plus family, Suzanne Hitz,
The BC Archives in Victoria, BC, The Malibu Tool
and Tackle Spring Group of 2003,
Ann Watson of the Sechelt Public Library,
The United Kingdom Hydrographic Office,
Tim French, Tom Luddesmeyer of the
Boeing Company Archives, and Victory 'Chip' Montgomery.

To the Men of the 2003 Malibu Club Men's Retreat –
Tom Hamilton did not invent the variable pitch propeller!
And it's the TRUTH!

Maps

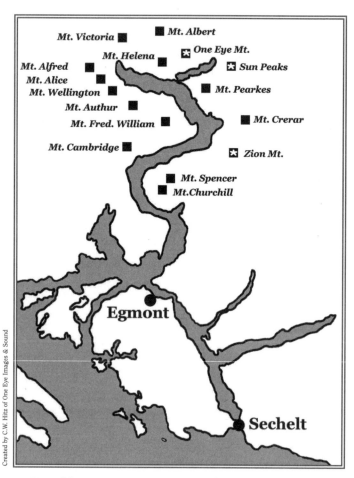

Map of the Jervis & Princess Louisa Inlet Mountains (2003)
(Not to Scale)
* Young Life's Beyond Name of the Mountain

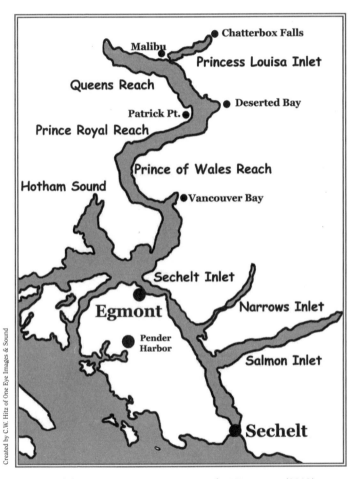

Map of the Jervis & Princess Louisa Inlet Waterways (2003)
(Not to Scale)

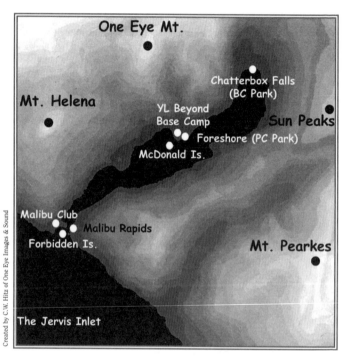

Map of Princess Louisa Inlet Place Names (2003)
(Not to Scale)

Created by C.W. Hitz of One Eye Images & Sound

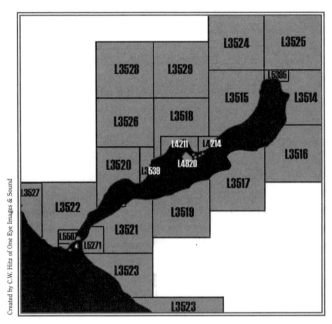

Map of Princess Louisa Inlet Lots (2003)
(Not to Scale)

Introduction

I have been passionate about Young Life's Malibu Club ever since I was a teenager attending Nathan Hale High School in Seattle, Washington, during the late 1970s. My near obsession was so obvious to everyone at school that a friend even wrote a song about it and penciled the lyrics in my high school annual, describing how I would wear a different colored Malibu tee shirt for every day of the week. This fascination with Young Life's Canadian property in British Columbia started ed when I first came to experience the Inlet known as Princess Louisa during the spring of 1978. A number of my high school friends, whom I meet through Nathan Hale's Young Life Club, were invited to Malibu for a spring workweek and we accepted.

Taken by John A. Wilson – Used with Permission

Chaz Hitz at Malibu (1984)

As Young Life's passenger ship, the Malibu Princess, moved through winding reaches of the Jervis Inlet some 100 miles northeast of Vancouver BC, my buddies and I saw for the first time the beauty and remoteness of the area. The camp, located on a narrow strip of land where the mouth of Princess Louisa Inlet is attached to the Jervis Inlet and accessible only by water or air, is isolated and seems far apart from the rest of the world. This only added to its mystery and fascination.

During that week I came to realize many new and exciting things related to this camp, to the Christian faith, and to friendships which still continue. I was hooked, and I tried to find every opportunity to volunteer my available time up at Malibu during the following springs and summers of my college years following high school. During each assignment I continued to learn something new about the Inlet, made new friends, and saw nature in action. Interestingly enough, I spent most of my time at Malibu working primarily as the Sanitation Engineer. In my opinion this is the best job at camp. At the time I felt I was doing privileged service as a volunteer on Malibu's work crew and summer staff. I got to know Malibu above and below the boardwalks far more than anyone should. This gave me a unique picture of the property. Nevertheless, the job was also far more important from a facility standpoint, for if I didn't collect the trash, who would?

My observation about the structure of the camp made more sense when I was able to apply the many stories and legends of the camp to the actual buildings. I believe that these tales have been told since the camp was first purchased from Tom Hamilton in 1953. Stories of deserted meals already cooked in the kitchen, yachts sunk at the dock where they were tied, and general tales of a swift and mysterious abandonment. I always wondered whether or not they were true. But I had other interests at the time and did not focus on serious historical research of Malibu or of the Inlet. This changed when I made a discovery in 1982 that would again ignite my interest and would culminate with the creation of this book. I found my grandfather's journal.

My grandfather, Dr. Clarence B. Hitz of Bellingham, Washington, had died before I was born. I only knew him through the stories and recollections of my parents and other relatives that were told at family functions and during holiday celebrations. He had kept a daily journal most of his adult life and was very detailed with each entry as to what he did, ate, or witnessed. It was a joy for me to read his writings as it brought to life a soul that I did not know. To my surprise, I found the passages of a family vacation cruise taken in the summer of 1941 through the Pacific Northwest waters of British Columbia. At that time my grandfather was Commodore of the Bellingham Yacht Club and owner of the yacht *JimBo*. He and his family, (which was also his crew!), including my grandmother (Doris), my father (Bob), and my father's older brother (my Uncle Jim), spent the summer months of 1941 cruising through the beautiful waters of British Columbia. I found that he had continued his journaling throughout that trip and had meticulously documented every detail of their journey. I was surprised and delighted to find that Princess Louisa Inlet was one of their destinations on that trip. His entry, on July 8, 1941, reads:

> "Up at 7 AM. Breakfast and left Vancouver Bay at 8 am and on up the Inlet (Jervis). Bathed in bright sunshine it was a beautiful sight. Then just a hidden narrow channel we went thru to Princess Louisa Inlet. The passage so narrow we had to lay off the entrance to allow the 100-ft yacht to pass out. We then lay along side the Malibu and visited the Trading Post and met Mr. Hamilton and the new Manager (blank) and also an old timer called Casper. After watching the tide rush thru the pass we then preceded up to McDonald's place mooring along his float. Met Mr. McDonald and enjoyed the eve. A beautiful moon light over the canyon walls."

From the Hitz Family Photo Collection

Dr. Clarence, Bob, Doris, & Jim Hitz at Malibu (1941)
(From left to right)

He continued with next the day's entry of July 9, 1941 after spending the day at Chatterbox Falls swimming, rowing, and generally enjoying the area:

From the Hitz Family Photo Collection

Boating at Chatterbox Falls (1941)

"Back to the floats again. In the evening, after dark this crowd all gathered on the beach about a fire in front of McDonald's house. Where he told Indian stories and many songs and there was a coronet and accordion playing."

My grandfather's passages of those two days at Princess Louisa Inlet mentioned many of the same names and people I had heard so much about during my time at Malibu. This was an intersection between an area I knew well and to a relative whom I had never met.

Doris Hitz at Malibu (1941)

I graduated from Western Washington University in Bellingham, Washington, (where my grandfather had lived and worked) in December of 1984. I had a decision to make which most young people have to make after earning a degree. Where would I find a full time job to support myself? This meant the work at Malibu was no longer an option since it was an all-volunteer crew. It also signaled that my summers at the Inlet were over and, for a time, this was hard to accept. However, two months after graduating from Western I was hired by the Boeing Company, and since then I have worked on many interesting and rewarding projects and jobs related to commercial aircraft. I have also supported the Young Life organization and their Malibu Club throughout these years with both my time and finances, and in 1998 I joined the Princess Louisa International Society as a lifetime member in order to help support their many endeavors to preserve the Inlet. In short, like many people before me my life had entered a new phase, now of supporting what had meant so much to me. So it was not until 1997 that I seriously started to research the records and details of the history that Princess Louisa Inlet has witnessed and those people who have established their names at the Inlet for time ever after.

From the Hitz Family Photo Collection

Dr. C.B. Hitz & Dr. Sutherland at Malibu (1941)
(left to right)

There have been many books about this area, but mostly they are related to how to get there, and what to see when one arrives and what to do. These books also address some details of the early history that have helped as a starting point for this book. But frustratingly, they did not provide specific particulars into how the events happened at Malibu and the Inlet. I wanted to know more of the real truth behind the stories I had heard concerning people and the Inlet itself. Specifically, I wanted to back up these tales that I and countless others have heard with records of proof concerning the actual event(s) or person(s). The Internet also became a valuable tool relating to the search of these records around the world and in the communication with academic professionals and scholars of British Columbia, early Canadian, American and English history who are experts in their fields. I also spent many hours in libraries, museums, archives and government agencies in Canada, the United States and England, researching specific records, books, manuscripts and maps to collaborate these stories. The academic professionals were also able to assist by providing insight into the specific time or place I was interested in. I interviewed a number of people throughout the US and Canada, who were either a part of or indirectly involved in the history of Malibu and the Inlet. That was the most enjoyable aspect of the research project, because I heard first-hand accounts of these interesting events. It was, in a sense, like finding lost treasure and it was similar to finding my grandfather's journal. I also appreciated the help and leads I received from others who assisted in the interviewing when I was not able to be there personally. There were often many times during my research that would seem as though I had reached a dead end. But I have been continually amazed how these pieces of information were resurrected by an off hand remark during an interview, a small slip of paper, or two words in a document or a book.

Nevertheless, this research has not been able to capture every single story there is concerning Princess Louisa Inlet. One point of view that will not be told in this book is that of the first inhabitants of this area, known as the Sechelt natives. I had an interview set up in November of 2002 with the Elders of the Sechelt First Nation Band to hear the first-hand stories associated with Princess Louisa Inlet. Many local people had suggested to me that in order to fully understand the natives of Princess Louisa Inlet I would need to talk with the Elders of this band and I had hoped their stories would be included in this book, for it is both a necessary and a very interesting chapter of the Inlet. They were a part of the area long before any of the European explorers arrived. I was scheduled in at the end of one of their regular meetings, at which time I made my introduction and request. The Elders responded by describing Princess Louisa Inlet as a very sacred and spiritual place to their people. They told me that they were reluctant to share any of their stories of the Inlet, as many others in the past had benefited from these stories at cost to their own people, I assumed both in terms of finance and recognition. In the end they were apologetic, but decided they would not share these specific tales of Princess Louisa Inlet for my book. Although I understand their concerns, their decision is disappointing. I appreciated their candor and honesty however, for their discussion brought up points I had not considered and I will abide by the Elders' wishes. And I will not include any of the specific Sechelt stories. Any references to the Sechelt band will be stated as 'the local native people', or as 'the Sechelt First Nation', 'the Sechelt tribal band' or as an endnote briefly describing a term or situation in which the Sechelt's have been involved as background information. This will also include other First Nation tribes of British Columbia and of the United States mentioned in this book. If the reader would like to learn more about some of the Sechelt stories associated with Princess Louisa Inlet and this group of people, they may refer to the book sanctioned by the Elders titled "The Story of the Sechelt Nation" by Lester Peterson, published by Harbor Publishing for the Sechelt Indian Band in 1990 (ISBN #1-55017-017-1).

This book is the culmination of many long hours of research, investigative work, personal interviews, writing, editing, and the many other tasks those who have written a book know. But I believe it is one of the most detailed works concerning and confirming the many stories and legends of Malibu, or of Princess Louisa Inlet, as depicted by the facts found in documents, memories, drawings, photographs, and stories of the actual event(s). I hope that you, the reader, will be able to see my passion for these two places and I hope that you enjoy this book. Anyone who has worked at Malibu, has anchored at Chatterbox Falls, or has only heard about this place, will enjoy this book. I also realize that many of you, after finishing, may have additional stories, photos, film, or something you would like to share related to this place. Please feel free to contact me. These may be helpful in bringing to light aspects I missed during the initial research and writing and for inclusion in future editions. I know I did not capture everything about Princess Louisa Inlet and the Malibu Club. Some information cannot ever be found in a library or archives, but is in the memory, or in the pages of unpublished journals, or in the photo images of those who have seen and witnessed the majesty and beauty of Princess Louisa Inlet.

The physical place where Princess Louisa Inlet lies is small in the overall scheme of the earth and, if given the chance, would be hard to spot from space. Only if one knows where to look can it be found, as it is part of a vast landscape and can be blurred within the far-reaching beauty of the rest of the earth. But those who have visited Princess Louisa Inlet know exactly where it is and know how to locate it from above and on the ground. The Inlet has been a part of specific historic events that helped shape both the Pacific Northwest and British Columbia and that history is both interesting and required to accurately tell the story of Princess Louisa Inlet. Now let's go through the rapids to begin the journey into the Inlet.

Charles William Hitz (Chaz)
December 2002

CHAPTER

ONE

The Natural History of the Inlet

A Satellite
View of the
BC Coast and
the Jervis
Inlet (2003)

"We saw the marks of several bears and
sufficient indications of deer...
I do not include mosquitoes, which swarm
about in myriads, and torment one night and
day as mosquitoes only knows how."

SECOND LT. MAYNE
(HMS PLUMPER –1861 JERVIS INLET SURVEY)

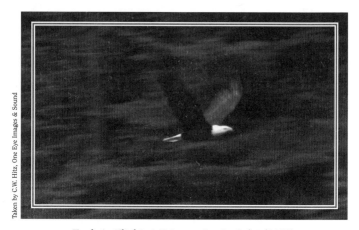

Taken by C.W. Hitz, One Eye Images & Sound

Eagle in Flight at Princess Louisa Inlet (2003)

FROM MALIBU, a pair of eagles circling together could be seen on an afternoon thermal near the entrance of Princess Louisa Inlet. Normally the pair perched on the highest tree growing on the island opposite the side of camp where eagles, out of all the many locations of the Inlet, seemed to permanently reside. These white headed birds, known as bald eagles, are revered as symbols of strength and freedom in Western culture. Suddenly, the profound silence of the area and the eagles' endless flight pattern shifted as they noticed an ungraceful and noisy cormorant starting to take off from the water. The cormorant's movements were similar to a float-plane taking off from a water runway, and just as loud. The bird gained its required speed by flapping his short wings, all the while running awkwardly on the surface till there was enough tension in the air to lift the weight of its body. The eagles both instinctively dove on the vulnerable and mobile prey, but the clever cormorant quickly aborted it's takeoff and nosed into the safety of the water. As cormorants are able to swim, it was protected underwater for the time being. The pair of eagles also abandoned their dive, only to resume their orbit until the prey came back up for air. The cormorant did as predicted, only to be pounced on again by the circling eagles. Again the cormorant dove for the safety of the deep. The action of both the eagles and cormorant played out over and over again for nearly an hour. All were acting their parts in Mother Nature's roles of hunter and prey, and each fought for survival: the hunter's need for food and the prey struggling to continue its life. The eagles waited patiently overhead, only to have the game end when the cormorant made a single fatal mistake. It may have been luck, or the skill of the eagle as a hunter, or even that the cormorant was just too tired to dive under the water again, but it hesitated for an additional second this time before diving to the depths, to be caught by one of the eagles. The sharp and wickedly shaped eagle talons functioned as they were designed to — by capturing and killing the unfortunate bird. A well-produced nature documentary would probably show the eagle majestically lifting off from the water with its freshly plucked meal, water droplets glittering like bright

Taken C.W. Hitz of One Eye Images & Sound

The Flight of the Hunter at Princess Louisa Inlet (2003)

white diamonds in the sun as it headed skyward. In actuality, this eagle chose to float unglamorously on the water's surface and prepare the meal as he drifted to the opposite shore of the Inlet. All the while the other eagle perched in a high tree above the beach and waited until its portion was ready.

THE PLACE

The scenario described is one of many that are performed over and over throughout the world according to nature's design. But in this place, at Princess Louisa Inlet,[i] nature's plays seem to have been uninterrupted and unencumbered by man for centuries.

On a geographical map, the Inlet is located approximately 100 miles north of Vancouver, British Columbia (BC), Canada, within the Pacific Northwest Coastal mountain range. Princess Louisa Inlet is also part of the Jervis Inlet, which forms one of the largest fjords within the extensive fjord systems on the west coast of British Columbia; a total navigable waterway exceeding 85 miles in length. The Jervis Inlet follows a zigzag course in a general northerly direction through the Coastal mountain range, starting from the Straits of Georgia up to the end or head of the Inlet where the Squawka River ends by emptying into the Inlet.

The Jervis Inlet has three specific arms, or reaches, that make up the meandering pattern it follows. The first arm, near the entrance of the Inlet, is called the Prince of Wales Reach and follows a northeast course from the Georgia Straits up past Vancouver Bay. It then turns to follow a northern direction, where the next leg becomes the Princess Royal Reach. The final turn is once again to the northwest and is called the Queens Reach. Here is where the entrance to Princess Louisa Inlet can be found, seven miles down from the head of the Jervis Inlet. The shallow entrance of Princess Louisa is specifically noted for the swift tidal current and the rapids it creates. Both the Jervis Inlet and the Princess Louisa Inlet are considered fjords, as their characteristic landscapes of steep and rocky shores give rise to sky-reaching mountains with no beaches. The high peaks, and the other distinguishing features that make up these types of fjords, create a beautiful and enchanting place to see and explore.

Image (1SS004-724-78) courtesy of Earth Science & Image Analysis
Laboratory, NASA Johnson Space Center (http://eol.jsc.nasa.gov/)

Princess Louisa Inlet from the ISS (2003)
(Arrow points to Princess Louisa Inlet)

If the land of the Jervis and Princess Louisa Inlets was seen in
orbit from far above the earth it would appear rough, craggy,
and unfinished. This isn't surprising, as this part of the continental landmass has gone through some of the greatest geologic and geographic changes the earth has ever known. The result
is an ever-altering appearance which has continued its evolu-
tion since it was first created. The best example of the terrain
would be to picture ice crystals forming on a cold winter window. When viewed from space, Princess Louisa Inlet's snow
capped mountains have a similar ice-like crystallization
appearance, and the similar lines of channels radiating outward
like features carved into the ice crystals on the cold window.
This similarity is due to a natural process called fracturalization. Fractals are imperfect, naturally occurring shapes that
help make up the dynamic patterns of many physical things,
such as a tree leaf's pattern, the shape of a snowflake, or that of
a mountain range. Regardless of the size, the same force applies
to the creation of the pattern or shape of a fractal, which is similar to a potter molding the clay with his hands as he rotates
and works the material into a vase or some other familiar

shape. The same fracturalization principle applies to Princess Louisa Inlet, for there are a number of molding forces at work that have shaped this area as well as most of the world, such as rotation of the earth, the slow geologic changes of the land, glacier retreats, and even the dynamic force of erosion. This chaos is what shaped the Coastal mountain range into the familiar maze of peaks, valleys, and Inlets. There really is no exact record or data that can show that these events occurred, just speculation and conjecture of known scientific facts, past stories, and tales of the First Nation people, the Sechelts, who were the first inhabitants of this area.

Image (STS045-152-52) courtesy of Earth Science & Image Analysis Laboratory, NASA Johnson Space Center (http://eol.jsc.nasa.gov/)

Princess Louisa Inlet from the Space Shuttle
(Arrow points to Inlet)

THE CREATION

The Jervis and Princess Louisa Inlets are primarily made of granite, more commonly known as bedrock. It is one of the hardest rocks known and was created within the interior of the earth in a hot molten state over 100 million years ago.[ii] This molten material was forced upward, but before it could reach the surface the rock was prematurely cooled. This created a sub-layer underneath the marine sediment and igneous rocks at the surface, hence the term bedrock. The hardened granite was subjected to various geologic forces of the earth for over many thousands of years, forcing it to fracture and split into crevasses, or deep fissures, in the rock. In time these fissures were filled in with softer plant and rock material. As the climate was subtropical during this period of the past, plants would thrive in the warm, humid environment. They would live, die, and decay in their natural cycle and thus become soil, creating many vast layers over time. The layers were then subjected to the same geological forces as the bedrock, turning the soft material into coal.

Taken by C.W. Hitz of One Eye Images & Sound

Bedrock Fracture at Princess Louisa Inlet (2003)

Rivers and streams abounded in the area, a natural offshoot of the subtropical, humid climate. After several million years these rivers had carved through most of the marine sediments, organic material and igneous rock to uncover the prematurely hardened granite underneath. The larger rivers were able to cut deeply into the bedrock and eroded it away in characteristic patterns. These water flows were eventually named the 'Jervis River', now known as the Jervis Inlet with its distinctive zigzag path, and a number of straight branch streams like the 'Sechelt River', the 'Salmon River', the 'Narrow River', and the 'Princess Louisa River'.[iii] These tributaries were much straighter because they flowed through the unrestrictive breaks in the granite. The offshoots are also now known as Inlets under the same names. Yet another force of nature, however, was responsible for permanently altering the bedrock and also for creating the Inlets of the Jervis and Princess Louisa Inlets – ice.

Image (STS047-42-34) courtesy of Earth Science & Image Analysis Laboratory, NASA Johnson Space Center (http://eol.jsc.nasa.gov/)

Princess Louisa Inlet and Queens Reach from Space
(Arrow points to PLI)

THE ICE GIANT

Geologists have calculated that the North American continent has gone through at least four distinct periods of glaciations during the last 1.6 million years, with the last ending a mere 10,000 years ago. During the last period, a gigantic ice sheet known as the 'Wisconsin Continental Glaciations' covered most of the North American continent. It spread as far south as northern Pennsylvania, Ohio, Indiana and Illinois and was comprised of two separate independent sheets; the 'Laurentide Sheet' in the east and the 'Cordilleran Ice Sheet' in the Pacific Northwest. The Cordilleran Ice Sheet started from the BC Coast mountain range and extended west of Vancouver Island and east to the Rocky Mountains of Montana. It also expanded as far south as Washington State's Puget Sound area and that of the Columbia basin, which it helped to create.

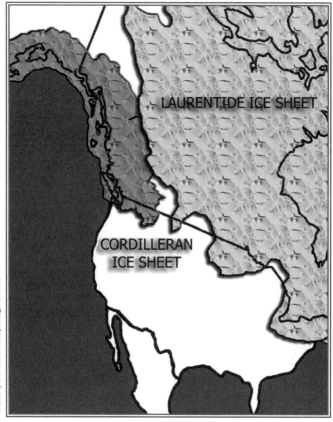

Created by C.W. Hitz of One Eye Images & Sound

Diagram of the Glacier Flow 10,000 Years Ago (2003)

An ice age comes about due to a number of changes in the earth's environment. The main requirement for ice is temperature – the colder the better. In most cases the temperature change is caused by shift in the earth's axis or something blocking the sun for a period of time, ash from a volcano, for instance. As the earth's surface temperature starts to cool, snow and ice begin to accumulate. In time the first lower layer gradually turns from old snow into glacial ice and, as each successive band of new snow is piled on top, more generations of older strata eventually turn to ice. As snow and ice accumulate, so does the weight, causing the ice sheet to move and, as it shifts, it carves into the earth's surface like a rasp smoothing a piece of metal. This carving action also works in reverse as the ice sheet begins to recede as it melts. About 7,000 years ago, warming temperatures caused the Cordilleran ice sheet to begin to recede towards the BC Coastal range. Reversal of the ice's movement from one direction to another helped to carve out the steep valleys of the fjords of the BC coast, including the Jervis Inlet and Princess Louisa area.

As a glacier moves it grates along the surface of the earth while, at the same time, melting water underneath the ice assists in removing debris. Normally a retreating glacier starts eroding from the top of the mountains, creating and shaping the peaks and eventually ending on the valley floors, littering them with debris. It is important to note, however, that the glacier removes the softer material overlaying the bedrock and not the actual bedrock of the old riverbeds discussed previously. In addition, the glacier actually follows the original direction of the old rivers as the ice retreats, these being the paths of least resistance.

It is known that the Cordilleran Ice Sheet did move south once more after its first retreat. At that time, 6,600 years ago, it moved to cover most of the Fraser lowland and the Sumas area, only to retreat once again back up north to its present location above the Arctic Circle near Alaska and parts of British

Columbia. Today the result of this eroding and retreating results in the form of the characteristic shapes of the Jervis and Princess Louisa Inlets. Both Inlets are typical fjords because of their U-shaped, cross-sectional profiles, with valley floors that are flat or slightly rounded and longitudinal in appearance. Each has shallow shoals or small islands around their entrances, sharp-peaked mountains created by the glacier's carving action and a scattering of small particles of stone to create a few beaches along the shore.

Taken by C.W. Hitz of One Eye Images & Sound

The Rapids at Malibu
and the Entrance to PLI (2003)

THE FLOODS

Water has also been significant in shaping the land around the Jervis and Princess Louisa Inlets. Scientists have determined that floods have occurred in the area not just once, like Noah's catastrophic flood depicted in the Bible, but several times over the centuries. Japanese archeologists have been able to ascertain, by examining the various layers of deposits in various shore digs on their native beaches, when various historical

Courtesy of Young Life – Used with Permission

The Power of the Tide at Princess Louisa Inlet (1999)

tsunami or tidal waves have dramatically impacted their islands. They have accurately determined from their research where and when these destructive waves originated. A number of them came from the Pacific Northwest as results of subduction (under the water) earthquakes. One earthquake in particular, measuring approximately 9.0 on the Richter scale, occurred on the night of January 26, 1700 off the coast of British Columbia,[iv] causing a tsunami to strike the islands of Japan a few hours later. The resulting wave caused massive destruction throughout many of Japan's coastal cities and inland waterways. The same earthquake also devastated the Jervis and Princess Louisa Inlets as well as most of British Columbia, not by a tidal wave, as the tsunami would flow outward from the center of the quake, but by a terrific surge of water. This phenomenon was horrific as the water level rose suddenly to a huge height, surging through the deep narrow Jervis Inlet with fantastic force. The Sechelt First Nation band residing in the area has numerous stories of its people running to the high mountains and riding out the flood in the many caves.[v] Other Pacific Northwest coastal tribes have similar stories tell of people being swept away and whales beached many miles up river valleys.

Scientists theorize that this type of flood, a sudden water surge, has happened not only in 1700, but actually many times before throughout the BC coastal areas and that of the two Inlets. The trigger location of these destructive waves is the 'Cascadian Subduction Zone' located many miles off the BC and Washington State coastlines, under the ocean in very deep water where two massive tectonic plates have intersected. The first is the 'Juan de Fuca Plate', which is being pulled and pushed under the other, known as the 'North American Continental Plate.'[vi] The subduction zone is so massive that it starts from the tip of Vancouver Island and runs all the way to the northern California border. Friction and strain between these two large plates builds up and, over time (between a 300 and 500 year period), releases its stored energy in the form of an earthquake. The liberated energy travels through the water in all directions like gigantic ripples in a pond, the oscillating energy of the tidal wave. Tsunamis are most destructive when they reach the shallow water of the continental shelf of any land mass, where they increase in both size and strength. The energy is dissipated as it crashes onto shore in the form of the huge breaking wave we know from scientific fact and hollywood movies. This is what struck Japan in 1700, causing so much damage. Since the Jervis Inlet is so deep and narrow, however, the water surges in these waterways instead of forming a wave, as the energy has nowhere to go but out and over, similar to a bucket full of water being jostled. The water is sloshed from side to side because of the confined space and the energy just dissipates over the side. It is very possible that more events of this nature will continue to occur and will affect both of the Inlets as well as the majority of the Pacific Northwest in the future.

THE MARINE ENVIRONMENT

Princess Louisa and the Queen's Reach areas of the Jervis Inlet are like two intersecting lines. Princess Louisa Inlet is a small appendage attached to the Queen's Reach arm of the Jervis

Inlet and its narrow entrance is seven miles from the head of the Jervis. Each of these areas is surrounded and hemmed in by steep mountains jutting out of the water, with only a few beaches to see. The entrance to Princess Louisa Inlet is unique, for a few small islands and a finger of flat land jut out from the side of Mount Helena, making the channel only a few yards wide and about the same depth. Through this constricted passage flow large volumes of seawater passing in two directions four times a day, because of the tide. The tidal action from both Princess Louisa Inlet and from the Jervis side is such a massive and strong force that the water moving through the narrows of Princess Louisa Inlet's entrance creates rapids that flow as fast as nine knots.

The moon's gravitational pull and the orbit of the earth affect the movement of the tides; they are rising or lowering in a cyclic rhythm. Using a similar analogy, Princess Louisa Inlet is like a large bucket being filled and refilled four times a day during a 24-hour period. A casual observer can see the phenomenon and can tell if it is low or high tide just by watching the flow at the narrow entrance of the Inlet. If the tide is flowing towards Jervis Inlet, then it is going out (low tide) and releasing the water from Princess Louisa Inlet. High tide is seen as water flowing toward Princess Louisa Inlet, as though it is trying to fill it up. This has been the natural rhythm of life for Princess Louisa Inlet since it was created.

Aside from the tides, oceanographers know that the deep waters of the ocean are constantly renewed with oxygen and other nutrients necessary for marine life to thrive. The same is true for the Straits of Georgia and those of the Georgia Basin Inlets (Saanich, Indian Arm, Howe Sound, Jervis, and the Bute Inlets) of British Columbia. By studying three main properties of seawater (temperature, salinity and dissolved oxygen), scientists can determine the rate of renewal for a specific area. According to a 50-year study of these properties by the Fisheries and Oceans Ministry of Canada, the Jervis Inlet renews its deep water each year. The cycle normally begins during the latter months of the year, when vast amounts of denser water from the renewed Straits of Georgia mix with fresh water run-off, occurring during the major weather period when precipitation is at its greatest and the glacier melt has subsided into the Inlet. The Queen's Reach section is a vast basin, with the outer part at the mouth of the Jervis Inlet and the inner part near Patrick Point, and the other reaches are basins that are each a bit deeper than the previous one, almost like a gradual waterfall in reverse, hidden beneath the surface. Princess Louisa Inlet is considered one of the basins, the only difference being its shallow and narrow entranceway. Is this entrance a barrier to the deep water cycle that revives the Jervis Inlet each year? If so, how does Princess Louisa Inlet renew its own deep water? There is no conclusive data to help answer this question, for, again, Princess Louisa Inlet is more like a bucket than a basin. It holds a large volume of seawater coming directly from the Jervis. The narrows, the lip of the bucket, siphon the top level of water off the surface, depending upon the direction of the tide. Chatterbox Falls and the other waterfalls, within the basin both permanent and temporary, are contributing by adding fresh water to the mix. The fresh water's density is a bit lighter, so it tends to remain on the surface. Incidentally, this is the reason why the Inlet freezes over during the winter. One can only guess at how Princess Louisa Inlet renews its deep waters, for the tide can only bring in and take out so much surface water, restricted by the narrow and shallow entrance. The nutrients from the waterfalls add something, but logically this should make the levels of temperature, salinity and dissolved oxygen even higher in the Inlet. What would this do to the marine life that thrives in this water? Is Princess Louisa Inlet a vast nutrient basin?

Marine life does reside in the Inlet. There are accounts of many species of fish and aquatic marine animals there. The cycle of life plays out each day, whether a harbor seal is chasing the elusive salmon or a killer whale hunting the seal. One person at

Malibu remembers two killer whales swimming through the rapids into Princess Louisa Inlet after salmon or seal, while the rest of the pod (family group or herd) remained outside the entrance. The observer felt that the two whales in the Inlet seemed to be herding a school of salmon or seal out to the entrance and it was more than apparent that these fish were going to be caught (and eaten) by the living net of the other whales waiting at the entrance on the Jervis Inlet side. Marine biologists and other researchers studying these types of whales believe there is intelligence and a social order associated with these marine mammals. They were known for their aggressive nature, as observed by whalers over a century ago, accounting for their name.

THE WEATHER

The summer months from June to September provide Princess Louisa Inlet with warm and favorable weather, but the rest of the time the weather is cold, windy and wet. When a weather front moves into the Pacific Northwest, it tends to get locked into the area of the Jervis and Princess Louisa Inlets. During the fall and winter months fog tends to permeate the area on an ongoing basis and is a significant threat to marine and aviation

Winter at Princess Louisa Inlet (1982)

By C.W. Hitz of One Eye Images & Sound

Chatterbox Falls (2002)

navigation. Rain is very common. The large peaks surrounding the Inlets seem to cut into the guts of the clouds, forcing them to drop their loads and giving way to downpours that can last for days. It is for this reason that the Jervis Inlet area and British Columbia are blanketed with a cover of green trees up and down the coast. During the summer months the unique landscape causes warm and cold airs to converge at various altitudes to create many spectacular thunder and lighting storms. The geology of some parts of the Jervis and Princess Louisa Inlets consists of a material that seems to attract the electrical conductivity, or lightning, of the storm. There is a described lightning belt of the Jervis Inlet that runs from Deserted Bay to follow the Princess Royal Reach to the Britain River, with the end of the belt around the Powell River area. Forest fires are common as a result of these electrical storms.

Activities of life are played out in various roles and processes at Princess Louisa Inlet. The many actors, in the form of animals, perform according to the lines Mother Nature has penned for them through their environment. Anyone who has visited the area has a story to tell about to seeing a bear, mountain goats high in the hills, or witnessing some natural event that they will remember the rest of their lives. The plays continue on, but how they and their theater were created is necessary for the story of this place. The steady pace would all change, however when explorers from halfway across the world would strut onto the stage.

ENDNOTES

i   Peterson, *The Story of the Sechelt Nation*, page 44 & 82 . Although Peterson does not give a definition to the name of Princess Louisa Inlet, SWAYWELAHT, it means a 'warm and sunny place.' However, the Sechelt term for mountain goat is SWAYTLYE and the first portion of SWAY may indicate height or mountain. Another variation of the Sechelt name or description for Princess Louisa Inlet is SWIVELOOT which is said to be 'bright shinny water', but no mention of this term is found in Peterson's book.

ii Nobes, *The Magnetometric off-shore Electrical sounding (MOSES) Method and its application in a survey of upper Jervis Inlet, BC*. 1984. Pages 74 & 76. Over 1 million years ago, the Jervis Inlet was subjected to volcanic activity of the Cascade and Garibaldi volcanic belt which is part of the seduction of the Juan de Fuca plate of the Pacific Northwest Coast.

iii Keller & Leslie, *Bright Seas, Pioneer Spirits*, page 4.

iv Connelly, *In The Northwest: Don't look now, but scientists think the Big One is just about due*. Seattle PI, March 2, 2001.

v   Peterson, *The Story of the Sechelt Nation*, page 4 & 6. Peterson describes a massive surge of water flowed through the Inlet and was defiantly not caused by rain or melting snow. It was so vast that the Sechelt says they rode out this massive event at the top of a high mountain called MINATCH near Mt. Victoria.

vi Paulson, Seattle PI, *Major quake could launch deadly tsunami* January 22, 2001.

Taken by C.W. Hitz of One Eye Images & Sound

CHAPTER
TWO

The Exploration of the Pacific Northwest and the Inlet

The Entrance
to Princess
Louisa Inlet
(1979)

*"Marine surveying is undertaken with the view
of rendering the coasts or ports surveyed safe
for the purposes of navigation, and not for
laying out town lots or lines of railway."*

REAR ADMIRAL RICHARD C. MAYNE (1874)

Taken by C.W. Hitz of One Eye Images & Sound

The Jervis Inlet & Patrick Point (1984)

Captain Vancouver's disappointment was readily apparent, for his small crew of men in the Pinnace noticed it
right away. Two days before they had spotted the
entrance of what the Captain had thought might be the beginning of the fabled Northwest Passage which he had specific
orders to find. Instead, after three days of hard rowing and sailing up the three reaches (soon to be named the Jervis Inlet) in
the worst weather possible, they had reached the end of the
line. A mighty river flowed down from the mountains in the
distance to the point where they had set anchor and it was
obvious this channel would not go any further. All the effort
they had put into exploration of the area since they left the
HMS Discovery over a week before, and the bad weather they

had endured in the small open boat, were enough to discourage them completely. This was Captain Vancouver's second disappointment in trying to find the Northwest Passage and it was not to be his last. He would, however, find the finger of land that would later become Malibu, and incidentally, bypassed the narrow mouth of Princess Louisa altogether, only to have the Inlet be discovered by his own countrymen some 70 years after his death.

BACKGROUND

History shows that in the early 17th and 18th centuries the three major European nations of Spain, Russia, and England converged on the Pacific Northwest in the name of exploration and expansion. That was a time of post-enlightenment and imperialism, when the understanding of the world came through science rather than religion and the acquisition of land was accomplished through colonization and conquest. The explorers of the day used ships with sails made of canvas to master the wind and propel their vessels over the vast oceans to far-away lands of the unknown world. Ironically, with all of the large new continents to explore, all three realms ended up in what would become British Columbia at relatively the same time. It isn't so surprising when the causes for this exploration and expansion are examined. The first reason was the need to colonize. The second was to increase commerce by opening more trade and markets in the area for products such as fur. The third reason was to increase navigable trade routes to more easily accomplish the first two goals. And the final reason, and primary goal of all of the expeditions, was to find the fabled Northwest Passage.

The first Europeans to document and chart this area of British Columbia were the Spanish. They had occupied and plundered most of South and Latin America during the late 16th and early 17th centuries and established settlements along the coasts of Mexico and California. These settlements became the springboard for the many probing voyages undertaken up and down the coast. Their forays included many as far North as the Pacific Northwest and their colonies gave the Spanish the ability to supply provisions to any expedition far more easily than other European nations. The other countries were forced to outfit their expeditions in Europe, substantially limiting the amount of time spent in actual exploration since they were required to pack all of their provisions for the long trip out and back. In addition, the Spanish had the advantage of having built a fort at Nootka (a large protected inlet on the Pacific side of Vancouver Island), from which they defended their interests in the fur trade.

The Russian Empire, on the other hand, started their own explorations along the same coasts but from the opposite direction, beginning in the north and working southward. They used their settlements in Siberia and the regions now known as Alaska and the Inside Passage, (eventually purchased by the United States many years later), in the same way that the Spanish used their bases in Latin America and California. The Russians, however, were not able to explore as far as the Spanish because their main adversary, the British, continually harassed them (and visa versa), both militarily on the high seas and politically in Europe until the end of the Crimean War.

England was the last European nation in this game of exploration. Unfortunately the British had few settlements in South America and did not posses the outposts on the Pacific Coast that the Spanish or Russians did, limiting their ability to conduct expeditions easily and efficiently. To reach the Pacific Northwest the British were forced to sail around the world and this, incidentally, was reason why the British so desperately sought the Northwest Passage, a mythical connection between the West Coast and the East Coast of North America. English ships were forced to follow the long southern routes around Africa's southern-most point, the Cape of Good Hope, or South America's Cape Horn. These southern routes were known for their treacherous seas, unforgiving winds, and ungodly weather that would tax any ship and crew to their utmost. The mythical Northwest Passage, once found, would allow the British to avoid all of these hazards, be a safer and faster route between the two oceans and significantly decrease transportation costs between England and the Orient. Although the passage did not exist, interestingly enough one would be built nearly a century later in the form of the Panama Canal. However, at this time of exploration, the British Empire had become alarmed by its two converging rival empires, one from the north and the other from the south, into the Pacific Northwest and it became an important political and military issue for the English to gain control of the area. All disadvantages of strategic outposts aside through what they lacked in locations they made up in mobility in the way of a large navy.

THE BRITISH EXPLORERS

Britain ruled the oceans. The English had been a seafaring people throughout their history, as their land was a vast island and their empire could only be expanded by venturing out to sea. During the early 1700s their first and most famous explorer, Captain Cook, was sent by the British Admiralty to explore the world, thus beginning the empire-building for which the English have been known. Cook's ship, the *HMS Endeavor*, made three voyages around the world, but it would be during his second and third voyages that he would arrive in the Pacific Northwest. The Captain's routine of exploration in this area was simple: spend the summers in the Pacific Northwest and winter in the South Pacific where the climate was more tolerable. Unfortunately, it would be in the tropical paradise of Hawaii where he would finally meet his demise at the hands of a group of natives.

During Cook's last two voyages, a young man by the name of George Vancouver accompanied him as one of his apprentice midshipman. As a midshipman, Vancouver was responsible for many of the more mundane tasks on board the *Endeavor*. Nevertheless, he became highly proficient in the scientific practices of surveying and navigation. He also excelled in leadership and seamanship. And years later this young midshipman would become a great English explorer, just as his mentor had trained him to be. Vancouver distinguished himself and his country during his many voyages throughout the world, the Pacific Ocean and, most of all, the Pacific Northwest, where he would be the first person to name many features known today around the area of British Columbia and the Princess Louisa Inlet.

George Vancouver was born in King's Lyman, Norfolk (England) on June 22, 1757 and was the youngest of five children. Although he only reached the age of 41, passing away on May 12, 1798, he lived fully and began his training for his future at an early age. He entered the Royal Navy at the age of 13 and eventually became a midshipman at Cook's appointment. Following his return from Cook's fatal voyage, on December 15, 1790, he was promoted to Commander and given orders to explore the coasts of Australia, New Zealand, Tahiti, Hawaii, and the Pacific Northwest coast of North America. The competition between the big three European countries had become more intense during this period, resulting in Vancouver being issued specific orders to retrieve all the territories seized by the Spanish. Vancouver eventually accomplished this by ratifying a number of treaties called the Nootka Convention with Spain, which included the Spanish relinquishing their claims to the area. His orders included gathering accurate information about the establishments of other foreign nations in the area and making detailed surveys of the Pacific Coast in order to help determine the general lines of direction and distinction. In other words, lay the foundation for future surveying missions, show British strength, and find the Northwest Passage.

Vancouver began his Pacific expedition from England in 1791 in command of the *HMS Discovery*. The *Discovery* was built in 1789 and was a 340-ton sailing sloop of war with three masts and a crew complement of 100. The mighty ship was armed

with four 10 pound cannons along with ten swivel guns, and
was well equipped to handle any situation that might arise on
their voyage. However, long after *Discovery* distinguished herself during Vancouver's forays into the Pacific Northwest, this
gallant ship would became an ordinary armory scow and eventually a lowly prison barge before finally being broken up at
Deptford, England in 1834.

The *HMS Chatham*, an armored tender with two masts, would
later accompany the *HMS Discovery* during the Vancouver
expedition while in the Pacific Northwest. The *Chatham* was
significantly smaller than the Discovery, weighting only 135
tons, and was only lightly armed. She was under the command
of Lieutenant Commander William Robert Broughton, whose
orders were clear. He was to provide assistance and support to
Captain Vancouver during his exploration of the Pacific
Northwest. Eventually Broughton would be recalled to
England where he would ultimately turn over command of the
Chatham to one of Vancouver's most trusted officers,
Lieutenant Commander Peter Puget.

Courtesy of the BC Archives, negative # PDP00289 used with permission

Vancouver's ship the Discovery (1792)

THE JERVIS INLET SURVEY

In 1791, after exploring parts of Australia and New Zealand, Vancouver set course for the Pacific Northwest where Lieutenant Broughton and the *Chatham* would rendezvous with the *Discovery*. By the spring of 1792, *Discovery* and the *Chatham* had charted most of the Straits of Juan De Fuca and parts of the area they would call Puget Sound (named after Peter Puget). In early June of 1792, the two English sailing ships both laid anchor in a bay they named Birch Bay, now part of Washington State, after the types of trees the crew encountered while gathering supplies. After a night or two there Vancouver decided that the commanding officers of the two ships would divide up the exploration duties, using their small sailing boats for this as their size and speed would enable the crew to maneuver and investigate the shallower waters which the officers anticipated encountering. Additionally, they would be able to cover greater distances than those of the larger ships. Vancouver decided he would explore to the north and Lieutenant Broughton would head south. They would each have a week's worth of provisions and when they ran low, this would signal their return.

Early in the morning on June 12, 1792, Captain Vancouver, along with Lieutenant Peter Puget and some of the crew of the *Discovery,* set sail north from Birch Bay in *Discovery's* Pinnace with a smaller sailing yawl in tow. In four days they found and charted a number of points and inlets, such as Point Roberts, Point Grey, Burrard Channel, Point Atkinson, Anvil Island, Howe Sound, and Point Gower. These names are still used today and are noted on all current marine charts of the area. By the 16th the weather had changed from fair to bad, as noted by Puget in his log "Though the rain continues, it did not prevent our journey in the continent."[i]

Vancouver and his crew would also find a number of rocky inlets and the entrance to the Jervis Inlet. Vancouver noted this area as being "agreeably to our general mode of proceeding."[ii]

Captain Vancouver may have felt that he might have just found the entrance to the Northwest Passage, for he writes in his journal:

"The next morning, Monday the 18th, as usual, at four o'clock, we proceeded up the inlet about three miles in a north by northwest direction, whence its width increases about half a leaguer in a direction nearly North East to a point which towards noon we reached, and ascertained it latitude to be 50 degrees 1 minute, longitude 236 degrees 46 minutes."[iii]

It is interesting to note that the actual entrance of this Inlet, the Jervis, is located at 124 degrees west longitude. At the time of Vancouver's voyage the longitude lines ran north to south starting at Greenwich, England and then would ripple out in both westerly and easterly intervals to meet in the Pacific Ocean at 180 degrees. However, Vancouver interpreted Greenwich as the starting and ending point of the longitude lines and so, in a sense, he went in only one direction. This is the reason for the discrepancy in the longitude calculation in his log. Vancouver continues in his journal with anticipation of discovery of the Northwest Passage:

"The width of this channel still continuing, again flattered us with discovering a breach in the eastern range of snowy mountains, notwithstanding the disappointment we had met with in Howe's sound; and although since our arrival in the gulf of Georgia, it had proved an impenetrable barrier to that inland navigation, of which we had heard so much, and had sought with sanguine hopes and ardent exertions hitherto in vain, to discover."[iv]

However, in spite of his initial enthusiasm, Jervis Inlet would prove to be just as disheartening as his disappointment at Howe Sound had been. Today we know that that Vancouver could never have been able to succeed in fulfilling this portion of his orders, finding the Northwest Passage, and was doomed to failure before he had even begun.

The day that Vancouver discovered the entrance to the Jervis Inlet was also the same day that he and his men encountered a number of First Nation inhabitants of the area – the Sechelts. Vancouver noted them as being "civil natives,"[v] indicating contact had been made, but did not go into detail. According to Puget's log, they had been welcomed to one of the native camps but they had graciously declined. However some trading had taken place in an exchange of salmon for both copper and iron.[vi] All the while the native bands showed the utmost courtesy to the foreigners, but were as curious about these strangers in their country as Captain Vancouver and crew were of them and their land. Vancouver and his men set up a tent near what they called "Breakfast Point" not far from "Scotch Fir Point". Scotch Fir Point had earned its name a few days before by being the only place outside of Scotland they had found a few Scotch Fir trees. They rested at the camp for some hours until the weather improved. As was Vancouver's custom, they arose very early in the morning on June 18th 1792, and even though the weather had not improved, Vancouver decided to proceed up channel anyway. At approximately 11:00am, his hopes of finding the Northwest Passage were dashed as they came to the end of the inlet. Peter Puget describes this termination point by indicating the muddy flats where the Squwaka River terminated, along with a description of the remnants of a local First Nation band village[vii] located nearby:

"33 miles from last night sleeping place we at last came to the termination of this Inlet, which we found lined low muddy ground. There were also huts with 5 or 6 Indian inhabitants but they I believe were only temporary dwellings."[viii]

At approximately three o'clock in the afternoon, while making their way back, they stopped at the entrance of Princess Louisa Inlet near the finger of land where Malibu would later be built. Vancouver and Puget both write how terrific the rapids were through the narrow entrance and described how they had difficulty rowing against them. Vancouver notes that:

"About two leagues from the head of the inlet (Jervis) we had observed, as we passed upwards as the Northern shore, a small creek with some rocky islets before it where I intended to take up our abode for the night. On our return, it was found to be full of salt water, just deep enough to admit our boats against a vary rapid stream, where at low tide they would have grounded some feet above the level of the water in the Inlet. From the rapidity of the stream, and the quantity of water it discharged, it was reasonable to suppose by its taking a winding direction up a valley to the Northeast that its source was at some distance. This not answering our purpose as a resting place, obliged us to continue our search along the shore for one less incommodious, which the perpendicular precipices precluded our finding until near eleven at night, when we disembarked on the only low projecting point the inlet afforded."[ix]

In actuality, Puget, along with a few other men, was sent to investigate in the yawl while Vancouver and the others waited in the Pinnace. Puget and his men bucked against the outgoing tidal current, which was incredibly strong since the month of June produces the severest high and low tides as the moon and earth move into the summer solstice. Puget said it was too much for them and that they "were very glad to find our way out clear of the rocks." They beached their boats and made their way along the difficult shoreline to the rapids. This particular finger of land was very rocky and cavernous, with only a few trees. It would seem an ideal place for shelter as it would provide enough protection against the weather, which was a concern to Vancouver. Puget mentions seeing a number of abandoned native huts on this body of land, and also determined that the flow of water was not a river, but possibly another Inlet working its way further northwest. He also was able to ascertain that this area was also full of "salt water."[x]

When Puget and his men reported back with the news of what they had found, Vancouver was far more interested in the more pressing question of "was there fresh water?" Since it was June, the winter runoff behind the rock cliff had dried up, leaving the rocky point barren and possibly explaining why the native camp was empty. Both Puget and Vancouver don't mention it specifically, but this was most likely the main reason for not setting up camp at this spot. Instead they sailed further down to a bay, later to be called Deserted Bay, near another populated Sechelt village.[xi] Vancouver thought this would be a safer and more sheltered place to set up the tents for the night and, most of all, there was a fresh water stream near by.

The next day Vancouver decided to sail the 84 miles back to *Discovery*. Vancouver honestly admits his decision to return was because of the poor, wet and cold weather conditions. It was a little hard to be in an open skiff for this length of time and, he writes, "too much time to be exposed to the elements under these conditions and made way on the 20th."[xii] When they entered the Straits of Georgia, Vancouver began giving names to the main waterways and landmarks they had just encountered. In Royal Navy tradition he named the main inlet the 'Jervis Inlet' (in early charts it was named 'Jarvis') after his friend Rear Admiral Sir John Jervis (Earl of St. Vincent). "To this arm of the sea, I gave the name of Jervis's Channel (Inlet), in honor of Admiral Sir John Jervis." Admiral Jervis received this distinction for his victory over the Spanish fleet in February 14, 1792 at St.Vincent in the Caribbean, and was also awarded the title of Earl of St. Vincent. Captain Vancouver named the bay near the entrance of the Jervis Inlet after that very place the battle was fought, St.Vincent Bay.[xiii]

The very next day, on the 21st, the wayward Vancouver and his crew spotted the sails of a ship they thought was *Discovery*. Instead it was the Spanish ships the *Sutil*, commanded by Captain Malaspina, and the *Mexican* under the command of Galiano. The Spanish ships and their crews were also exploring and hunting for the Northwest Passage but under a different flag, country, and government. Vancouver and his men were welcomed aboard as guests to the warm

inviting quarters and hot food of their Spanish hosts, even
though they were 'enemies'. The encounter lifted the sprits of
Vancouver's men, and it was during this meeting that
Vancouver and Galiano started a friendship that would later
help bring peace and stability in the area between Spain and
England. However this first meeting was in the form of
exchange, particularly of information. Galiano and Malaspina
had both surveyed the same area and had also found the
entrance to the Jervis Inlet. They had named it Boca de
Moñino (Mouth of Moñino)[xiv] after a Spanish Admiral, but did
not explore any further. Vancouver had observed that the
Spanish only surveyed big bodies of waters and avoided the
arms and Inlets. It seemed to him that the English focused on
details, whereas the Spanish were concerned with more general aspects. The English were invited to spend the night, but
Vancouver declined. He was intent on finding his own ships,
which he did only one day later.

Vancouver and the Spanish did end up rendezvousing a few
days later under the friendship of trust that seaman seem to
share, especially in uncharted and unfamiliar country. They
stayed together until both departed a few weeks later. This
resulted in a number of superb charts being produced, detailing the Northwest coast of America by the combined efforts of
both the Spanish and English, defining a coast and a future
province of Canada.

In the mid 1880s, some 70 years after Captain Vancouver's
cruise through the Pacific Northwest, his book on the voyage
and the many charts would be an integral part of another survey undertaken by the Royal Navy. The new survey mission
would last more than a decade and would detail more of this
area, and specifically affect the Inlet and the Pacific Northwest
as we know it today. In addition, it would finally be the
Englishmen of this mission who would name and chart the
many islands, waterways, bays, and inlets that we know today,
including that of Princess Louisa Inlet.

The Royal Navy's interest in this latest endeavor was fueled by four specific and familiar reasons: first to show British military presence, second to keep English commercial interests active, third to examine possible colonization of the region, and fourth to produce accurate navigational charts. By this time the Northwest Passage was no longer an issue, as it had been proven to be nonexistent by the Lewis and Clark expedition (below the 49th parallel) and the McKenzie group (above the 49th parallel). However, the British remained interested in the area as the English presence had gained significant strength since the time Vancouver had first surveyed the area in 1792.

The British had forced out the Spanish as a military and commercial competitor through a number of negotiated treaties, known as the Nootka Conventions, but there were still formidable foes in the area. The Russians were active in the Alaskan region and posed a threat up north and a new adversary had appeared as a growing and alarming threat, England's own former colony, the Americas. The Americans were expanding just as fast as the English were on the North American Continent, but under the 49th parallel.

So yet again, by the use of their sea power, the British extended their political and commercial interests in response to American and Russian expansion. They developed various commercial and civil establishments that would support their ships in the area, giving them an advantage they had lacked in Vancouver's time. First, a British naval base was built at Esquimalt near present-day Victoria BC. Second, a coaling station was constructed north of Esquimalt at Nanaimo, where three large veins of coal had been discovered. Coal was the fuel necessary to power the new steam propulsion engines currently used on the Royal Navy ships. Aside from the naval aspect, in 1843 England's Hudson's Bay Company (HBC) had created a commercial infrastructure specifically for the trading of fur, and they also maintained the coaling station at Nanaimo for military and civilian steam ships. The Hudson Bay Company's chief director, James Douglas, later to be Governor of the Crown Colonies of Vancouver Island and British Columbia, had begun to seek out more potential sites for his HBC 's operations north of the 49th parallel. The Royal Navy was there to help him with his endeavors. The Navy, however, was facing a serious problem that could not be categorized as political, military, or even commercial. Rather it was natural. It seems Her Majesty's ships were running aground because of significant uncalculated tidal changes, hidden obstacles and unknown currents that created difficulties for even the most seasoned navigator. The need for accurate surveys of this area, and around the world, had become paramount.

In 1795 the British Lords of the Admiralty created the Royal Hydrographic Office in London, England. The Navy was losing more ships to grounding than to military action. As well, the Royal Navy had shifted from an exploratory mode to more of a protector role for the Empire and its interests, the products these colonies brought to England, like fur from the Pacific Northwest. Alexander Dalrymple, the First Hydrographer of the Royal Navy, began to assemble all available surveys, charts, and views recorded of all the coasts throughout the world. These included Captain Cook's notes, Vancouver's observations and other types of data, in manuscript form, from the Pacific Northwest and elsewhere.

The early maps were not worth much because they provided little useful information or details. They lacked such basic information as tides, islands, or reefs, but by the turn of the nineteenth century changes in technology and science allowed for more detail and understanding, greatly improving the quality of the maps. Dalrymple capitalized on this knowledge and new tools available to create the hydrographic maps, known as Admiralty maps, which became the specific navigational aids used when circumnavigating the world via the ocean. These were the precursors to modern marine navigation maps. The term 'hydrographic' defines the ability to transform data of the marine world into a meaningful graphical map.

Admiralty charts generally used the Gerard Mercator projection first introduced in 1569, which transformed the curved surface of the earth onto the flat plane of a paper map. To create this type of map, a survey mission was needed to collect all the necessary information including soundings (depth of the water), observations of landforms and other marine obstacles, specific location (latitude and longitudes), triangulation, and the naming of these points which would all be recorded in the surveyor's journal and sketch book. Astronomical observations also would be included during these surveys and were often used as reference points as they helped in other areas of scientific research, such as understanding mathematics, astronomy, oceanography, and physics.

Courtesy of the BC Archives, negative # B-03617 used with permission

The Officers of the HMS Plumper (Esquimult-1860)
(Left to Right Standing): Dr. D. Lyell, Paymaster W.H. 'Bull' Brown, Captain G.H. Richards, & Lt. Daniel Pender.
(Left to Right Seated): Sub Lt. E.P. Bedwell, 2nd-Lt. R.C. Mayne, Mrs. G.H. Richards, & 1st-Lt. W. Moriarty

Specific ships were either built or converted into surveying vessels, and manned with trained officers and crew who would all act as surveyors in addition to their more ordinary sailing duties. A typical survey season was during spring and summer months while the weather was warm and clear. During the off-season, while the weather was at its worst and actual physical surveying was impossible, the task of recording and transferring their data would be undertaken by the captain and officers of the survey vessel while in port. Survey of an area took time, and it would not be unusual to take several years to completely finish examining an area. Once completed, however, all projections and information would be sent back to the hydrographic office to be finalized, approved, and sent to the engravers for printing. Due to all these efforts, a specific chart of the area, a book of sailing instructions, and a catalogue of general charts were available for both the Navy and Merchant sailors of England.

As an example, in the summer of 1860 Captain George Richards and the officers and the crew of the *HMS Plumper* completed the survey of the Jervis and the Princess Louisa Inlets. They had physically surveyed the land, taken soundings data of both Inlets, recorded tidal information, and named the specific landmarks such as mountains, points, bays and beaches. The data was compiled into a rough paper drawing and sent on to England for printing. The result, after final adjustments and measurements were made, was printed in 1861 and titled "Fraser R, to N.E. Pt. of Texada I. including Howe Sound and Jervis Inlet" (see map on page 53). This is only an example of how detailed, simple, and useful these early hydrographic charts were, particularly in the Pacific Northwest and British Columbia. But the significance of this particular chart was that Princess Louisa Inlet was now named and mapped, including soundings of the Inlet, representation of mountains, native trails and sites, and even, by way of an anchor symbol, where Captain Vancouver had anchored some 70 years before.

The survey crew assigned to the Pacific Northwest, Captain Richards and the crew of the *Plumper*, also surveyed the entire coast of British Columbia in 1857 to 1861, mapping and detailing large areas of the now Canadian Pacific Northwest. In late 1861, Richards transferred his command to another survey vessel, the *HMS Hecate*. Lieutenant Daniel Pender would later become Captain of the *HMS Hecate* following Richards and finally finish the British Columbia survey around 1870.

In 1883, the Canadian Hydrographic Service was founded and in 1904 it took over the survey tasks and chart creation from the Royal Navy. It continues to this day as a ministry department under the Canadian government, but back in the 1850s British Columbia was still considered the frontier, a remote and unknown place. This was the nature of the survey mission as assigned to Captain George Henry Richards and the crew of the *HMS Plumper* in 1857.

CAPTAIN GEORGE H. RICHARDS

George Henry Richards was born in 1820 at Antony, in Cornwall, and entered the Navy at the age of 13. When he was 15 he was appointed to a surveying expedition on board the *HMS Sulphur*. Richards excelled not only as a surveyor but also in combat, where he would prove his courage many times in China and South America. He became adept as a negotiator, which would serve him well in the San Juan Island dispute of the Washington Territory many years later. These characteristics were noticed by the captain of the *Sulphur*, Captain Belcher, for he described the young Richards with the highest praise for he saw in this officer the skill of a surveyor and the bravery of a military man during the Boxer Rebellion.

Richards later saw more action on the southeast coast of South America, where he was put in charge of the *HMS Philomel's* small arms detail. During this time he was wounded in his left hand during one of many military charges during the action of the Oblegado on the Parana River, where he had made a number of assaults against the forts situated along the river. As a result of the attacks and subsequent praise from his commanders, he was promoted to the rank of Commander in 1845 and was assigned to the paddle steamer *HMS Acheron,* where he had a dual role as assistant-surveyor and second-in-command of the ship during the survey of the coasts of New Zealand from 1847 to 1851.

In 1852 his old captain, Captain Edward Belcher, appointed Richards to Belcher's own ship, the *HMS Assistance,* as part of a five ship expedition to the northern polar regions to search for the missing explorer Sir John Franklin. Unfortunately, the search and the ships had to be abandoned due to the extreme winter conditions, which locked the ships fast to the ice. Due to this experience Commander Richards became known for his skills in the arctic, as he made one of the longest and most difficult sledding treks of the time, under the harshest of arctic conditions, in order to obtain help for the frozen expedition. Again Captain Belcher would praise Richards for this endeavor. Richards became a Captain himself in 1854 and took command of the *HMS Plumper* in 1856 for the survey of Vancouver Island and of the coast of British Columbia. It would be a trip when he would show much "energy and zeal," and for which he would later be rewarded by being made Admiral of the Hydrographic Section of the Royal Navy and be knighted by Queen Victoria.

THE HMS PLUMPER

The *HMS Plumper* was laid down in Portsmouth Dockyard in October, 1847 per the specifications of the master shipwright Fincham, who had also designed the famous *HMS Arrogant,* and was launched on April 5, 1848. Miss Prescott, daughter of the admiral/superintendent of the dockyard where the ship was built, christened the ship "Her Majesty's Ship (HMS) *Plumper.*" It would be the fifth vessel in the Royal Navy to take on the name of "Plumper." A name for any ship in the Royal Navy was important, for it gave the crew a boost to their morale and pride

Courtesy of the BC Archives, negative #PDP00076
used with permission

The HMS Plumper at Port Harvey, Johnston's Strait (1862)

in the name of the vessel they served, and the meanings were generally manifold. The word plumper had two meanings in the English language at that time. The first meant to throw a heavy blow or apply a sudden direct action, in terms of a ship firing the first shot or surprising an enemy ship by its firepower. The second meaning of plumper was a political term. At the time there were still a few Royal Naval officers who entered parliament, and they were only allowed two votes in the structure of this political body of the English government. A plumper was when both candidates could caste the votes on behalf of the Royal Navy, similar to a proxy vote in today's terms.

The *HMS Plumper* was 140 feet long and was designed as an auxiliary sailing sloop (a ship with three masts), with the hull constructed out of solid oak. It was then completely sheathed in copper to protect against the wood-boring parasites of the South Seas and the Pacific Northwest. The *HMS Plumper* was one of the first ships in the Royal Navy to use the new type propulsion system, consisting of a propeller and shaft underneath the keel. Other types of propulsion designs had been developed in the Royal Navy with varying degrees of success, but it was the 'paddle- wheel' propulsion systems that had been the most successful. However, these proven designs were vulnerable to enemy firepower, so the designers opted for the under-the-keel propeller system. Since it was unproven technology, it was incorporated in the design of the *HMS Plumper* and other ships as a proof-of-concept. The *HMS Plumper's* system relied on a propeller and shaft placed below the keel and to the rear of the ship, attached to a steam single engine. The engine had two large 27-inch diameter cylinders with a 2-foot stroke. This engine would give the ship a nominal speed of 9 knots on a good day, using 150 hp as its maximum power output, was fueled by coal, and could hold 68 tons of the black fuel in its bunkers. The propeller looked like a bow tie and this design would be the Achilles heel of the ship, as the new technology was slow in evolving. The propeller would be repaired and replaced many times during its commission and it was a wonder it ever operated as well as it did. The steam engine with the under-the-keel propeller system was designed for auxiliary use only and could only be operated during calm seas, or in tandem with the sails, and only when conditions were right. In British Columbia, however, the many inlets and rivers the *Plumper* needed to survey required the power of the steam engine and her screw more often than her sails to safely navigate the precarious waters.

Coal was the fuel of the time for steam engines, and the Royal Navy had a number of coaling stations around the world. The Pacific Station ships like the *Plumper* received their coal from the veins found in Nanaimo. Coal is formed from the material of living plants and animals from many centuries, before being changed to black rock by unyielding geologic forces and time. The Nanaimo coal was found above the watermark and could easily be mined above ground by the Hudson Bay Company. A coaling wharf was built in such a way that the coal could go directly from the ground to the ships. For a navy ship, the best properties of coal were its ability to burn very fast in order to convert large amounts of water into steam quickly, to burn cleanly and not produce exhaust which could give away the ship's position to the enemy, and to not decay in storage. Coal also has the ability to flake off as dust in storage (the dust of most coal being liable to spontaneously combust, just as a hay bale will combust when wet). The coal from Vancouver Island, however, was mixed with shale and slate, which only yielded about 20% pure coal, and thus was significantly less desirable to the Navy. The actual coal mined from Nanaimo was thick with carbon and high in other chemicals like sulfur, resulting in fast decay of the material when in storage and producing very black smoke after it was burned. Usually that smoke was something a naval officer would dread, for it was an obvious way to give away the position of his ship to an enemy, but in the case of the *Plumper's* mission which was to survey, it didn't matter if the smoke was jet black. Plus the coal had to be used up before it decayed beyond its chemical strength. The *HMS Plumper's* bunkers could keep about 19 days worth of coal, or 68 tons. Therefore, although the quality was less than desired for the majority of the Navy's uses, Nanaimo coal was perfectly suited for the work this ship was required to carry out during the British Columbia coast survey.

The *HMS Plumper* would be commissioned three times during her service with the Royal Navy. The first commission was from 1848 to 1853 when it was placed in service around North America and the West Indies. The only note-worthy item during this commissioning was the witnessing of a giant squid swimming on the surface by one of it officers. The anonymous officer described this encounter in one of the editorials of a leading London newspaper.

"Not having seen a sketch of the extraordinary creature we passed between England and Lisbon, and being requested by several gentlemen to send you the rough one I made at the time, I shall feel much obliged by your giving it publicity in your instructive and amusing columns. On the morning of the 31st December 1848, in lat. 41 degrees 13' N., and long. 12 degrees 31' W., being nearly due west of Oporto, I saw a long black creature with a sharp head, moving slowly, I should think about two knots, through the water, in the north-westerly direction, there being a fresh breeze at the time, and some sea on. I could not ascertain its exact length, but its back was about twenty feet if not more above water; and its head, as near as I could judge, from six to eight. I had not time to make a closer observation, as the ship was going six knots through the water, her head E. half S., and wind S.S.E. The creature moved across our wake towards a merchant baroque on our lee-quarter, and on the port tack. I was in hopes she would have seen it also. The officers and men who saw it, and who have served in parts of the world adjacent to whale and seal fisheries, and have seen them in the water, declare they have neither seen nor heard of any creature bearing the slightest resemblance to the one we saw. There was something on its back that appeared like a mane, and, as it moved through the water, kept washing about; but before I could examine it more closely, it was too far astern."[xv]

It is interesting to note that scientists today still have not seen this type of creature alive. But it is past eyewitness reports like this, and other evidence, that have led to the conclusion that the giant squid does exists somewhere in the deep oceans of the world.

After only four years of service, the *Plumper* was recalled and refitted with new masts, re-rigged for sailing on the open ocean and was given a whole new propulsion system. The *HMS Plumper's* second commission lasted from 1853 to 1856. Her main mission was anti-slave operations off the West Coast of Africa. She was successful in the capture of a small slave ship in 1855, where the slaves were released and the cutter destroyed. Again, because of engine and propeller problems, the *Plumper* was brought back for refit. Her third and final commission lasted from 1856 to 1865, but this time her role had been changed to that of a survey vessel when Captain Richards took command of her. While still in drydock, it was found that parts of the ships were a 'bit rotten' and many additions were needed in order for her to succeed in her new mission. A large chart room was built on deck to help in the creation and organization of all the anticipated survey data.

As in the time of Captain Vancouver, tasks would be divided among the crew. The small boats were used for exploring, with several being deployed at once to maximize the survey time. The *Plumper* had five boats included in her inventory, ranging from very long boats with two sailing masts to the small rowing Dinghy. Some were even large enough to be given specific names. The *Shark* was the name given by Captain Richard to the *Plumper's* 'Pinnace' so as not to be confused with *HMS Satellite's* 'Pinnace' (meaning a small sailing utility boat), which was on station in the same area when the *Plumper* arrived in the Pacific Northwest. The *Satellite* operated in tandem with the *Plumper* during the British Columbia survey work. The other boats from the *HMS Plumper* were the Gig, Whaler, Galley, and the Dinghy. Each would be used extensively throughout the British Columbia survey.

Immediately following refitting, the *HMS Plumper* set sail for the Pacific Northwest. During her time in the area she became a prominent influence as both a survey ship and a peace keeper of the British Navy. Many landmarks and waterways of British Columbia were proudly named by the crew of the *Plumper*, and she remained on station in British Columbia until the *HMS Hecate* replaced her in 1861. The *HMS Plumper* was finally decommissioned in England on June 2, 1865 and broken up in 1866.

THE SURVEY

On March 11, 1857, Captain Richards and the crew of the *HMS Plumper* departed from Portsmouth and set sail for Rio de Janeiro. They would remain there for some time in order to repair a broken shaft and a leak that had developed in the middle of the Atlantic Ocean, but were able to sail the ship into port to have the repairs started. Once completed, the *Plumper* departed on July 9th 1857, reaching the Straits of Magellan on

July 29th 1857. The timing was unfortunate, as they encountered the heavy weather of the peak winter season in the southern hemisphere. After stopover in Valparaiso and Honolulu, she
reached the Straits of Juan de Fuca on November 9th 1857 and
docked at Esquimalt the next day, where Captain George
Richards was given his orders.

The instructions detailed what he and the crew of the *HMS
Plumper* were to undertake for the next couple of years. They
were to continue the survey above the 49th parallel and provide the necessary data for the creation of specific hydrographic charts and sailing instructions for the British Columbia
region of Canada. Captain Richards was also to serve as part of
the Boundary Commission, whose purpose was to help define
the final American/Canadian border. This was a project which
was to take many years and several crises before it would finally be established. Richards was to provide support and security to British subjects living and carrying on commerce in the
region as well, and was to show the flag and the ship's military
power during times of difficulty with natives and foreigners. In
four years at the Pacific Station in British Columbia, the officers and crew of the *Plumper* would steam and sail through
many miles up and down the British Columbia coast. The
ship's company included blacksmiths, caulkers, carpenters,
painters, and mechanics, all of whom provided the vital skills
needed to maintain the ship in a foreign location far from
home and supplies.

The crew of the *Plumper* would witness many extraordinary
events, both political and natural, during their time in British
Columbia, including astronomical displays, such as a comet in
the Fall of 1858 (Comet Donati on its return leg away from the
sun), the aurora borealis (also known as the Northern Lights),
and an eclipse of the sun in 1860. But all these paled in comparison to three political events, covering a two year span,
which embroiled the *Plumper* before they could even begin
their survey of the Jervis Inlet. These events ensured that the

ship and her crew would have a prominent place in the history of British Columbia and that of the Pacific Northwest.

The first event was the discovery of gold along the Fraser River in 1858. It created a stampede of Americans out of the Bellingham area trying to 'get-rich-quick' in the Fraser River area, similar to the gold rush in California many years before. There was not enough civil authority to keep order and security in the area, so the *HMS Plumper* was called upon several times by the governor of British Columbia in Victoria to subdue the riotous situations that would erupt near Hope, a settlement located many miles north of the mouth of the Fraser River. One time in particular, Captain Richards navigated the *Plumper* up the Fraser as far as Fort Langley. From there, Second Lieutenant Richard Charles Mayne, one of the survey officers, continued upriver to investigate and stop insurrections. By the time he finally reached the town, after many days of strenuous rowing, the situation had been taken care of by local officials and the young officer and his men were sent back. This was an example of the extra duties which the ship, the captain, and the crew were expected to undertake in addition to their surveying activities.

The second event of note was dealing with the northern native raids into the American settlements, in order to acquire slaves from the many tribes of the southern regions of the Pacific Northwest. Occasionally white settlers were also involved and sometimes killed. Although these types of raids had been a part of the native culture hundreds of years before the Europeans and the British arrived, they became a problem for the respective non-native governments now that their own citizens were involved. Law enforcement was required and Captain Richards was ordered to control the northern natives on the Canadian side. It was task he did not relish, as he felt the natives were being unfairly discriminated against and managed far too harshly. While Richards was very much a man of the Victorian age, he disagreed with the view that fairness and enlightenment were the exception when dealing people of color. It would be this excuse, of the native raids, that would result in the third situation, which was the San Juan Island boundary dispute.

An American lighthouse was attacked on San Juan Island during one particular native raid, which resulted in the US Army installing troops on the island with the purpose of protecting American settlers and property. Earlier, in 1846, the boundary between the United States and Britain was agreed by treaties to be the 49th parallel. The boundary line ran from the state of Maine to the Washington Territory, where it continued down the main channel between Vancouver Island and the U.S. mainland. But there were two channels, and that was the heart of the friction. Which channel was the one to be used, the Haro Straits or the Rosario Straits? The San Juan Islands were caught in the middle, because the British claimed the Rosario Straits as the boundary, which gave them the islands. On the other hand, the Americans looked at Haro Straits as the border and, therefore, the islands were on their side. In 1853 the Americans fueled the situation further by incorporating San Juan Island into Island County through the Oregon Territory legislature. The British protested this action as illegal, but American settlers began to claim land on the island as soon as the act was passed.

On June 15, 1859, Mr. Lyman Cutlar, an American farmer on the island, got his gun and shot a pig which was rooting in his potato patch. This had been the third time a pig from the Hudson Bay pig farm had gotten into his patch and he decided to deal with it, but afterwards Mr. Cutlar, feeling guilty, offered $10 to the Hudson Bay officials for the pig he shot. The HB official refused and told him it would cost $100. This was far more than Lyman could afford, and significantly higher than the actual worth of the pig. Tempers flared and each side went to its local government officials to deal with the situation. A few months later, on July 3, 1863, Captain George Pickett (the same confederate General who would lead the famous and fateful Pickett's Charge at Gettysburg during the American Civil war), with 66 men of the 9th U.S. Infantry from their post at Fort Bellingham, landed on San Juan Island near Griffin Bay. In turn, that same week, the Royal Navy force based at Esquimalt, under the command of Rear Admiral Robert Lambert Baynes, escalated the situation by a sortie of all the British naval forces to surround the island. In all, five Royal Navy ships (*Ganges, Tribune, Pylades, Satellite*, and *Plumper*) steamed over to Griffin Bay to show British strength and resolve. At one point during the crisis, Captain Richards was ordered to take the *HMS Plumper* and land Royal Marines on the island as an additional English response to the situation.

It would take months before the leaders of the respective nations realized that they were about to go to war in a remote corner of the world over a dead pig. Eventually tempers cooled and diplomatic protocols were factored into the situation. The island settled down under marshal law, jointly occupied by the English (at the English Camp on the north end of the island) and Americans (at the American camp on the southern tip), for many years.

Resolution was slow in coming, as the American civil war put a hold on the boundary issue. Ultimately, Kaiser Wilhelm I of Germany ruled in favor of the United States concerning a new international agreement and the San Juan Island situation. On May 8, 1872, the Haro Straits became the official boundary, rendering the San Juan Islands an American territory. Actually, the Kaiser wisely had asked that an unbiased decision be made by a council of a few German judges.[xvi] The German emperor did not care all that much for the English, as he was biased against the military and commercial servants of Queen Victoria and her empire. This was further exacerbated by the fact that his daughter-in-law was Queen Victoria's oldest daughter (The Princess Royal) and he did not like her English liberal views or manners.[xvii] The arbitrated ruling stood and San Juan Island officially became a part of the United States. But by this time, the *Plumper* and her crew had begun their surveying mission throughout British Columbia.

Courtesy of the BC Archives, neg #I-51762 used with permission

An Engraving of the HMS Plumper
at the Jervis Inlet (1860)

THE INLET IS NAMED

Captain Vancouver had been the last to document and survey the large Inlet he called the Jervis and had once thought to be the fabled Northwest Passage. Now the Jervis was going to be fully explored and documented by Captain Richards and the crew of the *HMS Plumper*. The *Plumper* had just returned from San Francisco's Mare Island, where repairs to her wood and copper hull had been completed. The repairs were required because the ship had run aground three times prior to 1860, twice near Waldron Island and again at the Nanaimo coaling station. After the last episode the ship had been purposely put on shore. Earlier it had hit an underwater rock near the wharf which had caused substantial damage to the hull, and there was fear that the ship would sink. So the *Plumper* was beached and laid on her side for nearly a month until repairs were made and she could finally be re-floated. However, the copper sheath around the hull had been compromised and was still in need of immediate attention.[xviii] It is interesting to note that while the American and English nations were at a mutual stand-off concerning the San Juan Island boundary issue, the *Plumper* was allowed to sail to the American port at Mare Island in San Francisco for repairs. This may have been a gesture of good will by the Americans to help a ship in a very remote piece of the world.

The repaired *Plumper* returned to the Pacific Northwest and to her surveying duties, and on July 2, 1860, the ship steamed up the Jervis Inlet and weighed anchor at the head of the Inlet to drop off the first team. Second Lieutenant Richard C. Mayne, Dr. Wood, and five Sechelt guides began their mission, as directed by Lieutenant Governor Douglas, to explore the country between the Jervis Inlet and the upper Fraser River. The river at the end of the Jervis was called the Laakine River then, and the Sechelts, hired by Mayne, were reluctant to travel in that direction. The natives had indicated that the terrain was too difficult and the flow of the river would be too fast for the group to follow at that time of the year and they suggested an alternative route to Howe Sound. Second Lieutenant Mayne did not pay any attention to them and began on his journey up the river only to be turned back for the exact reasons the native guides had raised.

At the same time the Galley was doing a quick survey of the area in preparation for another crew to take on the challenge of the detailed survey of the inlet. During the course of 1860 there was an exchange of letters between Captain Richards and his superiors at the Admiralty in England concerning the Jervis Inlet. It seems that Captain Richard's superiors felt the Jervis Inlet should be given a low priority among the survey assignments of British Columbia, because of its remoteness and lack of resources.[xix] Captain Richards disagreed with this assessment, but was nevertheless ordered to go to the Puget Sound region, after dropping off Second Lieutenant Mayne's group, in order to observe the coming eclipse at the lower latitudes. However, Captain Richards wisely organized two additional survey parties to spend a month doing the detail survey of the Jervis Inlet region at the same time. This would not compromise the orders and obligations required of him as a Captain in the Royal Navy, but would still enable him to complete the survey of the British Columbia coast in an area he considered important.

Lieutenant Daniel Pender was put in charge of the first survey party and was ordered to focus on the upper reach of the Inlet from Vancouver Bay to the head of the Jervis. Lieutenant Pender had just become senior assistant-surveyor, after the man who held the rank previously had died. He and two members of the crew were given 30 day provisions and were assigned to the *Shark*. The *Plumper* then steamed down to Vancouver Bay where another party, commanded by Lieutenant Bedwell, was also provided with 30 days worth of provisions and was detached in the Gig to explore and survey the lower portions of the Jervis.

Two days after the *Plumper* departed for Puget Sound, and following their failed attempt to hike up the trail from the head of the Jervis, Lieutenant Mayne and Dr. Wood paddled with the Sechelts in their canoes down the Inlet to the Sechelt village, TSOHNYE, at Deserted Bay. The party had met Lieutenant Pender of the *Shark* about midpoint down the Inlet and had followed him down to the settlement. Second Lieutenant Mayne conveyed his disappointment in the conduct of the Sechelts to his friend Daniel Pender, and was glad to be in the company of his shipmates. He had described to his friends the reluctance the native guides expressed concerning the trek up the river and that he had to use threats and insults to motivate the group. Second Lieutenant Mayne was still skeptical as to whether the surveyors would be able to perform their task with any help from the natives. The next day Lieutenant Pender and his crew of the *Shark* bid farewell to their companions, as they began their trek toward Howe Sound, feeling all the while that they were lucky not to be a part of Second Lieutenant Mayne's overland expedition.

They were right, for the first day that Second Lieutenant Mayne and his company climbed up the Deserted River they gained 4000 feet in elevation. The whole trip was filled with adventure, challenge, and many hardships both for the Sechelts and the Englishmen. According to Second Lieutenant Mayne they endured snow, mosquitoes, rain, thunder and lightning, all during July. The English also experienced first hand the Sechelt fear of the supernatural, specifically of thunder and lighting:

"the rain fell in torrents, putting out their fire, and drenching them thoroughly: and though I dozed off again their idea of supernatural agency in thunder and lighting kept them awake all night; and whenever I was aroused by a particularly loud clap or bright flash than usual, I heard their shouts of terror or excitement mingling the thunders reverberation."[xx]

However, his perception of the Sechelts would change as the trek wore on. The supplies of flour and other eating essentials began to get low, causing concern for the Second Lieutenant as he faced the challenge of not having enough food to sustain the whole group. In typical Sechelt good-natured fashion, the guides suggested to the Second Lieutenant and the doctor that they should have the food and that they, the Sechelts, would fend for themselves. The natives sustained themselves on the berries and other plants of the area for the rest of the trip. Realistically, the native guides probably did not care for the unfamiliar English food and were content with what Mother Nature provided. However, to Second Lieutenant Mayne, this stood out as a very 'favorable trait' for a native, showing unselfish concern for another individual, particularly an Englishman. This was considered to be a respectable act in Victorian society and left a very positive impression on the young Second Lieutenant concerning this First Nation band.

While Second Lieutenant Mayne was involved with his trek overland, Lieutenant Pender and the small crew of the *Shark* continued their survey of the upper portions of the inlet. They spent the month at the head of the Jervis and worked their way

down to Vancouver Bay. This was the dividing line for
Lieutenant Bedwell, who was ordered to survey the lower and
most southern reaches of the Jervis. It is obvious that
Lieutenant Pender and his crew were greatly affected by this
area, for it is not coincidence that they would name the many
mountains, waterways, and other aspects the Inlet after royalty, particularly after the current sovereign of England, Queen
Victoria and her family.

Unfortunately the original survey notebooks of Lieutenant
Pender and Lieutenant Bedwell were discarded after the chart
was finished, as it was customary not to keep their 'rough
notes.' This is regrettable, as would have been fascinating to
read. Nevertheless, some idea of the work and the many tasks
this crew had to perform in order to get an accurate survey can
be surmised from a publication Second Lieutenant Mayne
wrote many years later. It was a textbook on how to conduct a
hydrographic survey and presents many of the methods used
during the Jervis Inlet and the Pacific Northwest surveys, along
with others around the world.

The idea behind a survey was to get accurate and detailed data
transferred onto a flat piece of paper. This was done with a pen-
cil and paper and in the head of the surveyor, who used mathematics as his data language. A series of triangles were used to
calculate the distance of a point, as well as the height or elevation, as the formulas used could calculate the unknown
lengths. It was a very efficient, exact, and quick way to record
these types of surveys. First the base of the first triangle was
constructed as a center point and a measured line was pulled to
create the base of the triangle. A number of other instruments
were used to help determine the accuracy of the adjacent side
of that triangle, including sextants, telemeters, theodolites, and
micrometers, all cutting edge technology of the nineteenth century. Everything within this triangle was sketched in detail to
include the contours of the shoreline, islands, rocks, reefs, and
points that a ship's captain would need to know in order to nav-

igate through the area. At times it was necessary for Pender and his crew to climb the hills to observe and sketch these details. These many high vantage points also helped the accuracy for detailing the surveys. The triangles gave the crew references for making soundings of the Inlets. This was the method used at Jervis, as the 1861 chart of the Jervis shows the lines of depth levels in an angular format. The soundings were done by a knotted rope which measured in fathoms, which are calculated in six foot intervals, and a lead sinker. The crewman threw the lead weight away from the boat, letting it sink until it went slack. The measurement was noted in the book and the rope was pulled up to the surface and the sounding was repeated. Tides were also noted, but not on the chart. They were detailed instead as part of the table in another navigation book, where they had measured a strong nine knot current at the narrows.

Bedwell and Pender's crews were picked up by the *Plumper* at a prearranged time in mid-August of 1860, off Texada Island. The actual amount of time it took to complete the Jervis Inlet chart is not known, but it was drafted during the 'off season' during the winter of 1860, while the ship was moored at their base in Esquimalt. The soundings, points, triangulation, and other miscellaneous information listed and noted in their sketchbooks were transferred graphically (by hand) onto the actual chart, which was then sent to England by the periodic supply ship and was published by the Royal Engraver in the summer of 1861. It is not clear whether any specific individual made the decision, or if it was a consensus of the captain and his officers, to name the features of the area after royalty. But at least a clue about how Richards felt about the area can be gleaned from a passage written about the Jervis and Princess Louisa Inlets, where he states "Strikingly grand and magnificent' per the 1898 Sailing Pilot[xxi] (the marine navigational instruction book produced along with the chart). Regardless who made the decision, the names of the area surveyed were those of Queen Victoria and her immediate family. The arms of the Jervis were named for the Queen and her first two children

The Royal Navy Survey Map Engraving
of the Jervis Inlet (1860)

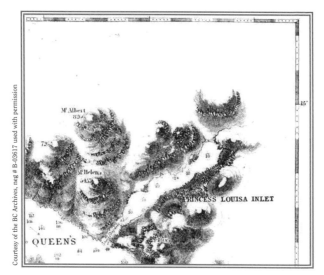

Courtesy of the BC Archives, neg # B-03617 used with permission

The Detail of Princess Louisa Inlet (1860)

(Queens Reach, Princess Royal Reach, and the Prince of Wales Reach). The high mountains around the head of the Jervis Inlet were given to Queen Victoria's additional children, Princess Alice (Mt. Alice), Prince Alfred (Mt. Alfred), Princess Victoria (Mt. Victoria), Prince Albert (Mt. Albert), and Princess Helena (Mt. Helena). Patrick Point is named after another son, Prince Arthur William Patrick Albert. Mt Fredrick William was named for the Princess's Royal German husband (also known as Fritz and son of the first German Kaiser Wehilm II) and Mt. Wellington was named after Arthur Wellesley, duke of Wellington, the Iron Duke, and the Victor of Waterloo. Princess Louisa Inlet was named for Princess Louise Caroline Alberta[xxii].

The publication and distribution of this chart showed mariners how to navigate and how to arrive at this remote and beautiful part of British Columbia, and was a most useful tool which introduced new settlers, trappers, loggers, and many other people to the inlet in the years to come.

ENDNOTES

i   Puget, *Log Book of Discovery*, page 54. First entry for June 16, 1792.

ii   Meany, *Vancouver's Discovery of Puget Sound.* Page 199.

iii   *Ibid.* Page 200.

iv   *Ibid.* Page 201.

v   *Ibid.*

vi   Puget, *Log Book of Discovery*, page55. Last entry for June 16, 1792.

vii   Peterson, *The Story of the Sechelt Nation*, pages 15 & 32. HUHNAHTCHIN was the Sechelt's name of a village and band at the head of Jervis Inlet.

viii   Puget, *Log Book of Discovery*, page 56. Last entry for June 18, 1792 & Peterson, *The Story of the Sechelt Nation*, page 31. Peterson indicates the Sechelt's' migrated from place to place because of seasonal, weather, and food patterns.

ix   Meany, *Vancouver's Discovery of Puget Sound.* Page 202.

x   Puget, *Log Book of Discovery*, page 56. The last entry along with a side note about the narrows for June 18, 1792.

xi   Peterson, *The story of the Sechelt Nation*, pg 32 & 41. TSOHNYE was the Sechelt's name of a main village and band located at Deserted Bay. It was a large area that ranged from the north end of Nelson Island to Princess Louisa Inlet.

xii   Meany, *Vancouver's Discovery of Puget Sound.* Page 203.

xiii   *Ibid.* Page 204.

xiv   Kendrick, *The Voyage of Sutil and Mexican 1792.* Page 130.

xv   Anonymous, *Illustrated London News*, April 10, 1849 .

xvi   Richardson, *Pig War Island*, page 147. Kaiser Wilhelm I was not the one who made the decision but rather an appointed panel of three judges that he selected that included the vice president of the Supreme Court of Berlin; a well known jurist commercial law; and Germany's expert geographer. The three took some months in seclusion going over the facts presented by the Americans and English. In the end, they decided in the American's favor.

xvii   Cecil, *Wilhelm II*, page 6. Kaiser Wilhelm I did not appreciate England and its liberal views. In fact, he was concerned and annoyed by his daughter-in-law, Vicky (Queen Victoria's oldest daughter), because of her idea and influence on his grandson (soon to be Kaiser Wilhelm II).

xviii   *HMS Plumper Log (1858 - 1861)*, Public Records Office (UK). Record Group ADM 53. Book # 6853. The Plumper is a grounded on May 9, 1858 off Waldron Is. Book # 6854 on November 29, 1858 indicates the Plumper was aground at Nanaimo near coaling wharf and from November 29 to December 3 the ship was beached in Commercial Creek to repair damaged copper. Every effort to re-float the ship was done by digging trenches under keel and to lighten ship. And on December 4, 1858 ship is a float. Book #6856: indicates the Plumper strikes another rock near Porter Pass on July 29, 1859.

xix   *Remarks Book of the HMS Plumper*. Page 485.

xx   Mayne, *Four years in British Columbia and Vancouver Island*, 1861 pg 201

xxi   Richards, *BC Pilot*, 2nd edition 1898, pg 222-223.

xxii   There have been many sources that indicate the Inlet was named after the mother of Queen Victoria, Princess Mary Louisa Victoria of Saxe-Coburg-Gotha. It would be safe to assume that the Inlet was named after the daughter, Princess Louise Caroline Alberta, rather than the mother of Queen Victoria because the officers of the HMS Plumper followed a pattern of naming the waterways and high mountains of the Jervis Inlet area after Queen Victoria's children. Also, Princess Mary Louisa's death was in 1861 after the chart had been published. However, no records during the research of this book indicate a name change after that time and nothing to indicate otherwise. Anyway the name of the Inlet remained the same regardless if the person it had been named after did change.

CHAPTER
THREE

Settlers, Societies,
and Parks
of the Inlet

The Buoy and the Entrance of Princess Louisa Inlet (2003)

"Yosemite, with a sea floor,
lay before us."

KATHRENE PINKERTON

Taken by C.W. Hitz of One Eye Images & Sound

Taken by C.W. Hitz of One Eye Images & Sound

Sailboat to Princess Louisa Inlet (2002)

The 32 foot sailboat, the *Recon*, had been waiting for about two hours outside the entrance to Princess Louisa Inlet. Bob and his crew, consisting of his wife and two boys, waited with a couple of other yachts for the tide to change and with it, the subsiding of the rapids through the narrow entrance way of the Inlet. Bob and his family were from Seattle and this trip had been six months in planning in order to visit this very spot. Bob and his wife had carefully arranged the trip to coincide with the boys school vacation and the good weather. He had heard about Princess Louisa Inlet from his many boating friends who had visited the area and talked of nothing but the Inlet's splendor. Finally, this was the summer that they themselves were able to have a boating vacation at Princess Louisa Inlet. Within in an hour, the violent white water rapids that had been raging through the shallow entrance to the Inlet had subsided to standing water, known as slack tide. 'Slack' is the term used to indicate a change in the motion and direction of the tidal cycle, in this case going from high to low. This was the window that the *Recon* and the other boats had waited for, and they began making their way safely through the narrow entrance of Princes Louisa Inlet. The water, which in the past hour had been a tidal chaos, was now amazingly motionless and flat calm. The line of boats glided one by one through the entrance of the Inlet, passing between the white and green marker buoy indicating a safe passage, and that of Forbidden Island.[i] Once passed, Bob made a sharp turn to the right (starboard) to align himself in the middle of the narrows. As the *Recon* glided through, the Malibu camp was on his port (left) side and jagged rocks lining the other side. His two small boys, engulfed by their bright orange life jackets, along with his wife, were on the bow waving to the people at Malibu, who had lined the railing of the pool's cement breakwater. They were so close that Bob thought he could almost reach out and touch them as he motored by. The *Recon* was the first in a long parade of yachts who followed his lead through the calm narrows. It was a picturesque scene, with Malibu's rustic dinning hall overlooking the pool and the entrance to the narrows. The dining hall's huge picture windows reflected the parading panorama unfolding below, with the blue sky and white cotton ball-like clouds capping off the backdrop. The small fleet then fanned out after passing through the narrow channel, with the faster motorboats pouring on the power to speed by the slower Recon. One of the boats flew the triangular pennant of the Princess Louisa International Society, indicating that they were a member of the group of committed yachters that had maintained the end of the Inlet for many years until the BC Park System took it over. The *Recon* quickly reached the center of the Inlet, marked by MacDonald Island. As they passed by, Bob saw a number of boats tied up at the yellow floats that had been placed there by the Parks Department some years before. He could also see a small park which bordered Malibu's Base Camp property on the side of the Inlet opposite the camp, including picnic tables and rest rooms for the weary seafarers to stretch their sea legs. "Maybe on the return" Bob thought to himself as he continued on his course to the falls. As they rounded the last canyon, his whole family gasped at the sight in front of them. A large canyon wall on their port side over-shadowed the termination of the Inlet. But the canyon seemed to wrap around and follow the contour of the shoreline. This landscape was vast with colors of green and gray, each repre-senting variations of the evergreen trees and the sheer granite rock. In the middle of this round vista was a single, massive waterfall. Bob noticed how loud it was even from a couple of miles away. Bob's family could also see the water originating from the top of the falls, hundreds of feet above them, where his boys were pointing. They could also see small boats con-verging at what appeared to be a dock. However, the boats turned out to not be all that small once they neared the wharf. There were motorboats and sailboats of all sizes and from all points of the world moored here. Fortunately, with the help of the park ranger, they were able to shoehorn into a spot in order to tie up. After securing the boat and talking with the Park Ranger, hearing some of the history of the Inlet and Chatterbox Falls and getting some safety pointers, the family decided to go exploring. They walked along a defined path that took them past a triangular shaped covered fire pit currently being used by a group of yachters enjoying their afternoon meal. Then they found a plaque commemorating the original members of the Princess Louisa International Society and the person that gave the property to the Society, a man named MacDonald. The boys were running ahead of Bob and his wife who had to stop to read the plaque, and they had to hurry to catch up. Then there it was, right up close, Chatterbox Falls, flowing at such a tremendous speed and creating the loud roar for which it had received its name. The water seemed to sparkle in the late afternoon sunlight. Bob knew, at that instant, that this trip at been worthwhile, as he snapped a pic-ture with his camera and relaxed.

Taken by C.W. Hitz of One Eye Images & Sound

The End of Princess Louisa Inlet
and Chatterbox Falls (2002)

SETTLERS

Since the initial survey conducted by Captain Richards and the crew of the *HMS Plumper* in 1860, Princess Louisa Inlet would slowly be visited and eventually settled. However, the majority of the non-native people who came to live at the Inlet were either running away from society, or were involved in some sort of business venture such as logging, fishing, trapping, or mining. Those running away took to the Inlet by either buying the land or by living on it without any legal right. Many of these people lived and worked off the land in order to survive, similar to the natives who had lived in the area many years before. They would hunt, fish, and trap for food and sell the excess to earn money to purchase items they needed that nature could not provide. Of these settlers, there were three that made their mark on the history of Princess Louisa Inlet. The Johnstone Family and their son, Steve Johnstone, a German immigrant named Herman Casper, and the most famous settler at Princess Louisa, James F. MacDonald, known simply as Mac.

The first recorded settler of Princess Louisa Inlet was a Mr. Charles Roscoe Johnstone who filed for a pre-emption on the north shore of Princess Louisa Inlet of Lot L4211 in 1910. He built a primitive house and garden to support his family. The house Charles built is in the area of the current park near MacDonald Island called the Foreshore, and close to where Malibu's Beyond Base camp now resides. It was a one room shake cabin with an open fire in the center, a double bed in one corner, and benches for their many children to sleep on scattered throughout the rest of the room. Charles had married his wife, Dora Ida, in Montana some years back and already had four children: Judd, Frank, Steve, and Ruth. The family continued to grow at their new home in the heart of Princess Louisa Inlet with the births of Jack, Ivan, Bruce, and Catherine (Kate). Sadly, Ivan died in the flu epidemic of 1918 and was buried at the entrance of Princess Louisa Inlet where Malibu now stands.[ii] It was not an easy life for the Johnstones, but it was an ideal situation for them, as they preferred to lived away from the modern world. They adopted the local native way of living and opted to follow many of the same traditions and methods the local Sechelt First Nation band had mastered centuries before. For example, the family often traveled through Princess Louisa Inlet and the Jervis using only dugout canoes they had fashioned in the same design used by the local natives. Paddling a canoe could, at times, be a little difficult, particularly at wintertime when the Inlet would freeze. Fresh water from Chatterbox Falls would reside above the salt water, only to freeze solid and cause the Johnstones to drag their boats across the ice till they reached clear water near the entrance of the narrows. If the winter was particularly harsh, the whole family would move down to the slate quarry, directly across the Jervis from the entrance of Princess Louisa Inlet at the foot of Mt. Arthur, for better shelter. When hunting, they liked the weapon of the bow and arrow, as it was easy to use, light, quiet, and cheap. But at times, the old .44 buffalo gun came in handy in times of emergencies, or out of sheer necessity. They would have a few visitors from time to time and some were welcomed as guests, while other were to be avoided. The unwelcome company came on the mail boat once a year, and sometimes the police or a timber ranger would be along doing their regular patrol. In a couple of instances, a truant official was on board looking for the Johnstone's children, because by Canadian law, they were supposed to be in school. The parents would hide the children until the official gave up looking for them. On most occasions, yachters would pay visits to the Johnstones, who would entertained their guests the best they could. In the summer of 1916, the 75-foot schooner the *"La Viajern"* out of Seattle made a stop to visit Princess Louisa Inlet.[iii] The Johnstone family acted as guides for hunting trips pursuing mountain goat, deer, and bear throughout the inlet. In the evenings, the visitors of the *La Viajern* were entertained by the

Courtesy of Marge Anderson – Used with Permission

Ray Anderson, Steve Johnson, Marge Anderson, Twila
Martinson, Nancy Hanson, & Henning Martinson (1957)
(From left to right)

stories of Johnstone's life at Princess Louisa Inlet. They were amazed at the Johnstone's self sufficiency, and at the good prices they received for the hides they sold. The Johnstones were all excellent hunters. They had to be in order to survive. To hone their hunting skills, Charles would sometimes have his sons go on 'wild man' hunts high into the mountains.[iv] They would go out for a week with nothing but some ammunition, matches, salt, a blanket, and the clothes they wore. The Johnstone family lived at Princess Louisa Inlet until the end of World War One, moving only when they began to feel crowded by a new logging camp moving in at Dessert Bay and another family, Charlie and Ethel Whittaker from Washington State, established themselves near Patrick Point on the Queen's Reach side of the Jervis inlet and began to hand-log the area. The Johnstones did not like close company, and the Whittaker's became permanent residents, remaining for nearly 40 years. The Johnstones moved up to Alaska, only to come back to the Sunshine Coast area some years later.

However, when the Johnstone's left, not all of the family went with them. Steve Johnstone had decided to stay at the Inlet and to live as he always had. He lived like a hermit, living on what nature provided in the way of animals, fishing, and various vegetation, and would trade for clothes and other hard-to-get food items from yachters and at Malibu. When Young Life took over Malibu, Steve took a liking to Potato chips and crushed pineapple, for which he traded logs he had peeled, which were used for the repair of the camp.[v] Steve first lived in a small shack between Malibu and MacDonald Island. He later moved into an abandoned cabin located on the opposite side of the Inlet from Malibu, originally the Canadian Government constructed a house for an official to live in while recording the tides. He would fish for salmon by rowing his boat with the fishing line wrapped around his waist and dragging behind him. When he felt a tug, he would bring in the fish hand over hand. He also continued trapping at Princess Louisa Inlet for food, selling the fur. But when his traps were not producing, he would cut firewood or work as a caretaker for the Gustavson's Lumber camp down at Deserted Bay. It was noticed that Steve was a little bit peculiar. He would go barefoot for most of the winter and on one instance he blew a hole in the floor of the shack while trying to kill a rat with a shotgun. He would take his yearly trip to Vancouver BC and returned wearing lipstick and nail polish on his fingers and toes.[vi] Unfortunately, in 1969, during one of his excursions to Vancouver, Steve was killed by a car while he was crossing the street.[vii]

Courtesy of Young Life – Used with Permission

Herman Casper (1957)

Princess Louisa played host to another individual, by the name of Herman Casper. Casper settled on the small strip of land where Malibu was later built. The general story of Casper states that he was a young Sergeant Major in the Kaiser's German Army during the First World War. It seems an officer started to harass Casper and it was more than he could take. Casper hit officer so hard that he knocked him out cold. At that time the punishment for hitting an officer was death, so Casper deserted and made his escape through Switzerland sometime near the end of the war. Somehow he made it to Canada and settled at Princess Louisa Inlet. Casper became a permanent fixture there , building a cabin generally known as 'Casper's Place'. This story about Casper has been told in every book related to Princess Louisa Inlet, but the real story relating to Herman Casper is somewhat different when examining the records relating to him.

On June 14^{th,} 1969, the man who settled at the Inlet, one Herman Alwin Harry Casper died at Saint Mary's Hospital in the town of Sechelt BC.^{viii} He passed away at the age of 82 and was buried in Gibson's Cemetery in an unmarked plot.^{ix} He had been a Canadian citizen for half of his life and had immigrated to Canada from Germany. Casper had actually landed in Canada at the port of Halifax on August 14th, 1928,^x where he disembarked from the steamer the S.S. *Seydlitz*, which had sailed from the German port of Bremen seven days earlier. Herman Casper was passenger number 26 on the roster and he came into the country with only $200 in hand. He had actually left his boyhood town of Frankenthal, Germany, where he had been born on February 4, 1887 to parents Moritz and Johanne Casper.^{xi} It can be assumed from the dates on the records that Casper probably had a rather rough childhood, for his mother had died when he was six years old. His father died in 1917, when Casper was approximately 30. It is not known if the man died in the war, or by disease, or old age. Regardless, Herman decided to immigrate to Canada in 1928. He had been a merchant and had decided to be a farmer in Canada with a friend in Winnipeg, Manitoba. The story of deserting and going to Switzerland are possibly false. It would be hard to substantiate that he was in the Germany Army at all, as most of the German military records of World War I were destroyed during World War II.

Although little is known about his farming venture, it is clear that it did not work out, for he ended up at Princess Louisa Inlet as a permanent resident. He probably did try farming, but it seems he may have drifted from job to job and eventually ended up in Vancouver BC. He almost certainly landed a job at a lumber camp working as a lumberman or as a cook. Prior to World War I, a German firm had set up a company in Sechelt BC where many Germans decided to stay. The German community was very tightly knit and their language was their bond. The Jervis Inlet and particularly Deserted River at Deserted Bay became a haven for German refugees during the First World War, so it is no wonder that Casper found himself in this area. As with everyone else, he fell in love with the place and set up his home. It is hard to determine how many years it took him to travel, and the exact year he settled at Princess Louisa Inlet, but most of the early publications in the 1930s describe him as already ensconced in his shack. So it would be safe to assume that Casper had settled in the early 1930s.

Courtesy of Young Life – Used with Permission

Mac (1967)

Casper was fond of cats and had many of them. Like Steve Johnstone, he lived a very quiet and hermit-like existence. However, everybody seemed to like him, for he enjoyed company and was very talented with his hands and with music. There is even a record that Mac made that is said to be Casper singing his famous 'Princess Louisa Inlet Waltz'. Actually, it was not Casper who was singing on the record, but someone else.[xii] This may have been because Casper would not have sold many records with his harsh, German-accented singing voice, so Mac had somebody else do the voice-over. In any event, most likely in Mac's typical generous style, the proceeds went to help out his friend Casper.

James Fredrick MacDonald, or 'Mac' to everyone who knew him, was a friend to Steve, Casper, and to many in the Pacific

Northwest yachting community. There have been numerous accounts written about Mac and the inlet through yachting books and magazines. The most notable book has to be M. Wylie Blanchet's 'The Curve of Time', a literary classic based on the adventures of a woman and her childrens' experiences on their boat, the *Caprice,* through the waters of British Columbia during the late 1920s and early '30s. In several sections Blanchet describes Mac as being from California, and building a cabin near their beloved Trappers Rock and the waterfall. Mac was also once a visitor to the Inlet back in 1919, and had been overwhelmed by the charm and beauty of the place.

James Fredrick MacDonald was born in Seattle on May 14, 1889 and grew up on Bainbridge Island. Mac's father died in 1893, leaving the young Mac and his mother alone. After Mac finished high school in 1908, he and a friend set out to explore the world. They would fund this adventure through lectures about the United States using color lanternslides. Admission was 50 cents and the two boys were able to fund their entire expedition of the world for a number of years. When they returned to the United States in 1910 Mac enrolled at Amherst College, only to transfer to the University of California in Berkeley and begin another trip to Europe in his junior year with a friend. While, he came to realize that the Pacific Northwest had everything to offer, times being what they were, Mac enlisted as an officer into the US Army as World War One was being waged in Europe. His training was at the Presidio in San Francisco, and he was commissioned a First Lieutenant of the 13th Infantry Regiment. He rose to the rank of captain and, when the war ended, wound up at Princess Louisa Inlet cruising with his uncle's yacht, the *Rambler,* as part of the new yachting crowd. He said that he had realized that Princess Louisa Inlet had more to offer him than most of the places he had seen or experienced through his travels around the globe but to buy his dream, he would need a large sum of money.

A number of books describe how he started working in the grocery business in the San Francisco area and eventually mining in the Pyramid Lake-Sand Pass area of the Nevada desert. However, according to one of Mac's sisters, he lived off the wealth of the family wholesale grocery business and, although his mine was legitimate, he would go there only for the picture opportunities while others did the work.[xiii] In many ways Mac and later Tom Hamilton (founder of Malibu), were one and the same when it came to promoting themselves and the Inlet. For example, Hamilton would tell folks he invented the variable pitch propeller when, in reality, he did not. Mac was the same, but in a slightly different manner. He was more of a storyteller and would 'adjust' a story to make it more interesting to his audience, even if it was not actually true. He did this most specifically when it came to native stories. They were both people who were larger than life and made the Inlet what it is today.

In 1927, Mac made a claim for a crown grant for property at the head of Princess Louisa Inlet. This was followed by a government survey of the property in question in order to assess its value. Needless to say, most of the land near the falls was vertical and the report mentioned that most the saleable trees had been logged (hand logged either by the Johnstones or the Whittakers) and assessed the value of the land to be about $420. Mac paid the amount and was recorded with the Crown Grant for lot L5385. At that time Mac renamed the falls "Chatterbox Falls" for it sounded as if it chattered all night/day long. He had achieved the dream of owning property at this place he had first visited with his uncle back in 1919.

In 1928 Mac started to design and build his home near the falls. Mr. McNaughton and his two sons from Pender Harbor built the structure, using large cedar logs, ranging in diameter from 15 to 20 inches in the construction. Mac's cabin would have a big living room, with a fireplace built of granite rocks. It also had a stairway to the second floor with two bedrooms and a bath plus lots of bookshelves, for Mac read a great deal. After the structure was completed more items were incorporated into the house, including an electrical generator. This machine would generate electricity via a hydro water wheel, where wooden pipes forced the water from a pool at the top of the falls to the generator near his house. Mac used this power for hot water and to light his cabin. He also built bridges and cut out paths for his many visitors to see the falls. Once, during the winter months when Mac wintered in Mexico, he let Steve Johnson house-sit for him. He was somewhat unsure as to whether Steve could handle the responsibility, but when Mac returned and found his cabin in good order, he felt his concern about Steve's ability had been unwarranted. That is, until he went around to the back of the cabin and found that most of the siding had been used as firewood while Steve was there over the winter months.

The actual date of completion of Mac's cabin was around 1930, and it remained until it was destroyed by fire in 1941. The story goes that Mac had married a woman from San Francisco. They honeymooned in Europe and then, while she returned to California, he went to the Inlet to ready the cabin. Mac got the cabin in order, then rented a motor launch to transport his sweetheart to the Inlet. But when they rounded the bend to where Chatterbox Falls and the cabin could be seen, all they saw were flames leaping in the air and smelled burning cedar, as his cabin was destroyed by the inferno. Their marriage ended shortly as well, and although they remained good friends it was still a bitter disappointment to Mac. To make matters worse, he could not afford another cabin and he had to settle on a float called the *Seaholm*. Like the great Captain Cook, who explored the same waters in the summer, then wintered in the warmer climates below the equator, Mac would follow the same pattern, living at the inlet in the summer and wintering down in Acapulco, Mexico.

Mac was a friend to everyone who visited him at Chatterbox Falls, especially the young. When Jim Rayburn, the founder of the non-denominational Christian Youth Association, bought Malibu in 1953, Mac became a frequent visitor to the camp. Mac would paddle over each week in his red canoe dressed as a native of the American Southwest First Nation bands, where he would put on a show for the young visitors. He would talk and entertain the students with stories of made-up native lore and demonstrate the native dances and customs of the American Southwest tribes (again, not those of the Sechelt First Nations who had been the original settlers of the area). The climax of his visit was the native fire dance, where parts of his body were lit on fire using alcohol. The last fire dance he did at Malibu was in 1971 and culminated with the curtains of the meeting lodge catching on fire.[xiv] Needless to say, safety outweighed entertainment and the fire dance ceased.

Banking over Macdonald Island and Base Camp (2003)

Mac would also come to Malibu to enjoy in one of his favorite pastimes – chess. A Young Life staff member remembered one particular time when Mac was at camp to play his favorite game and was also waiting for dinner. This particular day happened to be the day when the kids would hear about the death of Jesus. The dinner that night would be a beef stew, with the message about the death and resurrection to follow. When asked by the staff member how Mac was doing, his reply was "Stew and Sin tonight. Stew and Sin." Mac's last year at the inlet was in 1972, when he spent the entire summer as a privileged and welcomed guest at Young Life's Malibu Club. He resided in a nursing home in Seattle until his death in 1978.[xv]

THE SOCIETY AND THE PARK

The relationship between Tom Hamilton and Mac had always been a bit uneasy, especially after Mac's cabin had burned down. Tom and a hotel establishment had approached Mac to sell his property at the foot of the Chatterbox Falls shortly after the traumatic event, and Mac turned down both proposals as he felt that Hamilton had cheated him on the sale of the island back in 1940. Hamilton was a very experienced and shrewd salesman and Mac had learned this the hard way. In many ways Hamilton was focused on getting the land he wanted for his vast commercial enterprise and vision at whatever cost. All except Chatterbox Falls, which eluded him.

Mac owned that property and he wisely held onto it until 1953, the year Tom Hamilton sold Malibu to the Young Life organization. Mac felt strongly that the Inlet should be protected from any sort of commercial development and began to look for a way a way to accomplish this. He knew he couldn't do it alone and he searched for help from an outside source, approaching yachters of the Pacific Northwest, asking if they might be willing to help in this endeavor as they had a vested interest in the area as well. Mac talked specifically with many boating friends like Harold Jones, Horace McCurday, and other regular visitors to the Inlet, and the Princess Louisa International Society came into being shortly thereafter. In October, 1953, Mac deeded his property to the Princess Louisa International Society, a nonprofit organization set up under the Societies Act of British Columbia by the yachters of the Pacific Northwest, with an exchange of $100 covering the legal fees. As required by law, the Princess Louisa International Society organized an international board of directors consisting of an equal number of American and Canadian citizens, and elected officials such as a President, Vice-President, Secretary, and Treasurer. A membership structure was set up with yearly subscription fees and open donations in order to fund the non-profit society. It would be through this structure that Mac's dream and desire would be fulfilled – that Princess Louisa Inlet not be owned by one single individual, that any commercial development of the Inlet would be curbed, and that Princess Louisa Inlet would remain unspoiled for future generations to enjoy.

Close to the same time that Young Life took over the Malibu Club, the Princess Louisa International Society took over the title of Mac's property, Lot L5385 and a portion of the water surrounding Chatterbox Falls. It was recorded as gift transfer on the part of Mac, with a clause stating that in the future the Province could maintain the land as a park. There was also an unsuccessful attempt by the Society to acquire the surrounding lots (L3514, L3515, L3524, and L3525) around Chatterbox falls, but this land was to be held in reserve by the Royal Trust, after Tom Hamilton sold it because of the anticipated near and long-term future timber sales this area could provide by any future logging company. This would set the stage for an uneasy future partnership between the Society and the British Columbia Province.

Mac had a number of other ideas and tasks he wanted completed at the Inlet as part of the agreement once the society took over his deed. Mac's ideas were geared toward the benefit of those who would visit this picturesque area, for in his typical style he thought more of other people than himself when it came to the Inlet. The first on the list was for the Society to maintain the dock facilities and moorage floats around Chatterbox Falls. In 1964, even after a number of increases in the dues, the Society realized it would not have enough money to keep up the yearly maintenance of the dock and float along with all the other items Mac had on his list. So, as Mac had done ten years earlier, the Society turned to the Province of

British Columbia to seek its assistance, to see if they could help with the clause in the original transfer of Mac's property to the Society in 1958 and to contribute to the required upkeep in order to protect the Inlet from commercial development. On September 12, 1964, once again Mac's land, with his approval, was transferred to an organization in order to see the realization of his goals.

Through the Malibu Rapids at Slack Tide (1984)

This time, the recipient was the BC Provincial Government, through the Ministry of Parks, with the stipulation that the area be a public recreational area. The Princess Louisa International Society no longer owned the property, but was still to play a big role as a partner and would provide help when needed. The Society would find, however, that it would be both a blessing and a curse to have the BC Government involved. In early May 1966, a few park planners were given a tour of the Inlet. The planners were overcome with Princess Louisa Inlet and became intent on making the entire Inlet into a park. The Inlet would be the centerpiece of all the marine parks in the Province of BC and it would show the world that this Inlet was the typical fjord seen throughout the coast of British Columbia.

In an internal memo,[xvi] one of the planners on the tour, G.A. Wood, suggested that the following actions take place right away to begin the acquisition processes: first, that a detailed reconnaissance of air photos be used to define the boundaries in terms of the logging company's ownership of the land and second, to create a long-term policy of acquiring the land that Young Life's Malibu Club occupied at the entrance of the inlet. While his supervisor, R.H. Ahrens, Chief Planner, felt the proposal was a bit ambitious, he did feel it had merit. He was somewhat unclear as to the Malibu question, for he did not understand what the Society and the Parks Branch of the Land Acquisition Planning Office would do with the camp once they had acquired it. His options would be to either tear it down or to continue operating it on a limited budget.[xvii] Although it seemed unfeasible in the short term, the plan did have virtues for the long term.

During this same year, 1964, the Society and the Parks Branch expressed interest in obtaining the land known as the 'Foreshore', the flat land in front of Hamilton Island (Lot L4820, near where the Johnstones had first settled) and Lot L4211. There was an area of shallow water near the shore where a small reef and a number of rocks protruded, labeled as lot # L3534, which they were also interested in. The park did put in a number of mooring chains at the Foreshore to keep recreational boats safe and alternative moorage at Princess Louisa Inlet, but Tom Hamilton still owned all of it and he seemed intent on hanging onto the island. While many inquiries were made by agents on behalf of Young Life, and other commercial agencies, to see if Hamilton would part with his beloved island on behalf of the Society and the Park Branch, TF would not budge up until his death in 1969, when his estate was willing to sell the island and the surrounding lots of the Foreshore in an effort to liquefy most of his held assets. However, it was not until 1972 that the Society was successful in negotiating the price down to $25,000 from the original $35,000.[xviii]

By 1975 the Princess Louisa International Society was halfway through paying off the foreshore property (Lots L3530, L4820, L3534, and L4212) with the help of generous donations by Society members and friends. Once the property was debt free, the island was renamed MacDonald Island after the original owner – Mac.

MacDonald Memorial Cover (2003)

By 1975, the Parks Branch of British Columbia still maintained its policy of making Princess Louisa Inlet a marine and public park, with their specific goals of recreation and natural history to help preserve the Inlet in its natural state. But the huge BC timber conglomerate of the MacMillan and Bloedel Logging Company had acquired all the land around the inlet from Tom Hamilton in 1958, with the exception of that owned by Young Life and the Park Branch. The land at Princess Louisa Inlet was now part of the large BC lumber company's Tree Farm #19 and the Society and the Park Branch were concerned that they were about to harvest most of the worthwhile timber in the area. Obviously this would affect the Inlet both visually and audibly, so to curb this commercial rape of the land, the Parks Branch tried unsuccessfully to make Princess Louisa Inlet into a national park of Canada. This proposal was rejected by the

Canadian National Parks Board in 1973.[xix] Undeterred, the Parks Branch then proposed a new plan, focusing instead on offering an exchange of timber from the Garibaldi Park near Round Mountain to the lumber company in place of the land around Princess Louisa Inlet.[xx] However, a leading director of the Parks Department killed this plan outright and would not address the exchange and destruction of one area of public land in order to protect another.[xxi] In the end the Parks Department had to work with MacMillan and Bloedel on developing a logging plan which would best minimize the impact to the Inlet.

The Society felt betrayed, and this frustration would be expressed in a meeting between the Parks branch and the Princess Louisa International Society in Victoria, BC on January 10, 1975. The frustration may have been due in part due to the Parks Branch's ambitious policies, or its failure to curb the large lumber company from cutting trees out of the Inlet. It also could have included the barrier of bureaucracy in communicating with the BC Provincial government that non-profit organizations frequently encounters, especially when dealing with tax issues. But this dissatisfaction manifested itself over the Parks Branch's inability to handle simple tasks, like trash and major debris disposal after winter storms and during the summer months, for mounds of trash were noticed throughout the year. It was made all too clear by one of the Society's well-known members and officer, Bruce Calhoun, who stated firmly that he would oppose the sale of any more land (including the foreshore property) to the BC park system and he also expressed his profound regret that the Society had turned over Mac's land in the first place. Nevertheless, the Parks Branch and the Princess Louisa International Society prevailed throughout the many ups and downs of their partnership to continue to support the goals that Mac had penciled out many years before.

This partnership has been instrumental in seeing Mac's wishes related to the Inlet made a reality. Another of Mac's ideas was to have a covered camping area for yachters who were tired of the boat, especially during the rainy deluges common at the inlet. In 1970, George Heideman, an architect from Seattle and an avid yachter, designed a shelter with a native teepee motif to fit in with the natural surroundings. It was built on the site where Mac's cabin had originally stood. Heideman's design featured an octagonal-shaped building with eight cedar logs supporting the structure, and four closed sides alternating with four open sides around a stone base. Additionally it featured a sunken fire pit. It was built by John Bosch of Egmont, BC in 1972, and later donated by the Society to the Parks Department as a gift. Following Mac's death in 1978, it was renamed the MacDonald Memorial Lodge.

Taken by C.W. Hitz, One Eye Images & Sound

Mac's Memorial Plaque
at Chatterbox Falls (2003)

Finally Mac's specific wish to keep the Inlet untouched by commercial endeavors was close to being accomplished. The Weyerhaeuser Company, who bought out the MacMillan and Bloedel company and acquired its vast amounts of timberland throughout BC, including Princess Louisa Inlet, offered the Society the land around Chatterbox Falls, and was prepared to donate an additional lot to the Society if they could raise an unspecified sum by December 31, 2002. The board of the Princess Louisa International Society realized they would come up short and, once again, wisely sought the help of an outside organization with the resources and means to help in this large undertaking. The Nature Conservancy of Canada was the group selected to help with this task. Like the Princess Louisa International Society, the Nature Conservancy of Canada is a non-profit organization with the purpose of preserving important environmental parcels of land like old growth forests, native salmon streams, ecological wetlands and such throughout Canada. It was to be a perfect partnership, The Nature Conservancy of Canada and the Princess Louisa Inlet Society, who combined to obtain the necessary funds for this endeavor. In time the two groups hope to own the remainder of the land not owned by Young Life throughout the Inlet.

Today, the Princess Louisa International Society is working even harder to see that Mac's wishes are carried out, not just for his sake, but because of his ideals, and his desire to protect and share the inlet he loved. Although Mac is gone, the Princess Louisa International Society is an extension of James F. MacDonald himself, and has striven to support his wishes for the Inlet. The Society is doing a great job in achieving these goals, along with their partners, the Parks Department of BC and The Nature Conservancy of Canada. In tribute, the Society dedicated a memorial to James F. MacDonald by at Chatterbox Falls. It is a granite rock pillar with a copper relief of Mac's profile, and below it a plaque reads:

"James Frederick MacDonald
1889-1978
Laird of the Inlet
Gentleman
Friend to all who came here

Whose monument is this place
of beauty given by him to the
yachting fraternity of the Pacific

Northwest so that it will remain forever unspoiled."

Underneath both plaques is a circular plug of rock that was cut out so Mac's ashes could be interred symbolizing the steps he took to make sure that the place he loved would remain unchanged forever.

ENDNOTES

i   Petterson, *The Story of the Sechelt Nation*, page 62. The Sechelts would bury their dead in caves, trees, and the many small islands that are found around the Jervis Inlet, including the island at the entrance of Princess Louisa Inlet. Sadly, this site and others have been desecrated over the years by hand loggers and trappers who started appearing in this area after 1861. In 1954, Young Life was asked by the Canadian Authorities not to 'set foot' on this island for the reasons stated. Young Life has since called it 'Forbidden Island' in name and purpose – it is forbidden to go there!

ii BC Death Certificate – Reg# 1919-09-248571 for Ivan Johnstone. BC Archives Micro #B13115 & GSU# 1927143. Ivan was 13 when he died from complications of the flu epidemic of 1918. Ivan was buried near where Malibu was built. Properly, He would have buried him somewhere further back towards the rock fall and trees to keep animals and weather away from the grave site. At present, the grave has not been found.

iii Moss, *A Cruise into the Yachtsman's Paradise*, The Argus, Dec 1913. Page 32.

iv Southern, *The Nelson Island Story*. Page 65.

v   Campbell, *Young Life's Malibu*, pages 114-117.

vi Keller & Leslie, *Bright Seas, Pioneer Spirits*. Page 124.

vii *Ibid.*, No death certificate was found for Steve and the date or place can not be confirmed of his death. It is possible that he was listed as a John Doe by the BC authorities, for he may have not been carrying any identification at the time of accident. There have been other stories associated with Steve's death that place him at other places around the Sunshine Coast, but each collaborate he was hit by a car that killed him.

viii BC Death Certificate #69-09-009097 of Herman Alwin Harry Casper on June 14, 1969.

ix Located at Gibson BC Seaview Cemetery, unmarked grave site #72-A.

x   National Archives of Canada, microfilm roll #T-14816, Vol 11, page 200, Passenger List into Halifax 8/14/1928. Herman Casper is number #26 on passenger manifest.

xi Richter, Landkreis Bautzen Landratsamt, November 24, 1998, communication with a Mr. Richter indicating the various records related to the birth and occupation of Herman Casper and his parents plus sibling.

xii Schweizer, *Beyond Understanding*. Pages 212-220. An interview transcript between Schweizer and Norman Blanchard (a long time boat builder and enthusiast in the Seattle, WA area. Mr. Blanchard's boat yard built the yacht the 'Malibu' used by Tom Hamilton, as described in Chapter 4 of this book).

xiii *Ibid.* Page 212

xiv As witnessed by a number of people interviewed about Malibu's history. In particular, a former Young Life staff person who had to put out the flames, said it was a very serious situation since Malibu is a wood structure.

xv WA State Death Certificate #13020 for James F. MacDonald on June 5, 1978 and the Seattle Times Article announcing his death on June 8, 1978.

xvi BC Archives Collection # GR 1614, Box 27, file # 1-7-2-20: memo #1-1-2-20, dated May 26, 1966 to Mr. G.F. Macnab of the Lands Acquisition Planning Office (Parks Branch) from R.H. Ahrens, Chief Planner. Subject is Princess Louisa Inlet. There are two copies of this memo, the first is the original and the second is a photocopy with hand-written remarks made by Mr. Macnab.

xvii *Ibid.*

xviii *Ibid*, memo #2-7-2-20, January 13, 1975, from the Office of the Director, Parks Branch – Department of Recreation and Conservation by R.H. Ahrens (Acting Director). The minutes from the January 10, 1975 meeting between the Provincial Parks Branch and the Princess Louisa International Society in Victoria BC. Key points of the meeting were the acquisition of the Hamilton property by the Society and the dissatisfaction with the standard of maintenance of the park at Chatterbox Falls.

xix *Ibid*, last paragraph of meeting minutes where the National Parks Board of Canada did not have interest in making Princess Louisa Inlet a national park.

xx *Ibid*, memo #1-7-2-20-20, June 25, 1979, from G.F. MacNab, Manager Planning Section of the BC Ministry of Lands Parks and Housing (Parks and Outdoor Recreation Division), to G. Trachuk, Acting Director Planning and Design Branch: subject – timber Exchange- MacMillan & Bloedel. The memo contains the arguments, analysis, and recommendation for this exchange.

xxi *Ibid*, memo#2-7-2-20-20, August 8, 1979, from G.F. MacNab, Manager Planning Section of the BC Ministry of Lands Parks and Housing (Parks and Outdoor Recreation Division), to J.C. Leman, Regional Manager Lower Mainland Region. The memo informed subordinates that the swap-of-land deal was stopped. Also attached were the meeting minutes, #2-7-3-1-20 on June 26, 1979, where this decision was made.

CHAPTER

FOUR

Tom Hamilton and the Malibu Resort

Original
Hamilton
Totem Pole
and One Eye
Mt. (2003)

*"After all I have a certain amount of Canadian
in me, some of the first propellers I made
were in Vancouver, and my mother was
Canadian-born. I have a great interest in
Canada and I believe this resort will introduce
many influential Americans to this country."* [i]

TOM HAMILTON (1941)

Courtesy of Young Life – Used with Permission

The Malibu (1940)

"You can't leave until you have seen Princess Louisa Inlet" said an insistent Bill Boeing to Tom Hamilton and his family. The Hamiltons, along with the Boeings, were on vacation, cruising the waters of British Columbia (BC) on their newly purchased yacht, the Malibu. Boeing also owned a luxurious yacht called the *Taconite*. The boat was named after the mineral that made his father wealthy, creating the fortune which he had inherited. The *Taconite* and the *Malibu* were moored together near Campbell River, BC and the families were having a pleasant dinner on the *Taconite* at the invitation of Mr. Boeing. Although the Hamiltons were coming close to the end of their vacation cruise, they agreed to Mr. Boeing's suggestion regarding the side excursion to Princess Louisa Inlet and the next day both yachts set a course for the Jervis Inlet, arriving the following afternoon with the weather in their favor. As they entered Princess Louisa Inlet it was Ethel Hamilton, Tom Hamilton's wife, who fell in love with the area right away, particularly the small island halfway down the inlet. Tom is reported to have said "it's yours" and with those words, started something which would impact Princess Louisa Inlet for decades to come.

Courtesy of Elizabeth Hamilton Sunde – Used with Permission

Tom & Ethel Hamilton at Malibu (1946)

THOMAS F. HAMILTON

Thomas Foster Hamilton, TF or Tommy to his friends and family, was born on July 28, 1894 in Seattle, Washington. He was the oldest child of his parents, Thomas Luther & Henrietta Hamilton, and big brother to Edgar Charles Hamilton born a year later. Tom Hamilton's early interests included aviation, which began when he was approximately 10 years old. During the 1909 Alaskan-Yukon Exposition held in Seattle on the site of present-day University of Washington, the young Hamilton, now at the age of 14, had a job repairing hot-air balloons. This job would also allow him to ride what he repaired, possibly a type of insurance policy to ensure the balloons were fixed properly, which helped fuel his continuing interest in aviation. Also during this time, Tom and a school friend, Paul J. Palmer, established a partnership and called their company 'Hamilton and Palmer.' Their office and factory were located in their respective parents' garages and on kitchen tables. The two built and experimented with various biplane glider designs of the time, creating working craft which they tested themselves.

In 1910, after finishing their experiments with the gliders the two moved on to building propeller-driven aircraft and at this point, there was a disagreement between Palmer and Hamilton. The former was no longer involved with the company and was totally removed from the partnership, causing Tom to change the name of the company to the 'Hamilton Aero Manufacturing company.' In 1911 Hamilton teamed up with Ted Geary, a young yacht designer, (later to design and build Hamilton's *Malibu*) in order to create a number of unique seaplane designs. The total number of known aircraft built by Hamilton's Seattle Company is estimated to be around 10 to 25, built from 1909 to 1914. Unfortunately, the exact number is not known. His planes used the standard designs of the era, along with his own unique ideas incorporated into each aircraft.

Courtesy of Elizabeth Hamilton Sunde – Used with Permission

Tom Hamilton at the Controls
of his Early Aircraft (1910)

Those early years for Tom Hamilton were very much building years for this remarkable individual. Even at an early age he was able to comprehend and build complicated flying machines. Although he dropped out of high school and had no additional formal education, he was able to manufacture and sell these aircraft, all before he was 16 years old. The Seattle Times newspaper reporters referred to him as the 'Whiz Kid' when it came to aircraft. During this time, while Hamilton's company was going strong, he became acquainted with another aviation fan, Bill Boeing. Their friendship was to last throughout the years, both personally and professionally. Hamilton also is recorded to have played a significant role in the creation of the Boeing Company by introducing Boeing to Conrad Westervelt, a young Navy Lieutenant Commander who would later become a direct partner, at a club in Seattle in 1914, the same year Boeing took his first flight with Eddie Maroney in his Curtis Hydroplane on July 4th.

Not only was 1914 important in aviation history as the beginning of the Boeing Company, it was also a pivotal year for Hamilton. That year a number of wealthy businessmen from Vancouver, BC approached him for a specific and urgent reason. They were looking for someone to build airplanes for the non-profit and private 'BC Aviation School Ltd.' that would teach their Canadian sons to fly in the Great War (World War I) which was being fought over in Europe. Tom accepted the invitation and immediately moved his whole operation up to Vancouver, BC, and established the 'Hamilton Aero Manufacturing Ltd.' The contract was to build four planes to be used for training purposes in the school. However, only one airplane out of the four contracted was ever completed, because the only biplane, patterned after a Curtis tractor design with two seats, a six-cylinder engine and a tricycle landing gear, crashed in a muddy field outside of Vancouver after only a few months of training students. Prior to the destruction of the aircraft, however, out of the 12 students training to fly at the school, two were able to graduate and went on to fight in the war with the RFC (Royal

Flying Corps, the precursor to the RAF). The rest were integrated into other aviation training programs and transferred to the war. In the meantime, Tom Hamilton had become very interested in the physics of propellers and had begun making inquiries about his possible involvement in the war effort for the United States. His timing was excellent, as it was 1917 and the U.S. had just entered the war and the need was great for experienced people to help the country establish an aviation industry in order to support the overseas effort.

From the collection of C.W. Hitz

"The Maiden Milwaukee" The Hamilton Metalplane H-18
at the Ford Air Races (1927)
(Tom Hamilton is nearest the wing)

The US military was interested in Tom Hamilton's aviation background, and requested that he come out east and work in a company that produced propellers for the government. At that time the US military kept most of their aviation resources close to Washington, D.C. and not in the remote part of the Pacific Northwest where Boeing was established. A Milwaukee, Wisconsin woodworking firm, the 'Matthews Brothers Furniture Company,' was in need of an experienced person to run their new aviation division, as they had just signed a large military contract to produce wood propellers for the Navy and

Army air forces, so Tom Hamilton left the Vancouver, BC operation and became the Matthews Brothers Furniture Company director of aviation in 1918. However, once the war ended, Tom bought their entire inventory of wood propellers and again started his own company, the 'Hamilton Aero Manufacturing Company' in Milwaukee, Wisconsin. Tom was still only in his twenties and around this time he met and married his secretary, Ethel Inez Hughes, a Milwaukee native. The Hamilton family spent the next ten years in Milwaukee raising their four children; Ethel Mary, Kathryn (Kitten), Tom Luther Hamilton II, and Lawrence (Larry). During this period TF not only began his family, but also managed to help establish Milwaukee as one of the nation's major aviation hubs and continue his life's work in aviation.

The pattern of Tom's life had been established. At the beginning of his time in Milwaukee, propellers and sea-plane pontoons were made of wood. The material created some serious problems, from decaying due to exposure to seawater to propeller disintegrating at certain speeds. Tom Hamilton once again was in the forefront of the industry, being one of the first to use the new aluminum metal 'Duralumin.' In 1927, once again on the cutting edge, he produced one of the first all-metal aircraft, called the Hamilton Metalplane H-18, christened the 'Maiden Milwaukee,' or sometimes known as the 'Made-in Milwaukee'. The Maiden was built by another company Hamilton had set up in 1927, called the 'Hamilton Metalplane Company.' And it did well, winning several prestigious air awards plus earning the distinction of being the first US all-metal plane air certificate in the United States. It also was the first plane ever to be designed to haul mail in addition to passengers, maximizing the revenue for the airline(s), and it was cheaper to build than its major competitor, the Ford Motor Company's Tri-Motor known as the 'Tin-Goose,' since Hamilton's plane used products produced in Hamilton's other factory. Over the life of the company, Hamilton produced probably 27 to 40 aircraft but although his product was superior, it was outstripped by the Ford Motor

Company's marketing ability which claimed it was safer to fly with three engines than one.

A saving grace for the Metalplane Company came in the establishment of a 1929 holding company called 'United Aircraft and Transport Company' (UA&T), which was formed by a number of well-known aviation executives such as Mr. Boeing of the Boeing Company in Seattle, WA, Mr. Fred Rentschler of the Pratt & Whitney Company, an aircraft engine manufacturer in Connecticut, and other aviation manufacturing companies and airlines formed to make up a very powerful and profitable corporation within the US aviation industry. UA&T began to expand by incorporating a number of other aviation companies under this holding company, absorbing all of the Hamilton Metalplane Company's patents and assets into the corporation. It is interesting to note the possibility that many aspects, manufacturing techniques, designs, and ideas that originally belonging to the Hamilton Metalplane Company may have been used in development of other historical Boeing aircraft, such as the Boeing 247, Boeing's first all-metal monoplane, and the famous World War II bomber called the Boeing B-17.

At this time, Hamilton became president of United Airports, a division of UA&T, and was in charge of building a new airport in Burbank, California. He moved his family out to Beverly Hills and eventually established a permanent residence at Lake Arrowhead, California until his death in 1969.

During this time period, UA&T also decided to merge Hamilton's propeller company with its largest competitor 'Standard Steel Propeller Company' of Pittsburgh, PA and move to that location. This resulted in possible patent conflicts, while Hamilton and Standard Steel had incurred by developing propellers using new metal materials and by the introduction of a revolutionary new design called the variable pitch propeller.[ii] When Hamilton was made aware of the possible merger by UA&T he agreed, but only if his name took precedence in the new trademark, making it Hamilton-Standard. An agreement was reached and the new company was to become famous for the development of its variable pitch propeller, designed by Standard Steel's chief engineer, Frank Caldwell.[iii] Hamilton was fond of saying (incorrectly) many years later at gatherings in the social circles of Hollywood, and at his resort in British Columbia called The Malibu Club, that he was indeed the developer of the variable pitch propeller.

The mergers of both of Hamilton's Milwaukee companies allowed him to reap the rewards of becoming wealthy through his stock investments. However, he would lose most of this fortune in the 1929 stock crash and in other ideas he invested in at the time. When the Burbank Airport opened with a huge fanfare in 1930, Hamilton was ready for a new endeavor. And frankly, he needed the cash. He turned his attention towards Europe, becoming a foreign representative for 'United Aircraft Export Company', another company under the umbrella of UA&T. He set up operations in Paris and quickly established many contacts at the top echelons of various political, military, and corporate groups throughout Europe, Asia, and the Middle East. Not surprisingly, he became president of the company in 1936. The job was uniquely suited to his abilities and exactly what the corporation needed. He was known as the 'Yankee Peddler', a man full of 'salesmanship' and even was labeled the 'master-entertainer.' Hamilton's skill and experience helped the UA&T survive financially at the same time the United States, as well as a good part of the rest of the world, was embroiled in the Great Depression.

Hamilton was successful in the export position and became very shrewd, intelligent, and savvy concerning the European political games being waged in the 1930s. As a result, he saw the war (World War II) coming long before many of the top US business and governmental leaders did. A clear example that he understood the worsening European situation was shown in a meeting of the executive committee of United Aircraft which Tom had specifically returned from Europe in order to attend.

The talk turned to politics, and especially the rising German leader, Adolf Hitler. Hamilton stood up and said, "don't discount this fellow Hitler." [iv] He acknowledged that Hitler had a comical look with a Charley Chaplain moustache but warned them that Hitler was very powerful. He had many people behind him in the German military and political establishments of that country. Hamilton continued by indicating that Hitler's power and direction was vast and should not to take it lightly.

Hamilton also tried to convince the US Congress of the seriousness of doing business with countries like Germany, Japan, and Russia, but was ignored. He continued in his foreign sales position, which was so perfectly suited to his talents as a marketer, until France was overrun by the Germans during their blitzkrieg in 1940. At that time Tom Hamilton, his family safe in California, and his staff had to make an unorthodox escape out of Europe through Spain.

Tom Hamilton was a man of ingenuity and unusual talents. He had the ability to see something and detail it out in his mind, knowing it would work before manufacturing even began. He was successful with many of these ideas, especially in the aviation field where he helped stimulate technical advances within the industry helping to create its golden years. Sometimes these ideas would seem outlandish to the point where of being funny. For example, he mentioned to his wife and niece, while on a trip to Europe that he wanted to give busy corporate executives a way to travel and work, plus have a great vacation with the family. Tom thought he could provide a motor van and a hostess who would act as secretary, babysitter, cook, maid, and travel guide at a modest price. Hamilton's wife and niece thought it was one of the most ludicrous ideas he had ever had, for it would not be all that pleasant for the poor woman who'd have to endure that kind of employment. But many of Hamilton's ideas were forward thinking and could be seen as just ahead of their time.

Tom Hamilton as a successful businessman had obtained several fortunes during his lifetime. Aside from his unique ways of thinking and his undeniable genius, which combined to make him thrive in the business world, he did have an opposite side which could be frustrating to anyone around him. No matter what proposition he came up with or began, it would often be completed by someone else. He was a designer and thinker, but not very good in the execution and daily details in getting the plans off the ground. But his airplanes did fly and his designs did work, and as a result, he was a success at just about everything he did.

From the Collection of C. W. Hitz

The Malibu Club from the Air (1947)

TF enjoyed the 'good life' and was as passionate about his leisure time as he was about work. He spared no expense on his hobbies, any more than he did on his business ventures. He enjoyed painting, but his main enthusiasm was yachting. Tom had been a boating enthusiast from his days as a teenager growing up in Seattle on the shores of Lake Washington. His first major yacht purchase was the *Vagrant*, a sailing yacht purchased from Commodore H.S. Vanderbilt, which he used it to entertain clients and celebrities while in Europe. He was known to hire students from the University of Washington to crew for him in Europe during their summer vacations. Sadly, the *Vagrant* was in Marseilles, France prior to the German advance in 1939 and was destroyed when the Germans entered the city.

Hamilton's escape from Europe during World War II signaled yet another turning point in his life. Once safe, he decided to focus his talents in an entirely new direction and, after being introduced to the Princess Louisa Inlet by Mr. Boeing, he decided to build an exclusive resort for his family, friends, and guests at the remote and breathtakingly beautiful Princess Louisa Inlet.

MALIBU

Princess Louisa Inlet and the Malibu Club became TF's new adventure. The original idea had begun as a simple cabin on the island his wife loved but, in typical Hamilton fashion, it evolved into something more. It would be an achievement in design and planning for Tom Hamilton. It would allow him to enjoy the majestic place with his friends and family. But it would end in total financial failure and abandonment, similar to other ideas and projects he had started in the past.

After Mr. Boeing had introduced him to Princess Louisa Inlet in 1938, TF set in motion a plan to begin the development of the inlet. He wanted the place to become a 'Mecca for Millionaires.'[v] It was to be patterned after Jasper National Park, another area similar in its size and beauty. Hamilton's plan for Princess Louisa Inlet was to be accomplished in several phased steps.

In the first step Hamilton bought just the island from Mac and it was purchased for $18,000 in December of 1940. He immediately named it after himself – Hamilton Island. But he saw a potential in the Inlet and began to think beyond just a small cabin on the island. Hamilton knew how to run and make a business profitable despite himself, and he was gifted in matching talented people to the right job, so just prior to the purchase of the island he set up a company to manage and maintain all the operations he envisioned at Princess Louisa

Inlet. The officers and directors of these companies included Tom and his family as well as other prominent Canadian associates. 'Hamiltair Limited' was established in August of 1940[vi] and would ultimately be the umbrella company for the whole Canadian and American enterprise. Obviously the idea of 'just a small cabin for his family' was only fleeting.

The next step was to purchase the additional land he would need to build his dream resort(s). On June 16, 1941, Tom Hamilton applied for, and was granted, permission to purchase 9,381 acres of lands surrounding and adjacent to Princess Louisa Inlet in the Sechelt Forest Reserve, for a total of $6,000 (CAN) from the Canadian Government.[vii] In actuality what Hamilton purchased was the property that made up the entire Inlet, except for the small piece of land McDonald owned at Chatterbox Falls. Tom financed most of the construction out of his own pocket. He had estimated the development cost for his pleasure resort would be in the neighborhood of $75,000 but, in actuality, when completed it would approach one million dollars. He would spend thousands of dollars more on advertising to attract people to both his resort and his charter business in Canada. Once again the actual mechanics of putting an idea into operation hindered Hamilton for something else would move him in another direction. Nevertheless, building the actual resort continued on.

Construction started in early 1940 on the finger of rock at the entrance to Princess Louisa Inlet. Hamilton employed over sixty people from Vancouver, BC and the surrounding districts to work in the large scale project. The first task was to burn Casper's shack. It was so flea infested from of all of Casper's cats through out the years that it was not salvageable, nor did it have a place in Hamilton's vision. However, Hamilton's cause became Casper's saving grace by way of MacDonald. In Mac's style, the actual story of TF's purchase of the point of land was altered to say that Hamilton bought the property from Herman Casper at the entrance to Princess Louisa Inlet for $500. In actuality, Casper was a squatter and had no documented claim to the land and in fact MacDonald probably influenced Hamilton to pay Casper as part of the negotiation concerning Tom's purchase of the Island from Mac. This gesture on TF's part not only gave Casper some needed cash (possibly more money than he had ever seen in his life), but also in Mac's true style, secured him a full-time job through Hamilton as caretaker at the resort, which would allow Casper to remain at his beloved Inlet.

The second step in Hamilton's plan, following the burning of Casper's shack, was to build the Trading Post or Store. Hamilton patterned it after the old Hudson's Bay Post so as to make shopping an adventure. At the same time, he built a large lounge known as Big Squwaka, for recreation and other activities when the weather turned stormy. This was followed by an adjacent room, or library, called Little Squwaka. Three small lodges for guests were constructed skirting the shore of Princess Louisa Inlet and were called Sioux, Siwash, and Sequoia Lodges. As an afterthought, Hamilton had a boathouse and an extra lounge built nearby to help entertain the anticipated yachters who frequently visited the area. Continuing on, three smaller cabins were built, along with a storage shed and First-Aid hut for emergencies. And finally, the dining room was built prior to the grand opening in the middle of the summer in 1941. It is interesting to note that while a few cement foundations were poured for some of the smaller lodges, in the majority of the first building, and those that would be forthcoming Hamilton would use the exposed bedrock as their foundational base, as Young Life would later find out to its detriment.

The initial construction phase beginning in 1940, took nearly a year and half to build the resort at the entrance of Princess Louisa Inlet. The cost was $96,000, higher than anticipated. The slow pace of building and the huge expenses were attributable to a number of factors. First, TF designed all of the buildings himself and did so without the aid of drawings. This would drive the construction workers crazy. Additionally, at certain sites construction would be all but completed, only to have to be restarted or substantially modified because Hamilton had come up with another idea or design that absolutely had to be incorporated. Another reason for the slow pace of building was the local timber mill's inability to meet Hamilton's demand for lumber and materials. TF eventually started his own mill and was able to supplement the local mill's supply limitations with logs off his own property. The fourth and final problem faced by the workers at Princess Louisa Inlet was the weather. The most favorable weather conditions were during the early and late months of summer, a period that lasted only about four to five months each year. Otherwise the weather during the fall and winter months would hinder more than help the construction effort, for it was just too wet, cold, and dangerous to safely continue. Summer would be the only season to accomplish all that Hamilton wanted for his resort.

By the spring of 1941, after the main construction of all the structures of the resort was completed, Hamilton started on the final details where basic necessities were installed, such as water and electricity. Galvanized water pipes were laid from the camp to Helana creek, about a mile and half from the resort, in order to provide fresh water. Diesel generators were installed to generate the electricity needed to run the kitchen, lights, and other necessities of modern life at the resort. Hamilton had plans to build and install a hydro generator (of his own design) to harness the natural (and free) energy for the camp, but unfortunately, the cost of building the hydro generator proved to be too great and the technology too unreliable for the idea to be feasible at that time. Fuel was cheap and plentiful in the 1940s, so Hamilton relied on the diesel generators to produce all the needed power.

Work also began on the aesthetics of the resort, which included native carvings and totem poles. Tom hired Mr. and Mrs. Bud Graves, well-known Vancouver BC artists, to do the art work for

Indian wall motifs to be carved in some of the small lodges and a number of coastal natives were hired to carve the totem poles for the camp. It has been suggested that each pole carved by these people has a specific story or a legend to tell but sadly, these meanings, except for one, have been lost. Joe Matthias, a chief from a native band, carved the highest (62 feet), and most dominant totem pole at the resort, which still stands today.[viii] This totem pole depicts the story of Tom Hamilton and his family. The

Taken by C.W. Hitz of One Eye Images & Sound

The Main Totem Pole at Malibu Carved by Bud Graves (2001)

base of the totem has a carved symbol of a Hamilton Standard three bladed propeller, the carved shape of Tom's interest and success. Tom is the next character carved above the propeller, followed by depictions of his wife, children, and mother then finally the Thunderbird is at the top of the tall pole.[ix] Unfortunately, as magnificent as all of the carving and poles were, the native theme used at the resort was that of the American Southwest instead of the indigenous tribes. Hamilton knew most of the guests would come from California and that the Southwestern theme would be more familiar to

TOM HAMILTON AND THE MALIBU RESORT

them, so he used it extensively throughout the resort, although the style was far from the actual traditions of the local First Nation band, the Sechelts that had first settled and lived in the same area so many years before. Today most of the current stories about the natives of this area are variations of incorrect stories which are told to yachters and high school students who visit the Malibu. These native tales were either made up or modified by Hamilton or MacDonald, and were meant to entertain, with just a few facts interwoven. But the majority of these tales are just pure fiction.

Once the construction was finished, Tom finally settled on the name of his resort, naming it after his yacht the *Malibu*. Hamilton's friend and earlier partner in building airplanes in Seattle, Ted Geary, had designed the *Malibu* and she was constructed at the Blanchard Boat yard in Seattle in 1928. The original owners, May Rindge and Rhoda Adams of Los Angeles, had named their new boat after their ranch in California near the famous Malibu beach. Hamilton had purchased the *Malibu* in approximately 1938, while still in Europe. Her purpose was to be his primary yacht for cruising around the Pacific Northwest coast. Hamilton also owned the *Vagrant* at this time, and as she was based in Europe, he used her for sailing the Atlantic and Mediterranean oceans. He used both yachts to entertain his many clients in the States and around the world while working as a sales representative for United Export in Europe.

The Malibu Club resort would be the crown jewel in Hamilton's vision for the whole Inlet. Malibu was to be one of three resorts situated throughout the Inlet, each resort having its own theme and location. The Malibu Club would be at the entrance of the Inlet, with a native theme. Further down Princess Louisa, at the next point of land over, a Swiss Village would be built, featuring a number of Swiss chalets. The Scandinavian Village would be where Hamilton Island lay at the foot of Old One Eye Mountain (the triangular-shaped peak),[x] or Mt.

99

Hamilton, as Tom called it, looked down upon the Inlet. This was the location where TF planned to install a ski tram so his guests could ski at the glacier next to his mountain. Obviously, dreaming is one thing and actually doing it is another. The ski tram would have been a challenge to build and was finally considered not feasible.

Courtesy of Young Life – Used with Permission

Hamilton Touring his Guests
around the Inner Harbor (1948)

The Malibu Club was Tom Hamilton's idea, and its concept was exclusivity. It would be expensive, and developed only for those who could easily afford it. He wanted to attract the rich, famous, and attractive in particular, the well-known Hollywood movie stars and directors, rich industrialists, captains of industry, and chic popular socialites who were exclusive by nature, expected the very best and were willing to pay for it. Malibu was to be a club conducted along the lines of private membership. But Tom was also intent upon developing the Malibu Club into a seasonal recreational place for yachters and their families, as most tended to make a vacation of their cruises much like the author's own family did in July of 1941. The plan was to allow families and others to be there as guest-members of the Malibu Club during that first season. After the first year they would be invited to become permanent members, paying for an annual membership. The memberships would include access to all the stores, lodging, and yachting merchandise at Malibu.

Courtesy of Young Life – Used with Permission

T.Hamilton, Ken Murry, Mrs. Cummings,
L.Hamilton, & Robert Cummings (1948)
(Left to Right)

Tom Hamilton was part of this select community and he worked hard at promoting and showing off his resort in order to attract the high-paying customers. He was excellent at marketing and selling aircraft parts, and promoting the resort proved to be no different. Brochures and other advertisements were sent to boating magazines and other publications throughout the Pacific Northwest, showing off the beautiful scenery and people having fun recreating in the sunshine. Tom visited yacht clubs throughout the Pacific Northwest and personally invited them to his resort. He also made it a point to state that he had, indeed, invented the famous Hamilton

Standard Variable Pitch Propeller, which although not true, sounded good and made for excellent PR for the Club.

The marketing blitz concerning Malibu was at full speed prior to the official opening in July 1941. The local newspapers of Vancouver, BC ran stories and pictures of Tom holding a large salmon at the Inlet. (In reality the fish was caught down in Pender Harbor). Tom also promoted the fact that his roots were Canadian, his mother having been born in Ontario. Unfortunately, he also expounded how great the weather was at Malibu, forgetting that many of his guests were from Southern California. The actual weather would come as something of a surprise to them, as they expected it to be just as warm as it there, conveniently forgetting that they were significantly farther north.

The official opening of the Malibu Club in Canada resort was on July 16, 1941 and the theme was the 'Malibu Potlatch'. It was a festive time, featuring native dancing, log rolling, a clambake, and lots of entertainment. Overall, that first night and the remaining summer proved extremely successful for the Malibu Club, as Hamilton's marketing storm had brought many yachters and celebrities to the resort. The future looked bright and hopeful for Malibu Club and Tom Hamilton's vision of the inlet. Unfortunately, the surprise Japanese air attack on the US Navy fleet at Pearl Harbor on December 7, 1941 changed everybody's plans for the future, including Tom Hamilton's.

America and her allies entered the great world struggle against imperialism and fascism. The allied countries mobilized with the goal of winning the war in Europe and in the Pacific. Sacrifices were made and endured by all, worldwide. The American and Canadian Navies pressed all pleasure craft into military service for the duration of the war and Tom Hamilton gladly donated his yacht *Malibu,* as well as the other Malibu Club boats, to the cause. Tom also became a 'dollar-a-year' man, providing his knowledge and experience to the war effort by working at the Hardman Aircraft Company in Southern

California for only one dollar a year. This company produced many of the parts needed for the famous Boeing B-17 bomber of the mighty US Eighth Air Force. This was something Tom was extremely proud to be doing for his country, as he had seen first-hand the tyranny of Nazism while he was in Paris as a sales representative for United Aircraft during the 1930s.

Courtesy of Young Life – Used with Permission

T.Hamilton (sitting) and Guests at Malibu (1948)

Sadly, many Americans and Allied personnel lost their lives during this conflict, and the Hamilton family was not immune. Tom's only brother, who had died at the young age of 25, had had two children, Betty and Charles Harold 'Major' Hamilton. Major had quickly volunteered for military service shortly after the attack on Pearl Harbor. After serving courageously and participating in the Battle of the Coral Sea,[xi] which had the distinction of being the first naval aircraft battle in history, Major lost his life in a training accident on January 13, 1943 and he was buried at the Honolulu military memorial in Hawaii. The family was devastated by the untimely death of this fine young man. Major and his sister were an important part of the dynamics of the Hamilton family, first from the early years in Milwaukee, then at Lake Arrowhead and even at Malibu. To cope with his grief, Tom (a skilled artist) eventually painted a portrait of Major, which is proudly displayed today in Major's sister's home, along with all the medals and commendations he had earned.

MALIBU SEAERO

When the war ended, Tom Hamilton started his resort business back up by establishing two new companies, complete with new investors, to help keep the Malibu enterprise and resort alive. The first, begun in June of 1945, was called the 'Malibu SeAero Service Ltd,'[xii] and the company was designed to help build a charter aircraft business to help support the Malibu resort. Since Malibu was, and still is, accessible only by boat or by seaplane, it seemed a logical and most likely a profitable venture. The other company made Malibu an official legal entity,[xiii] and was filed as such at the end of November in 1945. Both of the companies were incorporated under the 'Societies Act' and would still be under the 'Hamiltair Ltd' umbrella but, most importantly, the changes included a number of new directors and shareholders. These new partners were friends and colleagues of Hamilton's, and were mostly made up of successful Canadians like Stanley Burke, president of 'Boeing of Canada' and Francis R. Graham, a prominent Canadian businessman. Tom also enlisted the help of his cousin Ed Green and a Mr. John C. Campbell of Vancouver, BC, to help Casper out as superintendents of the Malibu resort.

The war had depleted Hamilton's charter boat fleet, as all pleasure boats had been pressed into military service early on. Surprisingly, the US and Canadian military put these very boats up for auction as war surplus when the hostilities ceased, which was the very thing Hamilton was seeking. The Government was offloading the boats cheaply, as they were no longer needed and they were declared surplus property and fortunately, Tom Hamilton knew the right people in Canada and the US in to obtain these bargain-priced yachts for his resort at Princess Louisa Inlet.

Interestingly enough, Hamilton's first acquisition from the navy surplus was not a boat but an airplane. Specifically, a twin-engine amphibian (lands both on water and land) aircraft known as the Grumman Goose, available through the Canadian War Asset Corporation as a surplus item. This aircraft was part of FDR's original lend lease program to the British Commonwealth before America entered the war in 1941. The Grumman Goose was designed as a light flying boat, or amphibian utility transport aircraft, and it had the typical flying-boat appearance with a high wing, two-step hull, fixed under-wing floats, and two 405hp Pratt & Whitney engines. This particular aircraft served in World War II patrolling the coast of British Columbia where it was based at Pat Bay near Victoria, BC. After the war the 'Hamiltiair Corporation' bought the aircraft for $21,500.[xiv]

Malibu SeAero's Grumman Goose (1945)

This airplane was planned to be the first of many to be used as part of Hamilton's 'Malibu SeAero Company'. Tom and the board of SeAero figured it would be cheaper to buy the aircraft and maintain it themselves, than to keep chartering planes as they had been doing prior to the war. The SeAero Company would also be a revenue producer, as its main purpose would be to fly customers to Malibu and the other parts of Hamilton's envisioned entertainment resorts. The plane could be chartered out to other companies or individuals as needed. In reality, this would be the only aircraft purchased and maintained by the Malibu SeAero Company in support of the operation at Malibu and for Hamiltair.

Immediately upon purchasing the aircraft from the Canadian government, Tom contacted his partner Stanley Burke, president of 'Boeing of Canada', to refurbish the aircraft per Tom's specifications. The demand for military aircraft had dropped to zero at the end of the war and the Boeing plant in Vancouver, BC was badly in need of work.[xv] Stanley Burke heartily agreed to allow the aircraft to be refurbished in the Boeing plant and issued work order on April 26th, 1945.[xvi] The initial survey of the aircraft indicated that it would require a great deal of work to put it back into condition and to change it from a military plane to civilian. The engines and the propeller had to be removed and shipped back to the Pratt & Whitney Aircraft Co. Ltd in Longueil, Quebec for re-haul. The flight instruments needed replacement and the radios were upgraded. And because of the constant use of the aircraft in wartime and in a salt-water environment, the airframe, fittings, riggings, and controls of the airplane needed to be inspected and replaced if necessary. Finally, the aircraft was to be striped to bare metal and repainted. Now this was the issue about which Tom Hamilton was most concerned.

TF was obsessed with the look and presentation of the airplane, because it would be the billboard that would show the Malibu name from the air for all to see. This was apparent per the number of letters between Stan Burke and TF about the work to be done on this aircraft, specifically about the color of the paint and the logo. On April 30, 1945[xvii] Stanley Burke wrote Tom concerning the report from the Boeing General Chief Inspector, Mr. McKeown, that the reconditioning of the Goose was completed and it was ready for the complete paint job

Malibu SeAero Logo (1948)

Hamilton had requested. Tom Hamilton responded on May 9th, 1945 by sending the design he had sketched up for the logo of 'Malibu' and for 'Malibu SeAero' Company. This emblem was a Thunderbird, with lettering on the bow of the ship. In June he cabled again to Mr. Burke, stating his desire that the workmen not do an 'even job' on the writing, for the idea was to make it appear as authentic native writing. The words 'Malibu Sky Chief' were to be painted on both sides of the tail using the same type of lettering as used on the nose. Hamilton also wanted publicity photos taken with prominent BC businessmen next to the Malibu SeAero logo. He was very insistent about how the photos should be taken, and gave specific details describing each series. He stated that the first series of shots would be a three-quarter front view taken from the left front facing the cockpit so that the name 'Malibu' would be easily visible. The second series of photos would be side views showing the 'Malibu' on the nose and the final shots would be taken from the other side of the aircraft, so as to once again show the name 'Malibu' on the nose. Tom also requested a final series of pictures that featured that three or four attractive female models posing as intended passengers alongside the plane, and even through the entrance door. Again, the goal was to make the name 'Malibu' showed up prominently in the shot. Then TF finally requested that a number of photos be taken of the aircraft in the water alongside a mooring, or next to an attractive yacht for comparison.

Aside from all the concerns about how the aircraft looked, the work of refurbishing the Goose was completed on September 18, 1945 at a cost of $10,171.91 for all services and parts. The newly restored and shiny 'Malibu Sky Chief' was rolled out of the

Boeing factory and received a new Canadian registration of CF-BHL. It is also interesting to note that the company was issued the first civilian air permit following World War II from the Canadian air transport Board. They also received the commercial air service license (#45/2) to permit the company to operate a non-scheduled charter service carrying passengers and goods based to Princess Louisa Inlet only. Incidentally, it was also the only civilian license issued in Canada after the war. Hamilton had used his political connections again to get this prestigious and necessary transportation license, and he repaid of these connections by chartering his aircraft out to others beyond Princess Louisa Inlet as the permit stated. For example, a new dam and power house was being built up at Seton Lake, BC by the 'BC Electric Co' in 1948. The prime contractors used this particular airplane to haul the materials and men necessary, because 'Malibu SeAero' had the only permit to fly passengers and goods in BC. Other large companies of the area, like Bloedel, Stewart & Welch, MacMillan Export Co, BC Packers, and Power River Paper Co also used Malibu SeAero Sky Chief for the same reason. The Malibu Sky Chief also made its runs to Malibu when requested. Hamilton's aim was to provide speedy service from to Malibu from Vancouver. A complete hangar at the Vancouver BC airport was leased from the former Trans-Canada Airlines, coming complete with a maintenance dept. The hanger was also leased out to other companies, such as the 'Powell River Co', who made use of the storage, and to maintain their two Grumman Gooses. The Malibu Sky Chief served the club well for many years. It came to a sad ending, however, being sold after Malibu was abandoned. It crashed and was destroyed by its new owners on Jan 27th 1953 near Butedale, BC.

THE FAIRMILES AND OTHER YACHTS

Yachts, and lots of them, were badly needed at Malibu after the war. Tom Hamilton was able to secure a number of the vessels he needed for his resort and charter business through the American War Shipping Administration and the Canadian War

Malibu's Inner Dock with the Goose,
The Princess Louisa Inlet Fairmile, and Charters (1948)

Assets Corporations. He found that the majority were not in a condition to be used, but 'per his requirements' he did bid on and acquire some 20 to 35 boats of the best lots. He was awarded the 120-foot twin-screw diesel cruiser *Tara,* built in the 1920s by Nevins at the cost of $250,000. He also won the 148-foot steel sailing schooner called the *Vega* and a famous ferry from the Hudson River called the *Arrow.* The *Arrow* was built in 1924 and, after TF purchased it, was renamed the *Malibu Arrow.* The famous 55ft *Wahoo,* built by Consolidated Shipbuilding Corp of New York and the forerunner of the famous PT boats used in World War Two by the American Navy, also went to Tom Hamilton. A number of high speed cruisers and a collection of Chris-Craft boats, ranging from 34-foot express cruisers to the 55-foot sleek models, had also become part of Malibu's new fleet. The water craft would be given unique names, more fitting to the elite crowd Hamilton was hoping to attract, such as, the *Malibu Mala Bula,* the *Malibu Malablitz,* and the *Henrietta H.* (named after his beloved mother).

It would be, however, the purchase of the ex-'Fairmiles' fast motor torpedo boats that Hamilton's Malibu Club would be best known for. These vessels were originally planned as the versatile 112-foot 'B' class Motor Launch (M.L) as designed in

England by the Fairmile Company. Canada built at least 80 of these Fairmiles under license and had numbered them Q050 to Q129 respectively. British Columbia shipyards had built some of them for the purpose of providing escorts to convoys, for port defense, search and rescue, anti aircraft and submarine duties around the west coast of British Columbia. All of the Fairmiles were wood construction, 107 feet in length, and had two 450 horsepower engines in order to generate the power needed to turn the two propellers. The estimated cost of building these boats was around $195,000 (CAN) and, after the war, Hamilton got seven of them for $3000 (CAN) each. Then, much like he had with the Grumman Goose airplane, TF had the Fairmiles converted from a war configuration to a luxury yacht layout that would be able to handle between eight and twelve guests. After refurbishing, Tom Hamilton gave them names fitting the Malibu Club theme: the *Malibu Inez* (ex-Royal Canadian Navy 'RCN' Q129) after his wife's middle name Inez, the *Princess Louisa Inlet* (ex-RCN Q128), the *Chief Malibu* (ex-RCN Q127), the *Malibu Princess* (ex-RCN Q126), the *Malibu Tillikum* (ex-RCN Q125), the *Malibu Marlin* (ex-RCN Q123), and the *Malibu Tyee* (ex-RCN Q122). The *Princess Louisa Inlet* was the first to be converted and became the crown jewel in the Malibu Fairmile fleet. The others were converted in the following months and years after Malibu opened in 1945, as money and time permitted. Many of these boats were still in a war configuration, and stored at Malibu awaiting their conversion up until 1950, serving as spare parts for the working Fairmiles. Hamilton hired ex-military personal, who had worked in the navy to handle these craft, to crew and operate these luxury yachts.

The fate of the Fairmiles is a story mixed with tragedy and survival after their service at Malibu. The *Chief Malibu* now rests at the bottom of Princess Louisa Inlet, below Young Life's Malibu Inner-dock. At the time Hamilton's Malibu Club was abandoned, the *Chief Malibu* was left tied to the dock with all of the hatches open. At the end of the first winter the boat had filled up with rain and snow and had begun to list. By the time that Young Life had taken over in 1954, two years following the abandonment of the resort, the boat had sunk. From that point on until the early 1970s, the mast of the *Chief Malibu* could be seen at low tide. A number of items had been retrieved off the wreck by divers in the early 1960s, and Malibu has them on display in Little Squwaka lounge.

The *Malibu Marlin* was sold to a new owner in the United States and was renamed the *Toluca*. The *Malibu Tillikum* was also sold and has had many owners and names over the years, such as the *Yorkeen*, *Campana*, and the *Jormholm*. It is currently known the *Gulf Stream II*. There is an interesting side note about the Malibu *Tillikum* it, like the *Chief Malibu*, also sank due to open hatches in a bad storm. This occurred in 1946 while docked at its berth at Coal Harbor (site of the old Boeing plant) unlike the *Chief Malibu*, the *Malibu Tillikum* was later raised and pumped out, at a large expense to Hamilton. The *Malibu Tyee* was renamed the *Nancy H Seymour* and is now called the *Sogno d'Oro*. The *Princess Louisa Inlet*, the centerpiece of Tom Hamilton's Malibu Club, which had made regular runs up and down the Jervis Inlet, was sold. Unfortunately it sank in Pendreel Sound in BC in 1955. This was the yacht that had taken Hamilton and a number of Young Life guests to the hand-off of Malibu to Young life in 1953. Finally, the *Malibu Inez*, named after Tom Hamilton's wife's was sold to an unknown buyer after Malibu folded and is currently known as the *Huntress II* of Vancouver BC.

ADDITIONAL CONSTRUCTION

Hamilton not only increased the number of yachts at Malibu following World War II, but he worked on a number of additional buildings. 'Aztec Lodge' was the addition of two more floors to the Main Floor off the existing administration offices and stores of Malibu. The new Aztec Lodge had a total of three new stories, including an irregularly shaped frame and roof, and was sided with split logs around its exterior. The very top floor was called the 'Penthouse', for it had a large deck with

Taken by Elizabeth Hamilton Sunde – Used with Permission

Malibu's Penthouse Suite (1948)

a luxurious view that looked down on the Inlet. It included nine bedroom suites and five baths. The next floor down from the Penthouse was the 'Ground Floor', and had a deck walkway and included four bedrooms and baths for the guests on the Princess Louisa Inlet side, with staff quarters on the other side.

After completing the Aztec Lodge, Hamilton went to work on the construction of a lodge that would face the Jervis Inlet. He would call it 'Navajo', and it would overlook 'Indian Island', located at the entrance of Princess Louisa Inlet. It would be a two story rectangular building with an irregularly sloped gable roof and, in the middle, a triangular pinnacle arch, tee-pee shaped, stretching from the exterior of the structure out towards the inlet. There were four bedroom suites on the first floor, with six suites below. Each floor had large decks that overlooked the island and the Jervis inlet. Staff quarters were also added to the back, and each floor was connected by stairs for easy access.

A similar lodge was built that ran perpendicular from the Navajo Lodge but didn't have the fancy interconnecting decks or stairs. Instead, a large lounge called 'Sitka' was included, overlooking Princess Louisa Inlet. The lodge had three levels with eight rooms on the top section, three rooms on the middle section and an interconnecting interior hallway starting at the lounge area of Sitka. The third section was the laundry facility, located on the bottom floor. In addition, the dining room was extended in order to enlarge the current restaurant size, the power house was increased to handle larger generators and the boat house was enlarged as well. Hamilton had anticipated the need and desire for many returning service men and woman to do more recreational activities after the deprivations of the war. His friend and neighbor Conrad Hilton, of Hilton hotels, may have suggested to including large, hotel-like rooms to not only to handle the anticipated number, but to give a choice of the type of style and level of their stay at Malibu, similar to his hotels.

Taken by Elizabeth Hamilton Sunde – Used with Permission

Navajo and the Dining Hall (1948)

The second official Malibu opening was celebrated in July of 1946 and helped kick off the official summer season. Tom Hamilton invited a number of well-known industrialists and famous Hollywood celebrities to help promote his Malibu-Club-in-Canada. Once again the yachting magazines and local Vancouver, BC newspapers were full of news about the resort, and listed guests at Malibu each week for all of that summer and clear through the resort's closing in 1950. The Malibu guest book from 1946 to 1950 would include the names of such notables as Mr. and Mrs. B. Allison Gillies of New York (Vice President of Grumman Aircraft, and builder of Malibu SeAero's

Brenda Marshall & William Holden (1948)

aircraft), Conrad Hilton (owner of the Hilton Hotel chains), Ann Miller, Fred Murrey, Alexis Smith, Robert Cummings, Bing Crosby, Bob Hope, Brenda Marshall, William Holden, Barbara Stanwyck, Robert Taylor and C. David and Annette Weyerhaeuser, just to name a few.

Unfortunately, because of the weather and the remote location, not all of the guests enjoyed themselves. For example, Barbara Stanwyck was not impressed with her stay, mainly due to bad weather and Mr. Hamilton. At the time Ms. Stanwyck was one of Hollywood's highest-paid actresses and was best known for films like 'Annie Oakley', 'Ball of Fire', 'Double Indemnity', 'The Lady Eve', and 'Stella Dallas'. After two days at Malibu she asked the pilot to fly her out first thing in the morning. She was fed up! Tom had completely annoyed her, forever hounding her to pose for pictures for him at the Club. In addition, he had arranged for a photographer to meet her when she landed in Vancouver, BC. Tom had made it a point to photograph every well-known guest at the camp so he could market the high class cliental who came to his resort. Unfortunately, in Barbara's case, it made her crazy.

At times Tom Hamilton did drive some of his guests to distraction, and he also managed to frustrate his personnel. He was an idea person and tended to micro-manage his staff and, according to some of these hired workers, Malibu was in chaos when Tom was running the camp. When he was away and Mrs. Hamilton was in attendance, everything ran very smoothly.

This was very typical of the way Tom ran his businesses, from aviation to the resort. He wanted to manage every detail initially, but then would lose interest and go to the next project or idea in the same way. But he made a wise decision following the war, he hired a friend, L.B. Nelson, who was renown as a resort executive, to help run the overall operation at Malibu. Nelson had directed the operation of 166 hotels in Paris and London for the US Army prior to D-Day. Using his expertise he was able to bring Malibu to its peak in 1948 before turning operations over to TF's son, Larry Hamilton, who then ran the club until it was abandoned in 1950.

During the 1947 season, golf was added as a new recreation at Malibu. This seemed an odd choice, given the terrain of the area, until other reasons were considered. At the time only golf courses were able to easily acquire liquor licenses in BC, and TF wanted to be able to serve alcohol at Malibu. The golf course was built in typical Hamilton fashion. He designed and built a course complete with the required number of 18 holes, only no length was ever given for the fairways. Large amounts of fill and top soil were barged up to Malibu, with the fill used to level the rocky areas and the top soil to plant the grass seed, from the beach to the start of a boardwalk to the camp. A small clubhouse was built at the head of the boardwalk so people could get a drink, but in order to do so a golf membership had to be purchased and golf clubs rented. It became known as the 'Malibar', and was a typical cedar log building with a wide veranda. Inside the building featured a bar with a brass foot rail, just like an old saloon in a western movie. From the clubhouse, another

Courtesy of Young Life – Used with Permission

Golfing on the Malibu Greens (1948)

boardwalk was built on pilings, and skirting the rugged shore-line of Jervis Inlet in order to lead directly to the area where the golf course and tennis courts were located. The course itself was built in three tiers, following the slope upward. The first tier, near the Malibu bar, had a flat putting green where people could practice and socialize near the beach. The first hole was a few yards up from the putting green and bar, and all 18 holes followed a lazy S direction up and back, following the sloping terrain. The 18th hole ended near the first, and only a short distance back to the bar, in order to allow the golfers to quench their thirst after playing. During the summer months when the weather was nice and warm, almost everyone was actually out on the greens playing. It was one of the highlights Hamilton publicized in his advertisements, showing attractive girls playing golf with one the Fairmile yacht's in the background.

The bar was not only popular with the guests, as word quickly got around to the local loggers who thought it was a godsend in this remote part of BC. A story has been told about five loggers, who had been in the woods a lot longer than they cared to be, who decided that they wanted a couple of drinks after a hard day of work on the Jervis Inlet side. They all piled into a small boat and set course for the bar at Malibu. Once they reached the rapids, though they found their boat was unstable and unable to handle the current and everyone was pitched into the chuck. After all that effort they finally reached the bar, only to find that it was closed until summer as indicated by the caretaker of the camp who was a bit surprised to see guests climbing out of the water onto the dock.

A typical operating season for Malibu was short. The camp would open in mid-June and close the weekend after Labor Day in September, taking advantage of the best weather of the area. In the spring Hamilton would hire college students, mostly from the University of British Columbia in Vancouver, to work at Malibu as hostesses, waitresses, and dockhands. The workers were provided with crisp uniforms and were expected to always appear spotlessly dressed and well groomed. Appearances were extremely important, in order to give the camp the aura of class and professionalism required. The guests paid dearly to come to Malibu and the ambience reflected this, from the staff to the lodgings. Every detail was focused on the paying customer. Hamilton would personally hire the most attractive girls and the most handsome boys for jobs which required interaction with the guests. However, they were forbidden to mingle with any of them.

Despite the rules, stories indicate that the facts were otherwise. One regular customer of the resort would come each year with about ten suitcases, and it was thought that most of them contained liquor. This guest would always book the 'Penthouse' suite and she would stay inside the entire time, taking her meals via room service. It was rumored that the bus boys provided more than just room service. Some of the college workers and hired staff thought that Malibu was more of an exclusive brothel than a resort.[xviii]

To be a guest at Hamilton's Malibu was fun, entertaining, and formal. The accommodations were such that the visitors could

Courtesy of Young Life – Used with Permission

TF and guests at Malibu (1948)

select their room either facing toward the Jervis Inlet, (the 'Navajo' Lodge) or have a view of Princess Louisa Inlet and stay in the 'Sitka' Lodge. The rooms were luxurious with cedar siding, a bathroom with running water, and electricity. The furnishings were from an exclusive builder in Vancouver BC. The beds had Hudson Bay blankets which were specifically designed for Malibu, with the 'Malibu Club' logo woven into them. The rooms were designed to sleep one or two guests at time, and each room featured towels, pillowcases, and sheets all embroidered with the Malibu logo. On a given day, the guest(s) could sail, boat, fish, water ski, hike, hunt, read, shop, golf, or whatever they wished, as long as they could afford it. In the evening, dinner was a time of mingling and cocktails, where formal dress was required. Tom Hamilton would individually greet and seat each guest as they arrived for dinner, then the festivities would begin. French Chefs would prepare a banquet of interesting, dishes depending on the guests' tastes. They would eat on Malibu Club dishes, silverware, tableware, each branded with the totem logo. It was the time when everybody was together to enjoy a meal and the main entertainment of the evening. Dinnertime would also feature various bands and singers, that were flown up for entertainment and following the meal the programs would vary.

It is interesting to note that, although the many people who visited Malibu each week paid a high price to stay at the exclusive resort, Hamilton would not re-invest portions of this revenue into maintenance unless absolutely necessary. He was cost-conscious almost to the point of being a miser. Freight, both perishable and non-perishable, would be stored in the Vancouver, BC office until the next paying customer chartered the plane, and it could often be a week or two before it would be flown up to Malibu. One flight so over loaded the Grumman Goose that, when it landed at the Club, it nosed right into the water "like it was going straight to the bottom of the inlet"[xix] as reported by the pilot. The green water came over the nose and cabin of the airplane, but the Malibu Sky Chief did manage to make it to the dock to unload the cargo and the single guest. Another example of Hamilton's cost-consciousness was that he would not invest in running lights for the yachts, as he didn't deem it necessary to operate them at night.

Courtesy of Young Life – Used with Permission

The Malibu Dining Hall (1948)

ABANDONED

The saddest chapter of Malibu's history was when Hamilton literally abandoned the resort in 1950. For the next two years Malibu became a place where time stood still, as food was left in the pots and pans in the kitchen, tables were still set, and supplies were untouched in the stores and cabins, exactly as the day it was left. One yachter recalls seeing Malibu during this period where he remembered walking around the buildings having been left that way since the previous summer.

The question asked continually by so many, but never adequately answered, has been 'why was the resort abandoned?' There are three possible reasons as to why Hamilton just walked away from his million-dollar resort. The first and most obvious answer was financial, as has been mentioned. Tom Hamilton had a reputation for not spending money at Malibu unless it was absolutely necessary. Basic maintenance of the yachts and resort itself was preformed only when it could not be put off any longer. This attitude might have been predicated by the amount of money TF had had to put into the resort at the beginning, hoping to attract the type and numbers of clientele he needed to offset his building and startup costs. While there were no financial records related to the years of 1941 and 1945 to 1947, the records remaining for the years 1948 to 1950 indicate that Malibu was making a profit. In 1948 it was $5012.43, but a loss of $564.70 in 1949 and the resort made $4478.64, with no loss. But in 1950, the records show that the profit had decreased to $3870.97 with a loss of $295.47. This information clearly shows a growing downward trend of revenue for the resort. A good businessman would be able to spot the trend and make a choice – either change or get out.

The second possible reason that Malibu was abandoned was that Tom simply had lost interest in the Malibu project. Tom Hamilton was never really an operations person, nor was he ever keen on the details of maintaining the system that kept the camp running. His wife, Ethel, had been the person who organized and ran Malibu, and in past business ventures during their marriage. Unfortunately, Tom was no longer married to Ethel and that stability was gone. Frankly, the financial decline of Malibu could be attributed to Ethel's absence.

The third and most significant reason for this quick departure could well be due to a very serious polio scare. In the late 1940s, an infectious polio outbreak had left the BC province reeling, but by 1948 it seemed to be under control.[xx] The reality of going through another outbreak was unbearable, and the possibility of it starting again was very real, and it appeared to be beginning once more at Tom Hamilton's Malibu Club. In August 1948, the fun and entertainment at Malibu was interrupted late one night when one of the waitresses employed at the club was taken seriously ill. Sydney Diane Harris had been running a fever all day and finally collapsed at dinner. Diane was unconscious and shivering so violently she was wrapped in blankets to keep her warm. The Malibu nurse requested that she be flown to the hospital immediately, and she tried to contact Tom Hamilton, who was entertaining guests at one of the cabins and could not be reached. Instead, the nurse and another officer rushed her to the Sky Chief for a quick evacuation but the weather had turned stormy and the Grumman Goose could not take off. By the time the weather cleared, it was already dark and the Goose was not equipped for night flying. Instead the nurse and Philip Cook, captain of the *Malibu Arrow,* put her on board his boat to transport her to the hospital at Sechelt. Again weather and lack of running lights deterred them from reaching the hospital and they had to turn back. Back at Malibu a telephone radio link was made with her family doctor in Vancouver[xxi] and she lived through the night, to be airlifted the next day to a St. Paul's hospital in Vancouver, BC in hopes of saving her life. However, seventeen year old Sydney Diane Harris had died sometime during the flight and it was later learned she died from bulbar polio.[xxii] Polio, short for Poliomeubilts, is a virus that spreads orally. This type of virus attacks the central nervous system of the victim and kills nerve cells, which cannot be restored. The affected muscles will not function and become useless due to a process is called acute flaccid paralysis (AFP). There are other types of polio which attack the abdomen or the throat, but the most critical type is bulbar polio, which assaults the brain and causes problems with breathing, speech, and eating. Death can occur if the bulbar victim is not provided respiratory support, such as an iron lung (metal cylinders as a tool to help the patient breath) and this paralysis of the lungs is what killed young Diane Harris.

The next night Kathy Cook, a young woman from Vancouver, BC who had been visiting her brother, Philip Cook, captain of the *Malibu Arrow*, was playing cards onboard the boat with her brother and John Long. There was a nip in the air and Kathy unknowingly wrapped herself in the same blanket which had covered Diane Harris the night before. On September 11, 1948, Kathy was admitted to the hospital and where she too was diagnosed as having polio, which she had contracted indirectly from Diane's blankets. Her time at Malibu was a life-changing experience. Kathy was very ill and remained in the hospital for over three years where she had to be in an iron lung to assist her breathing due to the devastating effects of the disease. Following Diane Harris's death, George W. Spooner of the BC Ministry of Health, acting quarantine officer, immediately instituted fourteen day quarantine at Malibu.[xxiii] During this time, no one could get in nor could they leave Malibu until all the officials had checked and rechecked everyone for the deadly disease. The quarantine was lifted shortly afterward and operations at Malibu returned to normal. However, two years later in 1950, one of Tom Hamilton's grandchildren was afflicted with a mild case of this disease, only to recover a number of years later, without the devastating effects suffered by Kathy. Whether it was contracted at either at Malibu or from some where else, is not known, but it is possible that Hamilton feared that Malibu was infected. Only Polio could explain why Malibu was abandoned so quickly and completely, and a new scare in

1950 concerning his immediate family would definitely have a strong impact on Hamilton.

Hamilton knew this would be the coup de grace for his Malibu Club. The quarantine of 1948 was an experience he did not want to repeat, and he knew it would be bad for business. Particularly at a time when the numbers of guests were declining and one of his own grandchildren was suffering. He made his decision quickly and decisively, leaving the resort in waiting solitude.

As a single individual, Tom Hamilton undertook the idea of building a resort in one of the most beautiful and isolated locations in the world. As was typical of TF, his resort concept was one of unique vision and excess, flourishing for a few years during the summers of the 1940s under the name of The Malibu Club in Canada. Yet, typical again for this unique individual, the concept and idea lasted less than decade, only to be abandoned in less time than it took to build. And, like so many times in his past, Hamilton moved onto other, more interesting projects, leaving the resort behind and forgotten for a time. Malibu now lay dormant and empty.

From the Collection of C. W. Hitz

The Crowded Inner Harbor of Malibu (1948)

END NOTES

i Meek, *Jervis Inlet to Become Great BC Tourist Attraction*. Vancouver Sun, July 5, 1941.

ii Rosen & Anezis, *Thrusting Forward* pages 38-49. The Variable Pitch Propeller allows a pilot of an airplane to change the angles of the propeller's blades to move towards a direction that will either increase or decrease how it strikes the air (or Pitch). This gives the aircraft a more efficient way to move through the air than just a fixed propeller would. The Variable Pitch Propeller concept was not new to the aviation industry, for it was first proposed in 1871 by the French for Balloons and then by the Germans in 1909 for their dirigibles. However, due to the fact that most propellers of that time were made out of wood, it was not practical until metal propellers were introduced that had the strength to withstand the centrifugal forces of the propeller turning, the conversion of torque and speed from the engine, and the additional motion of the blades moving against various aerodynamic forces. In the mid-1920s aviation designers started to propose, design, and test a number of adjustable or variable pitch type propellers, but they were all based on mechanical means which meant substantial wear of the gears and propeller destruction during testing. Currently, there are four classes of aviation propellers: the fixed pitch, ground adjustable, in-flight adjustable & constant speed propellers. The latter two are defined as a variable pitch propeller.

iii US Patent (#2,032,254) titled the *Adjustable Pitch Propeller* was submitted by Frank Caldwell on April 21, 1931 and patented on February 25, 1936. Mr. Caldwell designed a hydraulic control device to change the pitch of the propeller blades, as opposed to a mechanically based design. He first filed the patent in 1931, and along with supplemental additions of devices to the original application up to 1936. This work was done through his time at Standard Steel, a company which later merged into Hamilton Standard in 1929, where he became Chief Engineer. Mr. Caldwell and his talented engineering team were able to create the "gear shift in the sky", in the form of this adjustable pitch or variable pitch propeller. Mr. Caldwell was awarded the 1933 and 1935 Collier Trophy for the controllable pitch propeller and a governor control to automatically adjust the pitch in flight (won in conjunction with Woodward Governor Company). Tom Hamilton was not the inventor, nor did he hold the patent of the Variable Pitch Propeller, but he was involved in the aviation industry during the early development of propellers with his Hamilton Aero Manufacturing Company in Milwaukee, WI and was involved in the propeller programs at a high level of development and marketing to other nations while part of United Aircraft and United Export.

iv Wilson. *Slipstream*. Page 209.

v Gilbert, *Malibu Club*. BC Digest, August 1946. Pages 29-31.

vi BC Archives. 1940. *Hamiltair Ltd*. In GR-1526, Reel # B-5506, file # BC-17230. Incorporation Documents: Microfilm.

vii Ministry of Environment, Lands, and Parks (Province of British Columbia) Crown Land Registry Services. Per O in C #827 – this land was purchased for $6,000.00 on 6-12-1941 with the desire to develop a pleasure resort at the expense roughly at $75,000.00. Also see the Appendix of this book entitled "Tom Hamilton Ownership of Property at Princess Louisa Inlet (1941-1952)."

viii During the winter months of 2003, this totem pole was reduced to 40 feet, for the years of exposure to the elements for over 60 years caused the mid and upper sections to decay much faster and it was easier to maintain the lower section than the top. As one worker put it "the only thing holding the totem together was the paint, everything else was rotten."

ix Hagstrom *Malibu Tour Talk,* 1954. Page 2.

x   Peterson, *The Story of the Sechelt Nation*, page 44. The triangular peak is un-named on modern maps and charts, but has been unofficially called One Eye at Malibu since Young Life took it over in 1954 (also called Mt. Hamilton when TF bought the entire Inlet and operated the Malibu Club). One Eye is the English meaning of the Sechelt term of the mountain called TUHKOHSS, which roughly means in English "Old One Eye". Supposedly, one can see a "sunken eye" below the peak looking from MacDonald Island and the peak is one of the Gods of creation standing watch over the Inlet, protecting it from other floods, according to Sechelt stories.

xi Johnston, *Queen of the Flat-Tops,* 1941. Pages 230 -231. An interesting and hair rising story of Ensign R.F. McDonald (pilot) and C.H.O.Hamilton (Major, who was radio operator and gunner) is described during the first battle of the Coral Sea in this book. Both Major and his pilot were part of the anti-torpedo screen for the *Lexington* and were involved in some heavy fighting. Returning from their mission, with the pilot wounded from the fighting and having missed the Japanese air assault on the USS Lexington, their Douglas Dauntless was misjudged to be Japanese by the Lexington crew and was fired upon as they were approaching to land. To make matters worse, their aircraft's left wing hit the deck of the aircraft carrier and flipped over the port (left) side of the ship and into the sea. They were picked up by a trailing destroyer. Major lost his life in a training accident a few months later, before the battle of Midway.

xii BC Archives. 1945. *Malibu SeAero Service Ltd.* In GR-1526, Reel # B-5527, file # BC-19404, Incorporation Documents: Microfilm.

xiii BC Archive. 1945. *The Malibu Club.* In GR-1526, Box 207, file # S-2987, edited by. Incorporation Documents: Paper. During this period, Hamilton also opened up a Hamiltair charter office in Newport Beach California. The office was the second step in a long range plan to have a charter business up and down the Pacific coast, beginning with Vancouver BC and Malibu, then the Newport Beach base for Mexico and California, and eventually adding operations Alaska.

xiv Boeing Company Archives. 1946. *Boeing Aircraft of Canada - Malibu SeAero, refurbishment of the Grumman Goose*, Box 9. File 3561/24. Sales Order dated April 20, 1945 from the War Assets Corporation of Montreal, Canada to the Hamiltair Limited Company.

xv *Boeing Plant at Sea Island May be Sold – if new contracts unavailable.* 1945, The Vancouver Province, September 10, page 1. The government had ceased all contracts and production and Hamilton's Goose was a needed boost to keep the production line open.

xvi Boeing Company Archives. 1946. *Boeing Aircraft of Canada - Malibu SeAero, refurbishment of the Grumman Goose*, Box 9. File 3561/24. Work orders #7138 & #7152.

xvii *Ibid.,* All letters concerning the color and logo of the aircraft consist of handwritten or typed missives, plus some telegrams.

xviii Tom Hamilton even met his second wife, Leora, at the Malibu Club, only to get a divorce some years later. (He and Ethel, his first wife of some 25 years had divorced prior to 1946.)

xix Williamson. 1998. *Experiences as a Pilot flying for Malibu SeAero Ltd*. Victoria, BC, August 13.

xx *Disease Record Remarkable* Vancouver Sun. September 2, 1948. Page 16.

xxi *Girl Sick only 3 days* Vancouver Sun, September 3, 1948. Page 44.

xxii *BC Death Certificate for Sydney Diane Harris* – Reg# 1948-09-008119. BC Archives Micro #B13198.

xxiii *Quarantine at Malibu Club*, Vancouver Sun Newspaper, September 2, 1948. Page 18.

CHAPTER
FIVE

Malibu
and Young Life

The Blob at Malibu (2003)

"By the grace God has given me,
I laid a foundation as an expert builder,
and someone else is building on it."

NIV BIBLE, 1 CORINTHIANS 3:10

Taken by Jason Koenig – used with permission

Taken by John Leaf – Used with Permissio

Joey's Malibu Welcome (1984)

Joey had been pestering the Malibu ski boat drivers all day. Out of frustration, they finally agreed to his request. Joey was going to ski the Malibu Welcome. It was the first weekend of September in 1985 and the latest camp of teenagers was about to leave while the next group was making its way up to Malibu on board the *Malibu Princess*. However, the Princess was not ferrying a regular camp, instead it was a group of potential and current Young Life leaders and staff, arriving for their annual training session called 'Leadership' at Malibu. A couple of Joey's friends were on board the *Princess* and he desperately wanted to show off a bit. Joey was part of the outdoor crew as a volunteer worker on Malibu's summer staff and he wanted to make a big splash (of sorts) before camp closed down in a few weeks. Suddenly a horn sounded long and true, indicating that the *Princess* had rounded Patrick Point and had been sighted from camp. Everyone stopped what they were doing and started to prepare the Welcome for the incoming camp. Traditionally, every Young Life camp has a Welcome to greet the teenagers and to give them a taste of what is in store for them for the upcoming week. However, a typical Malibu Welcome tends to be somewhat more spectacular than those of the other Young Life properties. It begins with the *Malibu Princess* stopping halfway between Patrick Point and Malibu, leaving the 250 young guests from all over the United States and Canada wondering why they have stopped in the middle of the Jervis Inlet. Out of the blue, three-ski boats appear, running at full speed with skiers in tow, and aiming for the *Princess*. The boats fly forward in a triangle formation, each with a large Canadian flag fluttering in the force of the wind. In a snap all three boats make a practiced turn in order to travel parallel to the *Princess*, which is now listing to one side because everyone has massed to see the action. The boats zoom past with spotters and skiers waving and yelling. Suddenly band music starts up, playing "On Wisconsin" from a previously unnoticed boat full of musicians playing all sorts of instruments. Those aboard who are not playing are shouting "Welcome to Malibu". The ski boats make another pass and then head toward Malibu's Outer-dock while the *Malibu Princess* powers up and sets course for the same location. This is the normal Malibu Welcome.

Malibu Welcome Past the Princess (1984)

Joey has suited up in his wet suit, along with a life preserver and gloves. The boats are in position, waiting for the *Princess* to stop at the prearranged point. After having made a lame splash as he entered the water, Joey is now bobbing in the water with his foot in the boot of the ski, holding onto the towrope of the slowly idling Ski Natique. In unison, at a signal given by the lead boat driver, all three-boat drivers push the throttles forward, instantaneously sending all three boats leaping. Joey and the other skiers begin to cut a wedge of moving water until each of them has gotten up on the step and is balancing his weight on the moving ski. They now have their arms inside the triangle-shaped handle attached to the towrope, and hang on. The view in front of Joey is moving fast now. He can see the driver, on the right side of the craft, facing forward, and the two spotters waving excitedly and taking pictures, but beyond the bow of the ski boat, Joey can see the stationary *Malibu Princess* full of people anticipating the Welcome. Joey is in a groove, high on the feeling of the moving boats, fluttering flags, and the lightness of moving fast over the water. The formation passes the ship and Joey waves coolly, letting out a yell. He hears the cheers and sees the flashes of cameras as he zooms by the *Princess* and feels a sense of pride of being a part of the famed Malibu Welcome.

The lead driver signals to everyone that they are about to come around again for a second pass. Joey knows the water will be rougher, as the wake of the ski boats has unsettled the otherwise smooth water of the Inlet. The drivers execute the turn flawlessly and Joey again raises his hand again to wave and is just about to yell, when everything suddenly changes. His ski catches and digs into the water, dramatically dousing all of his excitement and pride. Joey doesn't just fall into the water. Instead, he becomes a human projectile, arms and legs loosely flying in out-of-control circular motions until he finally slows down enough to make a spectacular entry into the water. A loud moan is heard clear out to the Outer-dock some distance away, as the witnesses on the *Malibu Princess* react to Joey's first and last Welcome. Joey, now bobbing in the water, takes a mental inventory of himself and his predicament and wonders somewhat dazedly if "anyone saw that?" The latter is confirmed, as he realizes that he has just wiped out in front of everyone on the *Malibu Princess*, and is greeted by the cheers, laughter, and finger pointing of every passenger on board, including his friends. "It must have been good" he tells himself humbly. The ski boat has circled around to pick him up and the driver asks if he is alright. Joey responds sheepishly that he is fine, only to have the driver add, heaping insult onto the proverbial injury, that he's "never seen anyone bite it like that before." "Thanks a bunch" Joey responds as lifts himself into the ski boat and adds "All part of the program." The ski boat then speeds up in order to catch the *Malibu Princess* which is once again underway and heading for the Outer-dock.

Malibu Princess is Welcomed at the Outer Dock (1984)

The above scene of liveliness and laughter is in sharp contrast to the Malibu Club that greeted Jim Rayburn of Young Life on his first inspection of the property. Tom Hamilton's exclusive resort had lain abandoned and neglected for over two years, exposed to the weather and all the elements Mother Nature could throw at it. Malibu was a home without a family, but all that would change in late 1952. Tom Hamilton had sold his interests in the Beverly Hills Hotel and was faced with a large capital gains tax payment. He desperately needed something to offset his gain, and Malibu was the ideal candidate for TF to offload, for he no longer needed nor used the camp. Malibu had to be sold, but to whom? Tom had tried to sell to a number of individuals and organizations in the Seattle and British Columbia areas, but no one seemed interested, particularly when the asking price was over one million dollars. Hamilton even tried to convince the association owners of aircraft owners of the Pacific Northwest into purchasing it, but again the asking price was too high.[i] Hamilton was bothered by this, not for sentimental reasons but because he was a businessman, and it was frustrating to him not to be able to get a return on an investment. He was at a point where he was desperate to sell his resort at the entrance of Princess Louisa Inlet to anyone, just to be out from under. Jim Rayburn would be that person. Rayburn, founder of the Young Life organization, a non-denominational Christian youth ministry, had just come from a tour of Malibu and was determined to buy it. He felt that, through God's will, Malibu was to be part of his many other Young Life Christian outreach camps.

JIM RAYBURN

Jim Rayburn was born to a Christian family from Newton, Kansas, and was brought up in a strict religious atmosphere. Jim was also an individual full of energy, vision, and leadership, electrifying everything he was involved with. Faith was a part of his life, but he found his parent's interpretation of religion stifling. He attended college at Kansas State University and was part of the Pi Kappa Alpha fraternity, where he learned to cut loose and have fun. At this time Jim still equated 'faith' with 'no fun'.

Young Jim Rayburn studied and worked toward gaining an engineering degree, with the desire of going on to graduate school in mineralogy. These plans would change though when he married his college sweetheart, Maxine Stanley, on September 11, 1932 in front of the justice of the peace in Harrisonville, Missouri. To make ends meet, Jim turned to

Courtesy of Young Life – Used with Permission

Young Life Founder – Jim Rayburn (1950)

preaching as a Presbyterian minister and started a small New Mexico church. During this time, Jim and Maxine's family started to grow and eventually they had three children: Elna Ann, Mary Margaret (Sue), and James C. Rayburn III.

Jim learned a great deal about his faith during this time, and about how God really worked. It would be the starting point of what would become his life's work, and the beginning of a larger Christian youth ministry organization which he would help start. Jim was known for taking young people on hiking trips, explaining geology and the gospel, both subjects he was passionate about. He had learned that the 'dos and don'ts' he had grown up with were not necessarily a part of the Christian faith. He felt that all people should have the opportunity to hear about God, especially teenagers, whom he found he enjoyed being with the most. In many ways, Jim seemed to hold a special attraction for these young people, and he had the knack of relating to them as equals.

In 1939, to help further his ministry, Jim decided to go to Dallas Seminary in Texas, where he would earn a Master's Degree in Divinity. During his first years at the Seminary, he and other students were challenged by one of his professors to start working with teenagers in the Dallas area, and Jim Rayburn, having both the experience and the charm, became the leader of this bunch. They began working in an established youth group called the 'Miracle Book Club', in Dallas, which would later be called 'Young Life', taken from the Young Life Christian Campaign begun in the United Kingdom.[ii] Within a year, other Young Life clubs began to spread to other towns, among them Galveston, Texas.

Monday nights became Young Life Club nights, because no classes were held at Dallas Seminary on that day, leaving Jim and the others free to devote the time to their vision. Jim and his other associates would pack into one car and drive to various Texas towns in the morning, where each designated leader would be dropped off at the local high school. Once there, he would hang out with the kids until club time in the evening. At the conclusion of club at about 9 o'clock, each leader would be picked up by the same vehicle for the return trip to Dallas, arriving in the wee morning hours barely in time to start their classes.

After graduation, Rayburn and his bunch, now called the Young Life Staff, continued their youth work and eventually created a board of directors to legitimize the non-profit organization. An operational staff was also put together to handle the details of administration, and was based out of an office in Colorado Springs, Colorado. Early on Jim envisioned the need for camps to help in his ministry. Partly because he loved the outdoors and partly because it helped his young friends 'get-away-from-it-all,' Jim made camps a priority for the organization, which resulted in three camps being purchased by benefactors then and donated to Young Life during 1950-51. The Star, Silver Cliff, and the Frontier Ranches, all located in Colorado, were the beginning. The three camps became very popular among high school student, although they were the typical camping experience most kids were used to, without much variation. Nevertheless, they were still fun.

The Young Life organization was also beginning to take root in the Seattle, Tacoma, and Bellingham, Washington high schools, but the cost and time involved in getting the Pacific Northwest kids to the Colorado camps in the summer was a hardship for both leaders and students. Rayburn knew, strategically, that his next camp needed to be in the Pacific Northwest. The opportunity came when Jim Rayburn, a fanatical sports fan, traveled to Seattle to watch the NCAA basketball play-offs at the University of Washington's 'Hec-Ed' gymnasium in March of 1952. The game was between the University of Kansas (Jim's home state) and St. John's basketball teams.

The Malibu Club from Above (1984)

While he was there, Jim took the opportunity to tour a few potential sites located in the San Juan Island area of Washington State. But it was not until he remembered a conversation about the Malibu Club resort through Bill and Else Campbell some months before, former guests in the late 1940s under Hamilton, sparked Rayburn's interest in the property was sparked.[iii] The Campbell's flew Jim up Malibu in their Seabee (N6401K, called the Miss University Chevrolet) before the big basketball game of March 1953 started. After their return, Jim talked about nothing but Malibu and its potential as a Young Life camp in the Pacific Northwest. Jim's staff thought it would be a mistake to buy this property. The money and time needed to get the place in order would be enormous. Even David Weyerhaeuser, part of the famous Pacific Northwest timber family and who also happened to be a supporter and board member of Young Life, thought it would be a big risk for the very same reasons. The staff also saw the enormous challenge associated with running a camp that could be reached only by boat or airplane. They envisioned the logistical nightmare of hauling passengers and freight from the mainland to the camp and back. And the maintenance required to put an abandoned resort in order, as well as the on-going future upkeep, was too much. All issues aside, Jim Rayburn was determined to make Malibu the fourth Young Life Property.

THE MALIBU CLUB

If Hamilton was the master builder of Malibu, then Jim Rayburn would be its soul. He would be the one to give the resort a purpose other than existing just for the rich and famous. It would be a resort for teenagers. It would set the tone for current and future Young Life camps, as Jim had realized that Young Life camps would have to be different from the typical youth camp. He saw, after touring Malibu and talking with Hamilton, that Young Life camps would have to be resorts for the young and entail a new, different, and exciting experience. Jim felt that Malibu was the next step and opened communications with Hamilton about a possible purchase in late 1952.

In the summer of 1953, Tom Hamilton was a guest of each of the three Young Life camps in Colorado and he saw first-hand how Young Life would use his resort.[iv] Hamilton was likely impressed not only with Rayburn, since they were both cut from the same mold as visionaries, but also with the whole aspect of Young Life's dealings with youth. Hamilton had always had an interest in young people, and had enjoyed being involved with setting up youth activities at his home in Lake Arrowhead, California. He even planned a couple of weeks dedicated to young people up at Malibu while he ran the resort. Rayburn later went back up to Malibu in order to survey the property and make plans, and Bob Campbell's Seabee was again pressed into service to haul Jim and his staff, including Bill Starr and Add Sewell, to Malibu for a second look before the negations began. Bill and Add both shook their heads to see the resort in such a deplorable state of decay, and the two men still thought it would be a big mistake to buy the property. Jim ignored them, however, for he looked past the present condition of the property in order to see the future, much like Hamilton had done.

The meeting to begin negations for the sale was finally set up at the office of Tom Hamilton's Los Angeles tax attorneys in November 1953. Jim Rayburn, Frank Muncy (accountant, Young Life staff member, and friend of Rayburn) and Young Life's representative lawyer, Vaughn R. Antablin, negotiated for three days with Tom Hamilton and his agents concerning the sale. Tom, being the experienced salesman, started out on day one by stating the highest possible price, one million dollars, an unheard of sum for a struggling ministry like Young Life. But Jim Rayburn was patient, and he was confident something would work out. And it did. On the second day they were told that the price had dropped to $400,000, and by the morning of the third day, Hamilton had further lowered the amount to $300,000. Frank Muncy, realizing that this was a great gesture on the part of Mr. Hamilton, urged Jim to take this "very generous offer." It must be noted that Mr. Muncy was correct, and even with TF wanting to unload the property, it was an extremely gracious gesture on his part. Jim Rayburn said he would give his answer in the morning and the meeting of the third day was adjourned.

Jim and Frank returned to their hotel room to discuss the matter. They prayed specifically about this transaction and afterward Jim made two phone calls to two specific donors to Young Life – one to an unknown businessman in Memphis and the other to an individual in New Orleans. According to Frank, these two calls produced $50,000 as a down payment for this new property.

The morning of the fourth day, Jim, Frank, and Vaughn returned to Hamilton's attorney's office and said they were willing to buy Malibu for $300,000, but only with the condition that he would accept $50,000 as a down payment and an IOU for $250,000. Tom Hamilton accepted the offer the morning of the fifth day, and had a legal agreement written up detailing the details of the transfer of Malibu to Young Life. By December 21, 1953, a schedule of payments to several escrow accounts was set up, with the understanding that the remaining $250,000 would be paid off before 1960. A mortgage agreement was then drawn up in support of the escrow accounts to pay for the remainder of the loan.[v]

A number of donors helped with this situation throughout the first years to help cover the 1954 payments. There were countless other faithful contributors who donated small and large amounts to help Young Life with the mortgage burden of Malibu. Eventually, Tom Hamilton would be the ultimate benefactor by declaring that the mortgage was "paid in full" well before the mortgage was paid off. Once again Hamilton had made a lasting impact on history of Princess Louisa Inlet, this time in the countless lives of the many young people who would visit the Malibu Club he first began in 1940. There are no dates associated with Hamilton's signature on the promissory notes, but they are estimated to be around 1955 or 1956. Nevertheless, the original negotiations, the deal, and legal paperwork were all completed on December 29, 1953,[vi] prior to the end of the tax year and enabling Hamilton to offset his capital gain expense. The sale of the resort resulted in Young Life owning a total of 638 acres of land on both sides of the entrance of Princess Louisa Inlet, including the 48 acres where the buildings stood, and an additional 589 acres on the other side of the entrance. But most of all, the Malibu Club at the entrance of Princess Louisa Inlet now had a new family. Young Life was ready to move in and build on what Hamilton had started.

Once the bill of sale had been written up, Jim Rayburn issued instructions to Bill Starr, Add Sewell, and a few other Young Life staff, including Tom Raley, Doug Coe, Carl Nelson, Bob Mitchell, and Ollie Dustin to start the process of getting the camp ready to handle high school students for the coming summer. It was January of 1954, and the weather was as cold and wet as anything Captain Vancouver and Lt. Puget had encountered some two hundred years before. Instead of an airplane, this time Bill, Add, and the rest of the team traveled up the Jervis Inlet on a rented fishing boat called the *Elsie Lee*. Ad remembers "typically miserable winter weather to take inventory. The boat was small, we were crowded in, but it was an adventure and coffee, tea, some good food, and the coziness of the cabin made the trip fun." [vii]

Once at Malibu they figured out the priorities for work for the coming year. The kitchen would take precedence, as it was in the worst condition, as it was nick-named the 'Black hole of Calcutta' by Ollie. [viii] The room had been left with food still in the kitchen sink and grease in the fryer. The decay of the whole camp was evident at first glance and it would be a challenge to build it back to the resort it had been known to be. The staff each took one building to pray, over asking the Lord for strength, resources, and guidance in this endeavor. In time these prayers were answered.

A second trip was taken in February of 1954 by Olli Dustin and Bill Starr, in order to inventory all the items in the camp, and these were compared to the thick inventory book done by Hamilton. They first needed to find out what had been looted from Malibu during the time it lay dormant and what items needed to be replaced for the operation of the camp. It was cold and tiring work for the small crew, but they managed to complete it in two days. Some of the people who still worked for Hamilton as caretakers of the property helped out in the inventory process as well. It has been said that Young Life was able to sell some of the items that it didn't need, to help pay some of the debt.

Rayburn set up a non-profit company called 'Young Life of Canada' to legitimize the sale and operation of his new camp and, in addition, the company would be used to hold Malibu in trust per Canadian law. Young Life of Canada eventually was incorporated under the Companies' Act in Winnipeg, Manitoba on May 18, 1954. Incidentally, it was the same act that legitimized the first incorporation of Malibu and Hamilton's other subsides related to the area in 1941 and 1945.

Taken by Elizabeth Hamilton Sunde – Used with Permission

Tom Hamilton (center) with YL Guest Onboard the *Yorkeen* (1954)

In March 1954, a college work week of students from the University of Washington and Seattle Pacific University started the physical part of getting the camp in order. Everything was worked on, inspected and repaired, including the 5,451 feet of steel pipe water line, floats and boardwalks. In addition, mattresses were aired and the many other tasks that were required to get the new camp ready for the summer were completed. During Easter of 1954, Tom Hamilton brought a number of Young Life staff and board members up for the official hand-off on one of his old converted Fairmile yachts now called the *Yorkeen*. Although he no longer owned it, he was able to borrow it for the occasion from the owner and friend, Fred Mckeen.

The first summer camp at Malibu was held in June, 1954. The Malibu staff was on a short budget and during that first week only 13 kids showed up. But they were treated to Jim Rayburn as the speaker, and to Bob Mitchell (a future Young Life President) handling the program. The ratio during those first two weeks of camp was more staff than campers and there was talk about canceling the rest of the summer so that the staff could continue repairs to make the camp operational for the next year. However, the number of campers seemed to pick as the weeks passed and Malibu was able to actually operate successfully, barely, during that first summer of 1954.

Taken by Jason Koenig – used with permission

Dancing the Night Away at Malibu (2003)

THE YOUNG LIFE ORGANIZATION

Young Life today, as well as in 1945 in Jim Rayburn's era, is a relational-based Christian, non-denominational, ministry focused specifically on young junior high and high school students. The ministry is one of the largest Christian youth ministries in North America today and has spread worldwide. It is still a non-profit organization, operating as a structured hierarchy similar to other large Christian organizations such as

InterVarsity. The Young Life organization is still based primarily in Colorado Springs, Colorado, where the administrative and president's offices continue to stand. Because of the large scope of the North American organization, the ministry is divided into a number of regional districts, each run by a vice president who provides assistance and support to his or her specific districts, and each district is divided into regions, each run by individual regional directors. These regions are further divided into still more specific urban or metropolitan areas and run by an area director responsible for the financial, managerial, and other requirements to make Young Life work for that particular area. Typically each area will have a number of volunteer college age and adult leaders who focus on individual junior and senior high schools Young Life areas and camps are funded through donations and fund-raising efforts. It takes a lot of time, energy, and money on the part of committed individuals and the committees to make these areas and camps work and this is especially true for Malibu, with its unusual needs and location.

The Young Life philosophy is that a leader earns the right to be heard by going to where the teenagers are. This is what Jim Rayburn believed back in the 1940s and it is still true today. A recent Young Life publication stated, "Young Life leaders will be at football games, the streets of inner-city neighborhoods, driving carloads of kids to the shopping malls or tutoring students in study centers after school."[ix] They are striving to befriend these young people and to understand their perspectives. They also want to help show them an alternative way of life through the Christian faith.

Youth of today are faced with so many distractions and concerns, that the choices they make at this stage of their lives will dictate the lives they will lead as adults. Jim Rayburn truly believed then, as do the Young Life leaders of today, that the answer lies in the Christian faith, specifically in the Bible, and God's son Jesus Christ. It is this model that Young Life leaders and the organization, use to show young people that there is hope even in today's world, just as there was 2,000 years ago in Jesus' time. A typical Young Life club will meet in a neighborhood home, with the leaders providing a social time of singing, skits, and a chance to hear about God's concern for them, known as a club talk. The many kids who attend a Young Life club really don't want to hear about religious things, but are more attracted to the fun and visibility a club offers. It does, however, give them the opportunity to learn what God is all about in a enjoyable way that they can understand. This is where a camp like Malibu comes into the picture.

Taken by Jason Koenig – used with permission

Disco Night at Malibu (2003)

Malibu provides a time 'to-get-away-from-it-all' and allows these new relationships between the high-school students and club leaders to be strengthened. It gives them a place and a week during the summer to focus on having a good time. These young students can be away from their normal environment, be it good or bad, and have an opportunity to examine new ideas. Malibu provides new experiences and thrills, such as rappelling, water skiing and other exciting water sports, as well as other adventures that some of these kids may never have experienced before. And each evening, just like back home, there is a Young Life Club where everyone meets in Big Squawka to sing, laugh, and have fun. There is always an assigned speaker who gives the club talks. The Young Life staff provides a hilarious and entertaining program that runs throughout the course of the week. The combination of program, club talks, the fun, and the incredible and unusual setting all combine to create unforgettable Malibu memories for each guest to take home at the end of their week. Today, more than 40,000 kids pack the 12 national properties owned by Young Life, and roughly 3,000 teenagers experience Malibu each summer. These numbers continue to grow.

Belly Flop Competition at Malibu (2003)

Along with the young guests who visit Malibu each summer for a week of camp, there are both paid and volunteer staffs who help operate and maintain Malibu during the camping season. Like all the other Young Life properties, these particular background jobs are necessary to allow the camping ministry to work and function at a lively and safe level for the teenagers who visit each year. The Property Manager looks after and maintains the physical property of Malibu, which includes the buildings, boats, new building and construction, operation, maintenance, safety, and enhancement to the property. The Camp Manager, on the other hand, looks after the people aspect of the program during the course of the summer. The Camp Manager is responsible for everything except the property, including all the staffing assignments, positions for work crew and summer staff, and acts as the liaison between the program staff and head counselors during their three-week assignments. In the past, a number of all-summer people were hired to do specific jobs and tasks at camp. Today they are known as Interns and they are at work in specific Young Life areas during the fall through spring seasons in a local club, spending their summers at Malibu. Essentially, they go where the kids are.

But the heart of Malibu, like all of the other Young Life camps, is those who volunteer part or all of their summer in order to help in the behind-the-scenes operation and program. There are two sets of workers: the work crew and the summer staff. The work crew is a group of high school students who have had a camping experience at Malibu or at another Young Life camp, and have a desire to serve. And serve they do, for they are the people who prepare the food, help with cooking, wash the dishes, and do the outdoor work necessary to support over 250 campers a week. The summer staff, on the other hand, is made up of college students who handle the more responsible positions related to the operation and program of the camp. Their jobs include the construction and outside crews, ski boat drivers, water ski instructors, office personnel, and house cleaning folks. The Malibu experience would not happen if it were not for the efforts and sacrifices these people make each summer and it is truly amazing to see how motivated and excited they are, every summer during each session. It is the dream of many CEOs to have their employees, show the same sprit in their jobs as these young people have at Malibu.

During the summer peak Malibu can host over 250 teenagers each week and the camp becomes very exclusive. This means that Malibu is no longer a public place to tie up and restock, or visit, as it used to be in Hamilton's time. Anyone wishing to have a tour of the camp can do so, but this is arranged by bringing a boat to the inner-dock, the Princess Louisa side, where the Malibu harbormaster will give the boat's skipper instructions where to tie up. Another volunteer, this time an adult, will escort the visiting party throughout the camp, explaining its history (hopefully they will have read this book) and giving the visitors an opportunity to view what Young Life is, and how it works. Afterward the skipper is encouraged to get underway, as the inner-dock is a busy place, filled with teenagers learning how to water ski, sea-planes delivering passengers and cargo to the camp and other yachters eager to get a tour. But this doesn't mean that private boaters can't enjoy the Inlet as well. Public moorage is available at the other end of the Inlet, near Chatterbox Falls, giving the yachters a chance to view the area at their leisure.

Taken by C.W. Hitz of One Eye Images & Sound

Profile of Young Life's Malibu Club (2003)

THE PROPERTY AND FACILITY

The Malibu Club has always been a unique feature at Princess Louisa Inlet. It was built and designed by Tom Hamilton out of his own imagination and experience. When Young Life took over the facility, it also took over the responsibility of maintaining and improving this unique spot, along with rebuilding it into one of the premier sites in the Pacific Northwest. Since 1953 the Young Life organization has invested time and money into keeping this property the crown jewel of all of their camps throughout North America. Through the years there have been many surprises to repair, improvements needed and additions required to keep the facility in working order, allowing the right blend of recreation and hospitality tasks and ensuring that the crew and guests are safely accounted for.

The designs of the buildings of Malibu are a result of Tom Hamilton's ideas, the need to promote the resort, and his desire to make money from the Inlet. The main buildings he built between 1940 and 1945 now make up the most permanent fixtures on the small finger of bedrock at the entrance of Princess Louisa Inlet. Besides designing all of Malibu's buildings, Hamilton named each of them after American Southwesteren native tribes of the California, Arizona, and New Mexico areas so that his guests, mainly from California, would recognize the familiar names. Once Young Life acquired Malibu from Hamilton, some of the names of the buildings were eventually changed to reflect the local Sechelt First Nation titles of the area. The Navajo Lodge became the women's/girls' dormitory, now called Nootka Lodge. Sitka Lodge became the boys' dormitory, retaining its original name. Hamilton's Aztec Lodge would be divided into its three floors, each having a new name. The second floor became Lilloet Deck (after another First Nation tribe and the name of a nearby river) and the top Penthouse floor became Swivolet Deck after the Sechelt name of the Inlet. The exclusive Victoria shop, 'George Strathe and Sons,' on Main Street became the 'Totem Trader,' where campers and yachters could buy Malibu merchandise and other items to remember their experience at the camp and the Inlet. The 'Photography Shop' became the 'Linen Nook' where all amenities for the rooms could be found, such as sheets, blankets, and cleaning supplies. The Barber/Beauty Shop became the infirmary, called the 'Medicine Man', where a camp doctor handled all medical concerns and emergencies. The Sports Shop remained, but later became the Main Office of Malibu, and was moved down to the lower deck underneath Big Squawka a couple of years later. Young Life built a soda fountain, called the 'Totem Inn', where teenagers could buy ice cream and other treats during their stay. Throughout the years the most famous item at the Totem Inn has been a large ice cream dish known as the Malibu Princess. A Malibu Princess consists of five scoops of different flavored ice-cream, and a number of toppings. The goal is, where many have tried and failed, to eat a whole 'Princess' in one sitting without getting sick. It is, and has been, a fun social event to watch, and those who succeed are well known for their feat during their week at camp.

In 1959 Young Life began improvements to the Malibu facility in order to increase function and add capacity. Over the years these changes would substantially alter the appearance of the camp. First, the Dining hall[x] was extended out from the original Hamilton design because of the need to handle more numbers than the original Dining hall could hold. A new boardwalk was constructed, wrapping around the extended hall and providing additional access to the rest of the camp and a swimming pool, Rayburn's priority number one at Malibu, was built by dynamiting away the rock between the Inlet and the newly remodeled Dinning hall. The new pool was leveled and lined with cement and a wall was constructed between the pool and the inlet to provide a barrier against the rushing rapids, creating the unique experience of swimming right next to the Inlet's mouth. This time, however, the pool was not filled with fresh water, but salt water directly from the Inlet. A number of new cement walkways were poured at this time, in order to facilitate

Taken by C.W. Hitz of One Eye Images & Sound

Looking Down Mainstreet at Malibu (1979)

access to the pool and other parts of the camp. Another fundraising drive was organized to find donations to help pay for these new additions. Ten years later, in 1968, the pool was upgraded, as over time large cracks had appeared in the bottom, allowing the Inlet access and causing the water level to ebb and flow with the tides. The pool was completely remodeled to include a new cement lining and chlorinated heated fresh water. This was accomplished by taking the cold fresh water and routing it through pipes to the power shack and on through heat exchangers attached to the diesel generators, thus increasing the water temperature. The warmed water was then piped to the pool to provide for a warmer and cleaner swimming experience. The pool would remain the same until another upgrade was required in 1997, when cracks again had developed which allowed the cold salt water to enter. This time, once the pool was drained, workers went ahead and leveled a portion of the rocky poolside in order to create safer entryways.

Of course all the needed improvements throughout the years cost money, and cash donations were, and are, a large part of the funding. But aside from the financial donations, other types of donation were accepted in the form of supplies, materials, and labor. For example, in the early 1960s Bob Rodgers, a fountain supply salesman, donated golf products at cost to help the sports shack provide enough equipment for the kids to play on the Malibu golf course. Another example was when the *Malibu Princess* was built in the mid 1960s and the Boeing Company gave surplus airliner seats, which provided seating room for the young guests on their trip up the Jervis Inlet. These are just examples of the many donations Malibu has received and continues to receive through the years. Donations, both material and financial, are an important part of keeping Malibu running.

Many other structural improvements followed the construction of the pool and the extended Dining hall. In 1964, a pumphouse was created to help meet the water demands of the growing camp and separate pipelines were installed strictly for fire suppression purposes, a constant concern for Malibu's wood structures. Improvements to the water line continued throughout the 1970s, and eventually included a new 12,000-gallon tank to give the camp more than enough of the fresh water needed for the kitchen, Totem Inn, and laundry. During this time the pipes had begun to be replaced, as well, with ABS plastic rather than steel as it was lighter, cheaper, and more durable.

But water was not the only utility that had to be upgraded due to Malibu's growth. The demand for more electricity also expanded and the original Hamilton diesel engines had to be replaced. History repeated itself, as hydro generation by use of a Pelton wheel was seriously considered once more but, as in Hamilton's time, the hydro plan was scrapped in favor of new diesel generators due to the lack of knowledge and reliable technology associated with hydro. Fuel was still relatively inexpensive. In 1976 a new powerhouse was built below the rock fall of Nootka, to allow for easy access and ventilation. The original Hamilton diesel shack became the plumbing shack once the diesels were removed to the new powerhouse, and this new powerhouse structure was later expanded in 1989 to incorporate the metal and wood shops. The original shops were located underneath Big Squawka and the constant loud noise of power tools disrupted the meetings held there. After the shops were moved, the old shop under Big Squawka was extended back towards the vacant shop in order to expand the Game Room.

In the years following these changes, Malibu would once again re-think the hydro possibility when high fuel costs became a significant issue. Peter Talbot, from Vancouver, BC, an ex-park ranger who managed the Chatterbox Falls marine park in the early 1980s, designed and built a prototype hydroelectric generation system as a proof-of-concept in the mid 1990s. He used this to power one of the cabins during the winter for a number of seasons. It was a success, proving that the idea and the technology worked, so in 2001, Malibu started working on building a larger hydro system across the Jervis Inlet at a river that flows strongly year around. This will provide the necessary energy, cleanly and cheaply, for years to come. The design work was finished in 2002 and, after a generous amount of money was donated in 2003, the project will be completed sometime in 2005.

Peter Talbot has also helped in the development of a better radio communication system at Malibu by building many of the parts and antennas for the High Frequency (HF), or ship to shore radio system used at Malibu during the 1980s and 90s. Today the installations are still in use but only as backup, since the modern satellite system that now serves as Malibu's primary phone and data communication system that was installed in 2000. Like Peter, there have been a number of other gifted and skilled people who have assisted Malibu, helping the camp in its many mechanical and electrical functions. Brian Anderson has provided his talents and assistance to Malibu since the late 1950s, helping to change and upgrade Malibu's infrastructure. For example, in the spring of 2003, Brian has been involved with the design of a well system where by Malibu can get its fresh water, rather than relying on the pipe system from Helena Creek in existence since Hamilton built the camp.

It is an ingenious idea and time will tell how well it will work. Many other people in the past have put their time and effort into this camp, but to name each person and what they have done not possible for the scope of this book.[xi] Malibu also benefits from the experience of these people during the two work weeks known as Tool and Tackle. The major tasks twice a year are accomplished with a week helping put the camp in working order before the summer season starts and another week to help prepare Malibu for the winter once the summer season is over. There are also college work weeks, where students from around the Pacific Northwest participate in helping Malibu with certain repairs or projects needed before the summer camping program begins. It is amazing to see the eager volunteers of all generations helping Malibu and its camping ministries function the way it does.

More structural changes included remodeling the original Sports Shack (next to the Game Room) into a Café in 2001, where a number of blends of coffee specific to Malibu can be purchased. The coffee blends are donated by an independent coffee producer, Brooke Payne of Cutters Point in Gig Harbor, Washington, specifically for Malibu to use in its service operations. The current plan is to next incorporate the Café into the Game Room, and display all sorts of Hamilton era items.

Sports and recreational activities have always played an important role in most teenagers' lives, and Rayburn was struck by the unique opportunities Malibu offered. Golf was already a part of the infrastructure, since the 18 hole course was set up by Hamilton in 1945. Young Life shortened the course when they took over, dropping the number of holes to 13 in order to facilitate maintenance. The original Sports Shack handled the storage and distribution of the balls and clubs for the campers to use. But the greens of Malibu needed to be maintained, so a golf shack was built in the summer of 1969 to be used as storage shed for all the supplies and equipment. It also marked the start of the trail up to Perspiration Point; the rocky ledge that overlooks Malibu and most of Princess Louisa and Jervis Inlets. Unfortunately, it is at the same site that the only camper-related death has ever occurred at the club while under Young Life's direction. In the summer of 1967, Ed Anastasio Jr. and his friend Norm Lebrett, both of Spokane, Washington, decided to hike up to Perspiration Point unsupervised. They had not reached the Point before deciding to start back down. Unfortunately they got lost, and somewhere on the way back Ed made a fatal decision to jump from a ledge to a large tree, thinking he could get to a lower ledge faster. The teenager was able to catch the tree, but realized too late that he could not get to the next ledge as planned. In trying to leap back to his original starting point he misjudged the jump and fell to his death, hitting the ledge beneath the tree, and another one some 150 feet below.[xii] Ed was killed instantly, as his friend Norm could only watch in horror.

It has been amazing to note that in Malibu's nearly 50 years of operation with Young Life, this has been the only death, especially when compared with the many deaths that have occurred at Chatterbox Falls over the years.[xiii] Malibu's safety record has been phenomenal. As a matter of record, this story is told to each camper that comes to Malibu to serve as a warning which seems to have been successful thus far.

Changes have continued, seemingly unabated. In 2000, golf was replaced with Frisbee golf because, over the years, the golf clubs and tees were damaging the grounds. In 1983, a ropes course was added to the woods near the golf shack to give campers a challenging activity to do as a group per their cabin assignments. The course was arranged some 30 to 60 feet in the air with many challenging obstacles to go through. In 2000, the course was revised with additional sections related to mountain repelling and rope work in a circular fashion around a set of steady cedar and fir trees. It has been a part of Malibu ever since.

Taken by C.W. Hitz of One Eye Images & Sound

The New Malibu Gym (2002)

Another recreational sport came to Malibu in 1968, when a single basketball court was constructed on the high glacier berms overlooking Malibu and the entrance to the Inlet. This entailed a lot of work since a basketball court is required to be level, and the location required more work than usual to achieve this. Dynamite was used to remove the granite berms and pulverize them into smaller chunks of rock, but the debris was too heavy to be manually hauled out by the workers. Instead backer boards, long narrow pieces of wood, were then erected above the rocky and uneven terrain to show where the court was to be built. The framing work of two by fours and beams was set among the rock debris of the berms and, once everything was level, plywood was laid to create the court. When the floor was solid and in place, the work on the surrounding barrier around the court, made out of chicken wire, could be completed and, finally, two hoops were added.

This single basketball court lasted a long, long time but was finally torn down in the winter of 2000 to make room for a three story covered gym, completed in the summer of 2001. It was said by the workers involved in tearing down the old 1968 court, that it was so solidly built that it took much more time to remove than was originally planned. It was worth it, though as the new Gym provides a three court covered recreational facility, including a weight training area and bathrooms. Below the gym level is an apartment for staff, and the bottom level houses the Beyond Radio Room. The entire structure was built along steel beam frames and took over a year and half to complete. Behind the gym, a cement utility road had to be constructed, in order to give the heavy construction equipment access to this site, as well as other potential sites in the future.

In 2000, the rocky ground near the pool was leveled and used to build a volleyball court, complete with sand and nets, with the added protection of high mesh nets to keep the balls in the court rather than in the inlet.

Taken by C.W. Hitz of One Eye Images & Sound

Looking Up Mainstreet at Malibu (1979)

Aside from the recreational aspect, Malibu has to maintain many other, more mundane functions just as other hotels and resorts do, in terms of sleeping quarters, sanitary arrangements, and food preparation. The ever-increasing number of guests made these on-going challenges important issues that had to be addressed. In the late 1960s, the need for pollution and sanitation control were dealt with as more campers visited the camp each summer and the Canadian environmental laws concerning the impact of waste vs. nature had been strengthened. In 1974 a grant was given to Malibu to build a new septic system. A new and larger septic tank was built, with a seawall protect it from the high winter tides and inevitable storms. This septic tank would treat all the sewage/waste from the camp, ensuring that treated water was not polluting the Inlet. This is an improvement from Hamilton's day, when he just dumped it straight into the Inlet. A large boardwalk was built above the septic tank to give functional access to the camp and the inner-dock, but the boat house, built in Hamilton's time, was removed to give more open space on the board walk.

More operational changes took place during this period. A cement skirt was built below the kitchen where an incinerator for garbage, affectionately called Ingrid, was installed. The camp's burnable garbage was now incinerated, but because of the location and the changing winds from morning to afternoon, burn times had to be strictly followed or the whole camp would be engulfed in acrid smoke. Today two propane incinerators have replaced Ingrid and so as not to 'smoke out' the camp, the incinerators are located on a dock away from the camp. The chambers are used to incinerator everything except the recyclable and non-burnable items, which are stored and taken to Vancouver, BC so they can be properly disposed of.

Young Life has had to keep planning, and re-planning with in regard to the needs of the camp and the various capacities it can hold. Over the years, new buildings have been added or old ones remodeled to keep up with the ever-increasing numbers of staff and campers. Haida, the old Malibu Bar during Hamilton's time, has been used in many capacities since its beginning as both staff and guest quarters, so in 1971, Treehouse was built to give extra living space for the staff that Haida could not handle. It would serve as the Malibu Manager's and family's quarters. Treehouse's design was based on four vertical logs that create a platform above the ground. In 1973, the lower part of Treehouse was filled in with additional guestrooms, with laundry facilities in the back. At the same time an additional cabin was added underneath Nootka, called Foc'sole, along with an additional cabin called Chimo for the cooks which was constructed up near what was then the basketball court.

Malibu's Sitka Dormitory (1979)

While most changes to the grounds and buildings were determined by the need for more space, others were more sudden and demanding in nature. In 1970, one of the girls working in the Laundry Room underneath Sitka remarked off-handedly to Bob Pritchard that in the morning when she started work her head would not touch the ceiling but by evening it did. Bob also noticed, when he was up in the Penthouse suite, that at one end of the three-story building seemed to bounce when he walked from one side to the other and, after some investigation, he found that both problems were caused by the beams Hamilton had used to secure the buildings. They were rotting and starting to fail as a base for the structures. Foundation work was started immediately on Sitka, as well as on Main Street. With major renovation work beginning, it was decided that Sitka was to be remodeled at the same time they shored up the foundations. The original Hamilton design of Sitka had a hallway running through the interior of each floor, with doors connecting to each room. In 1970 the halls were removed and the individual rooms combined, forming eight large dorm rooms. This allowed for more space (always important) for the boy's dormitory, and cement piers and bulkheads were added to shore up the sagging building.

Food storage and preparation also received a new building in this period. In 1968, there became a growing need to have an enclosed food storage area that was safe from the wildlife and midnight raiders, both human and animal. The new building was called Capilano, and its foundation was poured between Nootka and the Dining hall. Capilano would have two levels; the first dedicated to the storage of food supplies and the second the men's summer staff quarters. Capilano received an additional room for the male cooks in 1989. Women's summer staff quarters were in near the basketball court and were original Hamilton buildings called Uppers and Lowers, but the two buildings were finally torn down and replaced with new sleeping and lodging quarters, called Tilikum, in 1991. Other staff housing had been added through the years as the need increased. In 1969, during the same project in which the Golf Shack was constructed as was an A-frame house was built for staff. It included a single apartment and kitchenette, and was called Minatch. A few years later in 1973, a large house called Chilkoot, was built for the Superintendents of the camp. The most recent staff house, Kekuli, was built in 1993 and is located between Treehouse and Minatch.

Of all the structural changes that have been needed over time, possibly none was more important to the running of the camp than the upgrade of its docks. Since Hamilton's time there had been a dock to tie up to for the yachts and pleasure boats that visited the resort. When Young Life bought the property, the original Inner-dock was used until it was replaced with a donated barge, which had been re-decked and fitted with a ramp leading up to camp. Young Life also had another dock, built on the Jervis Inlet side, for loading and unloading as the camps became bigger and which later became the dock where the *Malibu Princess* tied up. This became known as the Outer-dock, and it was located past Hamburger point and the golf course. Having the dock on the Jervis Inlet side also eliminated the need to navigate the tidal rapids and more difficult route of the entrance to the Princess Louisa Inlet. Logistics became much simpler when the addition of a donated barge replaced the original Outer-dock in the mid 1970s. It was used as the dock for many years. A ski deck with a ladder was eventually built for this Outer-dock because a skier could be situated eight feet above the water level, providing for some of the most spectacular and painful water ski dock starts ever seen at Malibu. Unfortunately, the new Outer-dock had a tendency to leak, so a pump was installed along with the housing.

Both the Outer-dock and Inner-dock were later replaced between the late 1980s and the early 1990s, with cement float docks and aluminum gang-ways that were better able to handle the winter weather, and were lower to the water for easy access in or out of the boats.

Courtesy of Young Life – Used with Permission

The Jervis Express at Malibu (1958)

THE BOATS OF MALIBU

When Young Life first bought Malibu in 1954, the main mode of transportation for kids, guests, freight, and building supplies was by charter boat. During a typical week, two to three boats would be needed to haul people and goods back and forth from Malibu to Pender Harbor. It was a constant challenge for the Malibu staff, as many different companies were used throughout the years. The first company was the Tidewater Shipping Company out of Vancouver, BC, operating the *Jervis Express* (later renamed *Tournament*) and the *Troubadour* (used from 1954 to 1958). And the Coast Ferry's' boat, the *Island Princess* was used in 1959 along with the Harbor Ferry's boats, the *U-Chuck II* and the *Holly Burn* used from 1960 to 1965. By the mid-1960s, suitable charter boats used by Malibu were no longer going to be available and, without a charter contract, it seemed that Malibu might have to cease operations all together.

The Launching of the Malibu Princess (1966)

The solution to this problem was obvious, build a suitable vessel. But, as usual, lack of money was the main issue. Funding was just not available in the Young Life operations budget, so a number of successful fund-raising events were orchestrated throughout the Pacific Northwest. At the heart of each of these events was a scale model, built by Bob Prichard, of the anticipated *Malibu Princess* to help show what the donations would be used for.

The *Malibu Princess* was born out of a design by Philip F. Spaulding and Associates of Seattle, Washington, and was eventually built by Allied Shipbuilders Limited, of Vancouver, BC. The ship was designed to carry 250 passengers and seven crew members, and would be powered by two Caterpillar 325-hp diesel engines running two twin propellers for a maximum speed of 12 knots. When completed it would have an overall length of 126', a waterline length of 115', a beam of 32' 6" and a draft of 7' and 6".

The *Malibu Princess* was launched on Saturday morning, March 26th 1966, at the Allied's shipyard in Vancouver, BC. After she was christened and launched, she was tied alongside the dock so that those who had contributed to the building of this fine ship could give it a thorough inspection. In all, the *Malibu Princess* cost over $335,000. Thirty-five percent was funded by a Canadian Maritime Commission ship subsidy, five percent was from the sale of a donated luxury yacht called the *Westerly,* which was not suited for hauling passengers from Malibu to Vancouver, BC, and the remaining sixty percent was loaned from the Puget Sound National Bank in Tacoma, Washington, through the good offices of Mr. David Weyerhaeuser. Today the *Malibu Princess* ferries teenagers up and down the Jervis Inlet enroute to and from Malibu. When not providing this important service, it is often used as a tour boat as part of Malibu Yacht Charters, running regularly to Princess Louisa Inlet and the surrounding area for anyone interested in the area.

As Malibu is surrounded on three sides by water, it is only reasonable that water-based sports play a huge role in the activities of the camp. Water skiing in particular, has always been a popular activity, as the surface of the water at Princess Louisa

Tsuahdi, Squamish, Skwaka, and Chinook (1984)

Inlet is very warm and smooth. Hamilton had used many popular fast boats, such as the classic wooden Chris-Crafts, as ski boats for his guests. A couple of these boats as well as old wooden water skis were introduced to the camp, and Young Life has continued with this activity today. In the 1960s at least four ski boats were purchased for the summer's purposes. In the1970s four popular Ski Natique boats were sold at cost to Malibu, along with many of the new types of water ski gear. These boats had specific names, which were the same each year; *Tsuahdi, Squamish, Skwawka, and Chinook,* during the early 1970s and most of the 1980s. By the early 1990s Malibu made a switch to other types of ski boats and over successive years they tried out Ski Brendellas, Malibu Skiers, and MasterCrafts. Additional water sports were added as well, such as wakeboarding, tubing and the Caribe (the five person hot dog tube towed behind a boat).

Although much less glamorous than the water sport boats, workboats have been an integral part of maintaining the operations at Malibu, and throughout the years the Young Life Organization has relied on a number of donated and purchased boats to help with the maintenance and program. The

Nyjamiam or *Nyj* (later called the *Tillicum*) was one of the first boats used as a designated workboat during Malibu's early years. The *Nji* was a 30' cabin cruiser donated to Malibu by Dr. DuFresne, a mortician from Vancouver, Washington. Ray and Marge Anderson delivered this vessel, motoring the *Nyj* from the Columbia River, up the Washington Coast (Pacific Ocean), through the Straits of Juan De Fuca and the Straits of Georgia and, finally, up the Jervis Inlet to Malibu in early 1955. The boat saw service at Malibu until it was sold in the early 1960s. Another early workboat was the *Chinook*, an old Chris-Craft left over from the Hamilton years and included in the sale of the camp to Young Life. Even at the time of the purchase it was considered old, and getting parts to keep it running well was a

Courtesy of Marge Anderson – Used with Permission

Ray Anderson and the *Nyj* (1966)

problem. It took Ray Anderson nearly six weeks to get it operational after its long hibernation between the Hamilton years and Young Life's purchase. In 1963, after constant use at Malibu it was finally given to Ray, who in turn gave it to his son-in-law, John Cooke, who took it across the border on a trailer, hauling it to their property near Seattle at what is now known as Mill Creek. According to John, the Border guard took one look at the boat and said, "Canada certainly has no need of this boat and maybe America will have better luck with it." Indeed, for the *Chinook* was restored to its original configuration by Tom Parker, who now owns it and renamed it the *Malibu*. The *Skookum* was a 21' Correct Craft Boca Raton wood boat with a 150 HP Gray Marine engine gifted to Malibu by Mr. Walter Maloon of Cypress Gardens, Florida. The *Skookum* was used extensively until it was sold after many years of service to the camp. The *Princess Louisa* was another workboat used after the *Skookum* was sold. It was a 26' twin-screw sportster, with two 115 HP Gray Marine engines and it, too, was sold into retirement.

Throughout the 1980s, the Malibu Beyond program used a fiberglass landing barge called the *Peton*. It was built and donated by the Norman Dunn company of Vancouver BC and was used until 1990, when it was refitted and sold to another Christian outreach group on Vancouver Island. The money from the sale of the *Peton* was used to purchase the Beyond workboat, also called the *Skookum*. The Malibu Beyond *Skookum* was built by Gene Bellavance of Mitchell Island, based on a similar landing craft design like that of the *Peton*, but with the addition of a covered cabin. The new boat was powered by a 260Hp diesel, with a Model 273 Hamilton Jet, to get the Beyond trips from its base camp, located at Princess Louisa Inlet halfway down from the entrance near McDonald Island, to their launch point quickly and efficiently. Beyond Malibu doesn't use the *Malibu Princess* to transport trips from Egmont to Base Camp because it is not economically feasible or practical, so the *Malibu Papoose* was built specifically for this purpose, based on 51' fiberglass US Navy hull. It has been transporting Beyond trips since the 1970s and, like the *Princess*, is also used by Malibu Yacht Charters.

But the main workboat at Malibu has always been the *Cowichan*, affectionately called the *Cow*, a fishing boat fiberglass hull design built in 1975 by an unknown contractor for

Malibu. It has an open hull design, perfect for hauling freight and luggage, carrying the band during the Welcome, and the other necessary tasks in support of the Malibu program and facility. The current *Cow* was based on the design of the original wood *Cowichan*, which was used at Malibu in similar fashion during the 1960s. It is now on a beach in Egmont BC. Both versions of the boat feature an open control column and a bow overhang large enough to protect several workers during a rain storm. In 1990, a covered house was added to the newer model.

The *Cowichan* at Chatterbox Falls (2003)

The *Cowichan* is the most photographed boat at Malibu today, next to the *Malibu Princess*, and has proved its worth as a workboat. Other applications for this boat have been attempted over the years, with mixed results. For example, in 1981 during the Welcome for a work crew change, some of the summer staff thought the *Cow* might have enough power and torque to at least get someone up on a knee board. It did. For about five minutes. Then the boat red-lined and the engine seized up. Needless to say it was out of commission for two days as the engine was overhauled. Since then, knee boarding or any other recreational towing from the *Cowichan* has been forbidden. The *Cow* has also proved its worth as a steady golf platform. On yet another work crew change Welcome, a number of golf balls were shot from the *Cow's* bow platform across the *Princess's* bow, impressing everyone on both craft with the steadiness of the *Cowichan*. Nevertheless, hitting golf balls off of the *Cowichan* is now also forbidden.

THE PEOPLE

Since Young Life first purchased Malibu from Tom Hamilton in 1953, the property has gone through many upgrades in its 50 years of operation. These renovations could not have been possible without the dedicated generations of people who made the changes happen. Malibu has played host not only to the kids who have had the camping experience, but also to those who have had the privilege to serve on work crew, summer staff, as counselors, and as assignment staff or as property staff and it leaves an impression on anyone who visits, sparking a phenomenon known as the 'Malibu Experience.' It is something special and fantastic all at once, and they come away feeling as if they, too, own Malibu or at least a small piece of it. This excitement might be due to the programs they experienced or friendships that developed or a spiritual conversion, but as a result many people try to find additional ways of getting involved with Malibu and the area. The author of this book felt that way when he was in high school, and even today he welcomes any opportunity to return to the camp.

It would be impossible to list each and every person who has been affected by this place, or who has served here. The names of these people are just too numerous to record. However, that said, those who have served as Property Directors or have been directly involved in the Malibu operation are important and should be recognized, as they are the individuals who have overseen the many changes to the facility and are a major part of its history. The leadership, experience, and understanding that they have brought to this property have been both beneficial and necessary for making Malibu into what it is today.

The first Manager of Malibu was Add Sewell, per Jim Rayburn's direction. Both Add and his wife, Loveta, had been early participants of Rayburn's Young Life ministry in Texas and they helped bring the camp together in the first years both from a spiritual and administrative standpoint. Add was supported and helped by Bob Hagstrom, along with his wife, Diane, who served as superintendents of Malibu during the early years. As Bob settled into his tasks at Malibu, however, and he realized that the maintenance of the generators was a little over his head, he invited his friend Ray Anderson, with whom he served with in World War II, to come up and work on the generators and get them running properly. Ray knew his way around a marine engine from his work as an officer in the United States Coast Guard. Ray spent a couple of days at Malibu, working and getting to know the Young Life operation. Indeed, Ray had a Malibu experience while he was there. It is unknown whether Ray was captured by the beauty of the place, or the mission of Young Life, or maybe it was a little of both, but he called his wife, Marge, asked her to quit her job and to come up to Malibu to live and work. The Hagstroms and Andersons would be there until 1964, overseeing some of the many changes and daily maintenance Malibu required, and the skill and understanding that both families brought to Malibu was a miracle of placing the right people in the right positions at the right place. This type of phenomenon has happened many times throughout Malibu's history, and is a tangible indication of God at work. Ray turned out to have a marvelous ability to deal with troubled youth. This worked to Malibu's advantage and at times Ray was called to do more than just the maintenance and repair of the engines, boats of the camp. If one of the young guests did not want to participate in the Malibu program, or was just too rebellious, he or she would be placed under Ray's care and by the end of the week he or she would be a changed person. Ray was never too stern nor slack, but he had a way with teenagers that seemed to cut through the toughest exterior.

Courtesy of M.Anderson – used with permission

Bob Hagstrom & Ray Anderson (1958)

The next manager to take the reins of leadership at the camp was Frayne Gordon. He began his tenure in 1960, taking over from the Sewells. Frayne had been involved with the logging industry for many years as a troubleshooter and problem solver for many of the timber processes used by local mills and logging camps throughout the majority of British Columbia. He had come to Malibu on one of the workweeks in the late 1950s and ended up wanting to stay. He was told that he would have to take a significant cut in pay if he was to work at Malibu, but this obviously didn't bother him, for the next summer he was there as the Property Manager. But Frayne had a lot to learn, for Malibu always had three rules: the Right Way, the Wrong Way, and the Malibu Way. This was not just perversity; there was an actual method to the Malibu Way. Malibu's whole mission as a camp was to provide fellowship and learning for its young guests, including all of the work and maintenance performed by volunteers and paid staff. Involvement by all participants was mandatory, teaching each individual to work as part of a whole and to support one another. This not only developed the teamwork and camaraderie that made the camp function safely, but kept morale at a high level and provided an example to the campers. While Frayne was used to doing things himself, by the second week in the summer he had learned to delegate and lead. Frayne would spend about eight years at Malibu before moving on to Colorado for a stint on Young Life Property staff at the headquarters in Colorado Springs. Frayne died in the late 1960s while on staff in Colorado of a brain tumor. Frayne had been involved with something he was passionate about. He had helped Malibu through some of its early years by continuing improving and keeping up with the many demands and decisions that needed to be made in running a Christian youth camp in a very remote part of British Columbia.

The next person selected to take over as Malibu's Manger was Ken Parker. Ken was similar to Hamilton in many ways for he, too, was an idea generator, which was both a blessing and a curse to Malibu as camp. While many of his ideas were utilized and helped to enhance the Young Life experience at Malibu, occasionally, like Hamilton, his ideas would get in the way of the operations at the property. For example, when Treehouse was under construction and the roof was just about completed, using cedar shake shingles, Ken stopped the construction. He had a great idea to make the building chalet-like in appearance. This would have been fine, had completion of the original design not been so close. Again, as in Hamilton's day, this frustrated the workers, who stopped what they were doing and incorporated Mr. Parker's new design into the building. Regardless, Ken served Malibu well, supported by Vic Hookins and his wife, Nene, as Property Superintendents of the camp after the Hagstroms and Andersons left in 1964.

In 1972, Mike Sheridan took over from Ken. Mike was a corporate executive from Western Girl, one of the first temp agencies in the US, and had been recruited from New York City to take over the direct management of Malibu. In the past Malibu had incurred a number of loans, which had become large financial burdens, and there was concern about the infrastructure of the camp. With his experience and skill as a corporate executive in the business world, Mike was able to provide the vision as a leader to make the camp more self-sufficient, and he helped pay off the loans. He also began initiating necessary improvements to help the camp become what it is today.

Tim French took over from Mike Sheridan as Property Manager of Malibu in 1978. Tim had attended Malibu as a camper in 1970 and, sequentially, served on work crew, summer staff, and finally as an all-summer worker. In 1975, Tim would be the assistant caretaker with Jack Lewis, who had taken over as Superintendent from Vic Hookens, and Tim finally took over as Property Manager in 1978. The camp was nearly 35 years old by this time, and maintenance was not so much the pressing issue. Replacement of old, worn out equipment and structures was the mandatory concern. Tim was well able to deal with the major upgrades to the Malibu infrastructure, such as the instal-

Taken by Bob Prichard – used with Permission

Vic Hookins and Dumb Dumb[xiv] the Deer (1968)

Tim French (second from right)
and his Motley Summer Crew (1981)

lation of a new water line system, docks, boardwalk replacements, and a new telephone system. Tim also provided the talent and skill needed to run Malibu with a great deal humor and enthusiasm until his departure in the fall of 1985.

Gail Grimston shared responsibilities as the Guest Services Manager with Tim during the late '70s and most of the '80s. Gail was one of the first campers at Malibu, in 1954, and later joined Young Life staff in Vancouver BC. In 1973 she was the first person to serve as the new Guest Services Manager at

Gail Grimston (1984)

Malibu, started under the direction of Mike Sheridan. Several years later this post would become the Operations Manager position. She would eventually leave in 1986 and take another Young Life staff position, this time in Portland, Oregon. Gail still supports Malibu as a member of the many selection committees for the female interns, work crew and summer staff. It has been Gail's hard work, faith, and good nature over the years that have nurtured Malibu from its early inceptions to today's operation of the camp. Her influence is still felt today as a mentor, guide, and friend to most of the female staff of interns, summer staff, and work crew at Malibu.

Taken by John Leaf – used with permission

Frank Poirier (1984)

During 1980, the ex-park ranger from Chatterbox Falls, Peter Talbot, was hired as the caretaker of Malibu. Frank Poirier, a Canadian, took over Superintendent duties after Peter in 1981 and continued until the mid-1990s. Frank was suited for the yearly position at Malibu, for he preferred the solitude of the winters and only endured the crowded summer season. It must also be noted that he was also very gifted in wood carving, and created many of the new totem poles dotting the camp and the surrounding landscape for all to see and enjoy.

Courtesy of Young Life – used with permission

Kathy Murphy, Janice and Don Prittie (1981)
(Left to right)

After the departure of Tim, Don Prittie became the Property Managers of Malibu in 1985. Don and his wife Janice had been involved in Young Life in the BC area and were no strangers to Malibu, as they had provided dedicated service to the camp as Summer Staff volunteers in the 1970s. During Don's tenure a number of replacements to the buildings were undertaken, like the removal of Uppers and Lowers and replaced with Tilikum, moving the shop to the revamped power house, and many improvements like covered housings to the work boats. But the changes continued, with Kathy Murphy taking over from Gail as the Guest Services Manager (Operations Manager) position. Kathy would fill this role until her death in 1993 of cancer, with Jan Quiring taking the post shortly thereafter. Around the same time, after Kathy's death, Frank Poirier retired and Paul Bailey took over his position in 1994. In 1998, Don Prittie left his role as Property Manager, along with Jan and Paul shortly after. Steve Fisher served in a temporary capacity during the 1998 summer session until a permanent replacement was hired.

Harold Richert was selected to be Malibu's new Property Manager in 1999, along with wife Terri who handles the Trader, Carolyn Mortensen who handles many of the guest services and other operations of the camp, and Mike Lewis who continues support the many important upgrades like the new hydro plant and the Malibu Yacht charter down at Egmont. Harold's background has been in construction and his experience is being used heavily in support of the many projects and upgrades Malibu is currently going through, especially increasing the cabin sizes and additional facilities to help meet the future demand of teenagers who are anticipated in the future.

Terri and Harold Richert (2003)

MALIBU BEYOND

Malibu has always been a place of innovation. It should come as no surprise that the programs developed there are unique. The isolation of the area, and the landscape itself are conducive to taking the viewer outside of his normal world, and inspiring him to look at people and ideas just a little bit differently. This is the beauty of Malibu and the Princess Louisa Inlet, and was true for Second Lieutenant Richard C. Mayne, of the *HMS Plumper*, back in the days of the first explorations. In 1860 he was the first documented non-native to trek the Jervis Inlet. By order of the Governor of British Columbia, Mayne was required

Taken by Bob Prichard – used with Permission

An Early Beyond Trip on the Ridge up to One Eye (1974)

to survey and cross the country from the Jervis Inlet to Howe Sound. The trek was a challenge for his team and himself, crossing one of the most rugged and mountainous parts of the world. He changed during his time in the woods. His attitudes were different, especially concerning his native companions, as was documented in his writings.

One hundred and ten years later Barney Dobson, a Vancouver, B.C. Young Life leader, conceived of a similar trip. He had the idea of taking his high school kids into the surrounding mountains of Princess Louisa Inlet where they could go 'Beyond' the normal camp setting at Malibu. The Beyond trip was to challenge and encourage the participants in an environment that was way beyond what they were used to. A team of trained guides, who were experienced in mountain climbing skills and safety, took three trips, starting at Potato Creek over at Chatterbox Falls, during the summer of 1970. Their purpose was to see if the concept worked. It did!

By 1972, Beyond Malibu had become increasingly popular as an outreach Christian ministry. The numbers of staff, trips, and routes have all expanded since the summer of 1970. An old logging camp, near where the Johnstons had raised their family at Princess Louisa Inlet at the turn of the 20th century, was transformed into what is known as 'Base Camp', which makes use of the rustic facilities near the woods in view of MacDonald Island (formerly Hamilton Island). It started in the abandoned logging building as shelter from the weather and storage for the hiking gear. This land had been leased from MacMillan-Bloedel Timber Company since 1972, but it was not until 1997 that Beyond Malibu was able to secure property rights and ownership of the land.

A typical Beyond trip is a week, and begins at Base Camp. A specialized boat, called the *Papoose,* is used by Beyond Malibu to take the trip participants from Egmont, BC on up to Base Camp, bypassing the Malibu Club completely, where they become acclimated to their new surroundings and the challenges of the upcoming adventure. The group will meet their guides, get their gear and supplies, and learn where they will be spending the week hiking. The next day the group is ferried to their trailhead to begin their weeklong journey. Each group will hike a defined route, beginning at sea level and ascending through the thick cedar and pine forest to high alpine snowfields and glaciers, just like Second Lieutenant Richard C. Mayne wrote and complained about so many years before. The routine, aside from hiking each day, includes daily quiet times, a time to be by one's self to reflect, pray, and think, Bible studies and group discussions. Unity is developed within each group, as it shares the same experiences, hardships, concerns, joys, and food. There is always a challenge when hiking in such a natural backdrop, but the time spent will allow people to be open to reflection and growth. It is the ultimate adventure.

Experienced Beyond guides lead each trip. They are responsible for helping and teaching each of the novice hikers all the needed skills to safely transverse the many mountains of Princess Louisa Inlet. Malibu Beyond requires each guide to give a two year commitment. The newer guides are apprenticed by the experienced guides who, in their second year teach new guides the many routes, safety skills, climbing techniques, and leadership capabilities required in the woods or on the mountains or during a devotional. By the end of the week, the guides and hikers are working (hopefully) as a team that can conquer any mountain at Princess Louisa Inlet or everyday problems they may face at home. Also, like Malibu, there are summer volunteers who help support and maintain Base Camp and are an important element in the whole operation. If not for these people, none of the food would get packed, equipment sorted or distributed, tents cleaned or maintained, or any of the various other necessary tasks completed that are required by Beyond to keep the operation functioning. They are an unseen, but integral part of the program.

Since 1970 there have been a number of defined routes which a group can take. The access points are normally semi-used logging roads, which the groups use to ascend above the tree line into the high fjord country of Princess Louisa Inlet and the Jervis Inlet. Currently, there are nine routes in use, with one discontinued and another just coming into operation. The routes are named after the mountain or destination of that trip. The Sun Peaks route is above Chatterbox Falls, beginning and ending at the falls. The One Eye route ascents to the triangle shaped mountain the local natives called 'Old One Eye' at Princess Louisa Inlet. This route starts and finishes at Base Camp. The route called Albert focuses on climbing to Mt Albert. Perks is the route that works its way up Mt. Perks. The Frankenstein route wanders up to Mt. Fredrick William. Zion is the Beyond route named for the mountain near Deserted Bay and is a portion of the route Second Lieutenant Mayne and his survey team took in 1860. A Beyond route called Arthur focuses on climbing to the top of Mt Arthur, and the same is true for the Wellington route where the target is the top of Mt. Wellington. Grant is the new route in the Jervis Inlet area. El Doria is a route no longer used because there were too many insects to be reckoned with.

Taken by Bob Prichard – used with Permission

A Beyond Trip Close to One Eye (1974)

Similar to Malibu, the numbers of people affected by the Beyond program as participants, staff, and guides is extensive and those who are now, and have run, the Beyond programs deserve recognition for their services and efforts in helping to expand the Malibu Beyond program since the first trips in 1970. The first Director was Dave Buckley, who helped start the program along with Barney Dobson. Gordy Anderson took over around 1977, with Tom Buckly filling the position in the early 1980s. Art Kopicky replaced Tom two years later and was the Beyond Director till 1988. Rob Dyker and his wife Lori took over from Art Kopicky and are currently the longest running Directors. For over 15 years, Rob and Lori have worked to make the Beyond into the fun, safe, and successful adventure hiking program it is. The major accomplishments of the Beyond program during the Dyker's tenure has been the acquisition of the land where Base camp is located, and construction of the permanent buildings located there. They also set up a new Sea Kayaking program in the summer of 1998. Instead of hiking though the mountains of Princess Louisa Inlet and the Jervis Inlet, the campers kayak along the Salmon, Sechelt and

Narrows inlets of the coastal mountains of British Columbia. The Sea Kayaking program is similar to the hiking program, with trained guides who help the participants learn how to use the boats as well as run the program of the trip. The Sea Kayaking program is based out of the Egmont, Malibu office, and it expands the adventure opportunities available for those have had a Malibu experience and want something more.   In the 1980s a similar program was started, called Sailing Beyond, with three full size sail boats. The Sailing Beyond program folded due to a number of cost and support issues in the late 1980s.

Leaving the Malibu Club (2003)

The Malibu Club, like Princess Louisa Inlet, is just a place in one of the most beautiful parts of North America. But this specific place would not have happened if it weren't for people who believed in the purpose of Malibu and its other programs as a Christian Ministry in the form of Young Life. The history of Malibu's buildings and other aspects of its past is interesting, and necessary to describe. But Malibu, most importantly, is about people's lives being changed for the positive, in spirit and character, as young teenagers begin the road to adulthood. Countless young lives have been reformed, reborn, and renewed in this place. Individuals impacted by this setting have grown into people of stature and service, who have helped and continue to help our society, culture, nation, and the world. Those who have been in leadership positions, worked for a season and longer, or have volunteered their time to help maintain or build up Malibu, must be acknowledged and remembered. The generation that was a part of the early years at Malibu is now beginning to pass away. Recording their names in this book is only one way to remember them, for they have built a lasting legacy in Malibu itself. The next generation is moving in to take their place, and will themselves leave an indelible mark. This place is truly generational: may it continue for many other generations to come.

END NOTES

i   Campbell, *Malibu*, pages 19-20.

ii   Rayburn III, *Dance Children Dance*. Page 51.

iii   Campbell, *Malibu*, pages 22-29. Elsie Campbell describes in detail the events, conversation, and thoughts of Jim Rayburn's introduction and tour of Malibu.

iv   Young Life Real Estate Dept. *Malibu Legal and Miscellaneous Documents*. Legal Agreement, signed November 5, 1953 by Tom Hamilton and Jim Rayburn, on page one indicates Hamilton had visited Star Ranch, Silver Cliff, & Frontier Ranch and was in agreement of selling the property below the original cost "as a contribution to the worthy cause of the Young Life Campaign."

v   *Ibid.* December 21, 1953, Bank of America Escrow Instructions indicating $28,000 is to be paid toward the principle on December 28, 1953. However, no mention is made of the down payment.

vi   *Ibid.*, Short form of Mortgage Act dated Young Life's lawyer representative on December 29, 1953.

vii   Sewell, *The Beginning of Malibu*. Seattle WA, March 16, 1992.

viii   Dustin dl La Mothe, *Young Life of Canada – The Early Days*. Page 10.

ix   Young Life's web site at *www.younglife.org*.

x   Campbell, *Malibu*, pages 85-86. The Dinning Hall was designed by Harold Nesland and was completed by 1959.

xi   Those worth mentioning are individuals like John Kautz, Bob Pritchard, Bill Rose, Brono Dombrowski, and many countless others have volunteered their skills, talents, and time in helping Malibu to be what it is today.

xii   BC Archives Death Certificate of Edward Anastasio, August 8, 1967,. #1967-09-010630 & *Youth dies in plunge off Cliff*, Vancouver Providence, 8-15-1967. Page 9.

xiii   The official sign at Chatterbox Falls indicates 18 but newspaper research state up to 16 and a death certificate search is inconclusive for the places of death indicates Princess Louisa or the Jervis Inlet.

xiv   Dumb Dumb the deer was a local mascot of sorts at Malibu during the early 1960s. She had been found and raised by a local logging camp which fed her pancakes. She was given to Malibu once the logging camp moved out of the Jervis Inlet area and was a animal that thought she was a human or a part of the camp.

Taken by C.W. Hitz of One Eye Images & Sound

CHAPTER
SIX

*Icons
of the Inlet*

Front View of a
Beaver (2003)

*"The country in general produces forest trees
in greet abundance, of some variety and mag-
nitude: the pine is the most common, and the
woods are little encumbered with bushes or
trees of inferior growth."*

CAPT. GEORGE VANCOUVER (1792)

Taken by C.W. Hitz of One Eye Images & Sound

Tail-out from the Inner-Dock (2003)

"Clear" yelled the pilot as he switched the magnetos to 'on'. The DeHavilland Beaver sputtered somewhat as the propeller slowly cranked over. The man gingerly worked the throttle slightly in order to send the right mixture of fuel and oxygen into the Pratt Whitney radial engine. The sputtering turned into a quick crescendo, then burst into a loud explosion of noise as the right mixture was achieved to ignite in the cylinders, causing the engine to kick over and the blades of the propeller to bite into the air as the revolutions increased, allowing the aircraft to move away from the Inner-dock at Malibu. The orange and black striped Tyee Beaver, on floats, glided easily away after taking on its three passengers and their luggage. The three had just finished their assignment as program staff at Malibu during the summer of 1979 and were heading home. Two of the passengers sat on either side of the aircraft in order to get the best view from the large trapezoid windows at each of the side doors. These particular windows were not flat, rather they were bubbled to give better visibility for the passengers. The third staff member sat up front in the right hand co-pilot seat next to the pilot. The pilot worked the pedals to move the tail and rudders of the pontoons to steer away from two obstructing ski boats, which were circling a downed skier near Malibu's Inner-dock. He calmly managed the aircraft, using both hands and feet, all the while having a friendly chat with his new passenger beside him. A few minutes later, when the path ahead looked clear for the aircraft to make its run down the watery runway, the pilot then set in motion, like he had done a thousand time before, the sequence of tasks called the 'by the check list.' This included lifting the pontoon's rudders with a pull of the D-ring and securing it, easing the throttles forward and working the yoke a little as the engine noise and power increased. Everything vibrated in the plane, for it was pure torque and revolutions as the floatplane started its run. Faster and faster the Beaver raced down the Inlet with the nose coming down ever so slowly, allowing a level view for the pilot and his passenger. At this point the Beaver acted more like a fast moving speedboat than an airplane. Then in an instant, the aircraft was lifted into the air as the correct airflow over the large wings allowed it off the water, but not climbing for altitude. Instead the Beaver stayed low above the watery deck as it made a gradual 180 degree turn around the island that both Mac and Hamilton had called their own. The passenger in front turned to his friends in back and yelled at the top of his voice so as to be heard above the deafening sound of the Pratt Whitney engine, "Watch this and hang on." Both back passengers' eyes went wide and they looked at each other with a surprised expression as they pondered what was actually going to happen. The pilot only smiled, knowing this particular passenger had flown with him before and knew what he was in for. The Beaver now was gaining speed and was only a few meters above the water. The pilot directed his aircraft straight for the entrance of Princess Louisa Inlet and banked slightly as he entered the narrows. The orange streak that flew past Malibu's Dining hall was watched by an entire deck full of people, who knew who was at the controls of this aircraft and watched the spectacle in awe. The scene changed when the Beaver suddenly went from 'on the deck' to a 45-

degree pitch climb with its nose to the sky, over the island, past Malibu, and over the rapids of Princess Louisa Inlet. The passengers were excited and wanted to do it again, but the pilot only smiled and yelled back "next time" as he set course for their destination of Vancouver BC. The pilot was Blacky and this was his trademark stunt whenever he left Princess Louisa Inlet. Everyone knew about Blacky from Malibu to most of British Columbia, for he had become an icon.

Taken by C.W. Hitz of One Eye Images & Sound

Blackie past the Rapids (1979)

The definition of an icon in the dictionary means "represent or symbolize something or someone." In this case, a thing(s), or a person(s), an activity(s), or service(s) can symbolize a place like Princess Louisa Inlet. An icon is also a visual or verbal cue that the human brain will store and recall as related to this place.

Already this book has described a number of icons that are synonymous with Princess Louisa Inlet. These include people like Vancouver, Richards, Pender, Mayne, Hamilton, Mac, Steve Johnston, Casper, and Jim Rayburn, as well as entities such as Young Life, the Princess Louisa Inlet Society, and the Parks Department of British Columbia. Word icons like Malibu,

Chatterbox Falls, and The Rapids also bring to mind this particular place. There are a few more words, people, and objects that can help clarify more specific details related to Princess Louisa Inlet and the area that have not already been mentioned. These natural icons of Princess Louisa Inlet can be broken down into three basic parts: the sea, land, and air. These parts are further represented by the occupations, machines, and even a recreational pastime done or used at Princess Louisa Inlet.

The Inlet has provided ample trees to log, fish to catch, animals to trap, and minerals to mine. Fishing and animal trapping are significant to Princess Louisa Inlet, because hunting provided the profit during those early years and trap lines were mainly used to catch prey for their fur. However, as the animals' population naturally declined because of over-trapping and hunting at Princess Louisa Inlet, fish began to increase in types and numbers. It used to be that many types of fish could be found in both the salt and fresh waters of the Jervis and Princess Louisa. Now, because of many environmental and over-fishing pressures, this is no longer so. Today the main fishery of the Inlet is shrimp and the Jervis Inlet is particularly known for the type of prawns that can be harvested from its far depths. The fishing industry, however, is making a comeback, since fish farming was introduced in the 1970s to the lower Jervis Inlet region. But it has been the logging and mining occupations that are and have been the most active commerce icons of the Princess Louisa Inlet area. There are a number of records related to these occupations that have made it possible to trace the people and businesses associated with the trade through the Jervis and Princess Louisa area of the 20th century. These trades have also introduced a number of tools for the lumbermen and miners to help ease some of their manual tasks, and it would be these machines that would become lasting icons of the area. This chapter explores some of these miscellaneous bits and pieces of history that make up the icons of the Inlet.

Taken by C.W. Hitz of One Eye Images & Sound

A Classic Icon at Louisa (1982)

ICON OF THE SEA

The invention of boats and their many propulsion systems opened up the world. From exploration to fishing, boats have been used by man through the centuries. The Industrial Age introduced a new marine recreational pastime known as yachting. By the late 1800, many rich industrialists and other members of high society invested their wealth into fancy pleasure boats to both impress and explore. Yacht clubs were established around the world with a common interest of promoting the new pastime. In the Pacific Northwest many of them sprouted up around cities like Seattle and Tacoma in Washington State, and Vancouver and Victoria in British Columbia. During the late 1800s and early 1900s many of these yachts would cruise through the local waters and Inlets of the Pacific Northwest. Princess Louisa Inlet was discovered by the yachting circles of the time and became THE destination for those around the world to experience one of the most magnificent wonders of the world. This has resulted in many, many stories. Anyone coming to the Inlet remembers this portion of their trip and has something to tell about it, whether the tale deals with seeing Princess Louisa for the first time, or some sort of encounter with nature. These stories usually make for a good yarn by the campfire, and can be compelling, humorous, or even adventurous. Many of the best stories deal with the rapids at Malibu, the tide change, boats running aground, seeing a famous celebrity or boat, being chased by a bear, or even sighting a bald eagle. All have merit and help recall the memory of Princess Louisa Inlet to each person. Some of the stories about Inlet cruises have even been published and documented for all to enjoy. Today, there are many that visit this area in their own boats, a charter, or a tour because, like a hundred years ago, Princess Louisa Inlet has been passed on by word-of-mouth.

Singer John Denver at Malibu (1984)

Many famous and not so famous people and yachts have visited this place like the *Calcite*, the *Caprice*, *Taconite*, *Malibu*, and many other famous designs and owners have made the Inlet a place to be seen and known. For example, the movie star John Wayne would bring up his converted mine sweeper, *The Wild Goose*, each summer until his death. John Denver visited and sang at Malibu in 1984, when he was guest on a friend's yacht. Each summer seems to bring wind of famous Hollywood celebrities who are cruising up the BC coast and will eventually pay the Inlet a visit. Corporate executives make Princess Louisa Inlet a favorite area to hold a company retreat. The list guest seems to grow larger and larger each summer at Chatterbox Falls and at the Malibu Club.

Taken by C.W. Hitz of One Eye Images & Sound

A Big Yacht Through the Malibu Narrows (1981)

ICONS OF LAND

The symbol of the ax and handsaw are synonymous with the forests of British Columbia, as well as the Jervis and Princess Louisa Inlet areas. Both Captain Vancouver and Lieutenant Puget mentioned the vast forests they encountered in their early survey of the area in 1792. The first icons would be the picks and shovels used to mine specific minerals out of the ground in the Jervis and Princess Louisa Inlet areas, starting some of the first major businesses of British Columbia.

The Fraser River gold rush put the area on the map. It was the second rush since the California gold rush some years previously and was the pre-curser to the Klondike rush in Alaska many years later. The Fraser River started the gold fever and everybody wanted to stake a claim as quickly as possible. Major William Downie was hired by the Hudson Bay Company to search and find a direct route to the Caribou Gold Fields in 1858, starting from the head of the Jervis Inlet. Like Second Lieutenant Mayne he, too, was turned away because of the terrible weather he encountered, and the vast flow of the river. He eventually found a different route. Nevertheless, the choice of

Major Downie by the Hudson Bay Company was not by chance, for he had become a wealthy man from the gold he had found and mined in California. Because of his finds in that area, a town was named after him outside of Sacramento, California. In 1861, as discussed earlier in this book, Second Lieutenant Mayne of the *HMS Plumper* was ordered, also, to explore from Deserted Bay to blaze a path to find other possible gold veins in the area. It was journey full of hardship, but many of the region's names still used today are a result of his mission. Afterwards, there was a gold rush of sorts at one of the tributaries of the Squawka River, called Canyon Creek, at the head of the Jervis Inlet. There were a number of preemptions issued by prospectors looking for gold, starting in 1891 and lasting until approximately 1919, when these pre-emptors, or prospectors, failed to renew their claims. It is uncertain as to whether any gold was actually found in the area, but in 1933 an old-timer had a secret mine near the Beaver Creek location of the Jervis Inlet. It was known that each year 'Old Paddy Hatt' would bring out his gold in a rowboat. Unfortunately he died before he revealed its true location. Muriel Blanchet, the author of 'Curve of Time' would describe in her book meeting people who were looking for gold on some of the hikes they took from Princess Louisa Inlet.

As minerals go, however, it would not be gold that the Jervis and Princess Louisa Inlets would be known for, but rather a common mineral, slate. Slate is a metamorphic rock, changed by heat or pressure, and comes from the core rock of shale. Shale is the remains of dead plant life from the tropical climate that prevailed before the glaciers came. Slate was specifically used in roofs and chalkboards, and the Jervis and Princess Louisa Inlets had significant amounts of it. The local Sechelt natives used to make arrowheads and spears from it. In 1910, a slate quarry was established at Deserted Bay and was in operation until 1916. Another quarry was established before 1915, called 'Marble Mountain,'[i] which was straight across the Jervis Inlet from Malibu and operated for only a short time before it was closed down. Why it stopped production is unknown. Today, the vast amounts of rock in the mountains are hard granite, alternated with the layers of slate to make up the many interesting cliffs, ridges, and peaks throughout Princess Louisa Inlet.

Taken by Peter Talbot – Used with Permission

Logging Barge through the Narrows (1989)

As well as the minerals of the area, there is the ever-present resource of lumber. Although the land is very rocky and cavernous, there is a green carpet of trees on the steep slopes of the area. According to an official Canadian Government report in1918,[ii] the Jervis Inlet had about 21 square miles of agricultural land, and the rest of it was mostly high timber quality. In this report, it was estimated that the Inlet held about 6.5 million board feet of timber, with 35% of all trees being red cedar, 30% Douglas fir, and the remaining 35% a mixture of hemlock, spruce, pine, and cypress. The official report stated that the Jervis Inlet and Princess Louisa Inlet have a very "high quality of timber, especially of cedar, and has attracted loggers for a number years, in spite of the rather rough ground on which they had to operate." The report continued by indicating that, though many of the large trees had been harvested and re-logged from the shoreline on up, there still remained a virgin stand which had remained untouched. Fifteen years later, in

1934, another government bulletin further explained the increased demand for lumber, stating that "Many logging camps are situated along the Inlet, chief output being fir and cedar, and there is much hemlock utilizable."[iii] This estimate was the overall total output of timber that the Jervis Inlet could produce with 65 trillion feet of saw-timber (similar to the 6.5 million board feet in 1918), but it also reported an additional 2 million cords of pulp material and about 400 square miles being under known timber licenses. This included the many hand logging and floating logging camps claims that were established throughout the Inlet areas between 1918 and 1934. Incidentally, the 1934 report singles out Princess Louisa Inlet as being a very difficult place for any logging operation to make money, as the land was steep and barren, and lacked any valuable types of trees.

Two companies did take out licenses in 1907 to log Princess Louisa Inlet, Heaps Timber Company and Cook and Tait Ltd, only to move to more fruitful areas later. Heaps was the first company to log the north shore of 640 acres of the Princess Louisa Inlet where Malibu is now located. Cook and Tait harvested the south bank half-way up the head of Princess Louisa Inlet near Chatterbox falls. By the next year the licenses were not renewed because the land was too steep and barren.

The next person to take out a hand-logging license at Princess Louisa Inlet was Judd Johnstone and he was also the first documented settler of Princess Louisa Inlet, as he applied for a crown grant to own the land. A hand-logging license stated that the logger was required to use only axes and saws for harvesting their trees. Beginning around 1860, the practice of hand logging was preformed around the banks of the Inlet and the many waterways throughout the BC coast. A tree was selected, cut from the shoreline, and rafted together with others to be floated to the mills. However, once the prime shore trees had been harvested the hand loggers had to go deeper into the woods or up the steep slopes. The trees would have to be moved by hand jacks or by a team of animals, such as donkeys. It was hard work for the Johnstones, but it seemed to have sustained them through the spring and summer months that they resided at Princess Louisa Inlet. During the fall and winter months they would set trap lines to help tide them over.

The Whittakers were the next documented hand loggers, moving into a cabin that they built near Patrick Point. Two brothers also involved in the trade were Don and John McNaughton, as they switched from gold mining to harvesting trees in1908. In 1918 they were the first to use new technology in logging called the 'donkey' pull system using a steam engine rather than real donkeys to pull the cut trees. But most often the brothers preferred the traditional methods. Their sons eventually took up the trade and were known for their hand logging skills. They would be the ones who constructed MacDonald's cabin at Chatterbox falls. Mac's home was built using traditional hand logging methods.

The next known hand logger to settle into the area was a Norwegian immigrant, Herman Solberg. He and his daughters, Bergie and Minnie, took up the ways of their father and settled near Deserted Bay around 1928. They lived in the area till Herman's death in the late 1970s, at which time he sold his land for $16,000.[iv] His daughters stayed in the same area: Bergie lived on 172 acres near Sechelt on the Jervis Inlet near its entrance, and Minnie remained in the Deserted Bay area till her death in 2000. Both sisters lived the simple frontier life they learned from their father, much like that of Steve Johnston. They were known as dead-eye shots with a rifle and also for the many cougars they killed. Neither sister married but, according to Minnie, she had a child by a local logger, which was later put up for adoption.[v]

The most famous and successful hand loggers were the Gustavson brothers. Eric and Thure Gustavson had emigrated from Sweden to Canada in 1914 and started hand logging at Porpoise Bay. By 1934, in order to expand their operation, they

Taken by C.W. Hitz of One Eye Images & Sound

Frankenstein & Forbidden Island (2003)

moved up to the Jervis and Princess Louisa Inlet area. Logging technology was starting to change and, like the McNaughtons, they embraced the new tools and methods in their operation. This started a shift of icons in the lumber industry. The ax or saw were no longer the only icons; they now began to include modern machines like the steam donkeys, narrow gauge railroads, trucks, new techniques, and the chain saw. Eric and Thure Gustavson implemented this new narrow gauge railroad system in their logging occupation, which would become the most successful logging company using rail in the BC region at the time. The operation was located at Deserted Bay near the old slate quarry and their new railroad extended up into the valley. They had a mobile type camp which consisted of ten-man bunkhouses, a saw filer building, first aid and staff building, office and administration building, wash house, an outhouse, dining hall, kitchen, and a root house and meat cooler building. The roofs were rolled tarpaper and the walls were ship-lap with no insulation. But wood stoves supplied plenty of heat, and all of the chimneys were the Yukon type, one pipe inside the other for heat separation. All of the buildings were mounted on wooden sleds so they could be moved easily to a new location, either by rail or by barge, making the Gustavson's operation the most flexible of its day. The camp would be moved to a different site on the Inlet or up the shore as soon as the rails were laid. The Deserted Bay site continued successfully for many years until it finally folded in 1951, following the death of both brothers.

Tom Hamilton himself continued the tradition of logging, at one time logging the lumber off his own land to be used in the construction of his resort. As discussed earlier, he had not planned on doing this originally, but most the mills in the general area could not keep up with his need for the vast amount of wood resources he required. Hamilton ended up building a small sawmill and hiring a number of men to log his property for him. Twenty years later, like Hamilton, Young Life decided to mill its own wood. A sawmill was built on the opposite side of the entrance of Princess Louisa Inlet from the camp in the early 1950s, but after a few years it cost more for Young Life to harvest, cut, and process the wood than it did to maintain Malibu itself. The lumber practice was later abandoned and the only reminiscence of the original mill is the structure, which can still be seen today from the entrance to Princess Louisa Inlet, and is used as covered storage for the camp. All of the wood Malibu needs today for railings, boardwalks, siding, and other needs is manufactured offsite and shipped to the camp. It is far cheaper and causes less negative impact to the immediate environment. In 1956, Tom Hamilton was able to make up some of his loss on the sale of Malibu to Young Life by selling his remaining land to the Logger Cam Hudson Company of Mission, BC which was an umbrella company for three specific companies: Cam Hudson Logging, Tommy Bay Logging, and Louisa Bay.[vi] Eventually these companies folded because of the steepness of the terrain around Princess Louisa Inlet, with the exceptions of areas above Malibu and around Mt. Helena, where the only sizable growth is available. Not having the equipment and means to harvest the lumber, the company defaulted on its loans, and the Royal Trust seized the land.

In 1961, Macmillan Bloedel Ltd. developed an effective way of logging, by using poles to effectively transport cut trees from the steep terrain to the waterline below. The Bloedel Company was established in 1911 as the Bloedel, Stewart & Welch, formed by the Bellingham lumberman Julius Bloedel and two railway builders, Patrick Welch and John Stewart. Later it was shortened to Bloedel when Julius bought his partners out. In 1951, the Macmillan Export Company, established by Harvey Macmillan in 1919, merged with Bloedel to form the largest firm engaged in the production and sales of lumber in British Columbia. In 1960, Bloedel Macmillan acquired the Powell River Company to become one of the largest lumber companies in North America. The American lumber company called Weyerhaeuser bought out Bloedel Macmillan in 1999, becoming one of the primary lumber companies in the world. David Weyerhaeuser, who helped Jim Rayburn purchase Malibu for Young Life, was a part of this lumber family and a philanthropist involved in many Christian services.

Other machines helped the logging industry. The winch, also known as the 'donkey,' was steam powered and replaced the four-legged animal teams that used to drag the logs to the water. With railways, steam donkeys, and 27 meter steel towers added, the timber removal process for previously un-loggable trees became possible, and harvesting of the untouched trees from Princess Louisa Inlet began. A heavy skyline ran from the skidder to the top of the spar, and then to the back end of the area being logged, where the trees were already felled and bucked into logs. Another line, the mainline, pulled a carriage hanging from the skyline. The carriage was pulled out over the logs with a haul-back line, a set of tongs on the end of the mainline was attached to the log and the winch hauled in the line, lifting the log off the ground. This was known as skyline logging. At about the same time another system, called high-lead logging, was developed. A mainline ran from the winch through a block at the top of a tall spar tree, then out to the logs without the use of a skyline. The logs were dragged in over the ground and could be lifted over obstacles by applying a brake on the haul-back line while pulling on the mainline. This method was used at the Jervis and Princess Louisa Inlet and most of BC until a new technique was developed, using an icon of the air called the helicopter.

Taken by C.W. Hitz of One Eye Images & Sound

Hughes 500 Landing at Malibu's Outer-Dock (2003)

n 1977 and 1978, tests were conducted using helicopters to log timber in British Columbia, and by 1980 four operating helicopters were being used to log the steep terrain where the majority of BC timber grew. In 1984 one of those helicopters, a Boeing early model Chinook, began operating in tandem with a Hughes 500 at the Jervis Inlet area opposite Malibu. A floating platform was secured below the logging site at McCannel Creek, where living quarters, equipment, fuel, and landing platforms were used in support of the helicopters. The basic operation was simple. First, the smaller helicopter ferried the loggers or cutters to the site in the high elevation of Mt. Wellington, where they would cut and prep the trees for hauling. Then, hovering, stripped-down Chinook would lower a grapple attached to its bottom center fuselage for the ground crew to attach to the prepped logs. Once this was done, the large Chinook would pull up high to gain altitude, and then dive for the water with the logs in tow. As the helio neared the

The Propeller of an Icon (2003)

water the pilot would pitch up the nose to slow the speed of the helicopter and then released the grapple. This allowed the swinging logs underneath to continue their journey downward and plummet into the water with the assistance of gravity and motion. The water plume from the logs entering the water would be large enough to be seen a mile away. Release of these massive logs is a true feat of the skill and timing by the pilot, who controls the entry of the logs into water like a diver diving into a pool. If the release is too early or too late, the logs are pulverized into fragments and are worthless. The whole operation from mountain to water lasts just over two minutes and the maximum number of logs on the grapple at one time can be about four large trees.

ICONS OF THE AIR

It is not known who made the first flight into Princess Louisa Inlet, but it was probably flown in support of the many logging camps operating in the area in the late 1920s or 1930s. The many flying machines around British Columbia were now constructed of metal, including the propeller and pontoons, instead of the early fabric, wood, and wire airplanes. Today many types of float and amphibious aircraft have visited and provided services to Princess Louisa Inlet, including private and commercial aircraft like the Cessna 185, Grumman Goose and Widgeons, Dash 7 & 8, and the famous DeHavilland Beaver. Helicopters are also a part of this vast inventory of icons related to the air at Princess Louisa Inlet.

This Boeing Chinook, described earlier in this chapter, is a civil version of the military helicopter developed in the 1950s. It has been used extensively throughout the world, including by both the US and Canadian military. When it's used for logging, the Chinook is a stripped down version and all non-essential equipment is removed. Certain modifications are made in order for the aircraft to be used as a crane and to aid the pilot in his work, like the addition of bubble windows for the pilot and co-pilot, to give a better perspective of the ground. In early 1990, the Malibu Club gave permission for the Macmillan Bloedel timber company to log portions of their land in exchange for ownership of land rights further down the end of Princess Louisa Inlet. The timber company used the same technique that logged the McCannel Creek site ten years before, but now using the Sky Crane, or the Sikorsky S64E. This helicopter was designed during the 1960s for use in Vietnam to lift heavy loads like machinery and buildings into war zones. Two Pratt and Whitney turbofan engines provide the power to the main 72' diameter rotor to lift the tremendous loads. This lifting capability is almost like an elevator ferrying people up and down in a building. In logging, a 150-200 foot cable is attached underneath the helicopter. On the other end is a grapple, which is used to 'grab' and secure the logs till they reach the water below, similar to the Chinook operation described previously. Today there are in excess of 40 helicopters dedicated to logging operations in British Columbia alone, extracting more than 3 million cubic meters of timber annually. Heli-logging has made logging the steep terrain of the Jervis Inlet safer and easier.

Taken by Peter Talbot – Used with Permission

Ski Crain and Support Barge
at the Jervis Inlet (1989)

One of the most famous icons of Princess Louisa Inlet and that
of the Pacific Northwest is the DeHavilland Beaver. It is as sym-
bolic to Canadians as apple pie is to its American neighbors.
The Beaver, with its distinctive square body, tapered fuselage,
high and sturdy wings and the powerful throaty sound of its
propeller engine is recognized throughout the world as a work-
horse, or pickup truck, of the air. It was designed as a bush
plane right from the start. It's design originated from the
Canadian Aviation Company of De Havilland, located at
Downsview, Ontario by engineering teams who wanted to create and build an all-Canadian civilian bush aircraft right after
the Second World War in 1945. Prior to World War Two, this
same company also designed and built the Canadian Chipmunk
trainers, used by allied forces to teach their cadets to be pilots.
This team consisted of Doug Hunter and Fred Howard Buller
as the chief engineers, Jaki Jakimiuk as chief designer, and Dick
Hiscock as the Aerodynamicist. Incidentally, Fred Buller came
from Roberts Creek on the Sechelt Peninsula of the Sunshine

Coast not too far from the entrance of the Jervis Inlet. Fred's experience and knowledge of the Jervis Inlet, the surrounding area, and the landscape of British Columbia went into the rugged design of this aircraft, and the final configuration included long, narrow wings attached on top of the fuselage (so as not to interfere with docks), high lift flaps for Sort Take Off and Landings (STOL), oil spout inside near the pilot (to add oil in flight), doors for the pilot to have easy exit and entry, floats and wheels and most importantly, the Wasp Junior R-985 radial engine. After World War Two, Pratt and Whitney of Canada Ltd had acquired a stockpile of surplus of these engines which produced over 450 hp, and it would be this engine that would give the familiar appearance to the aircraft. The aircraft was called the Beaver, not only because of the way it looked, but also because it was traditional to name Canadian-built aircraft after Canadian mammals.

On August 16, 1947, the prototype DHC-2 Beaver took to the air for its first successful test flight, and would be the first of over 1600 aircraft being produced at the Downsview, Ontario factory during the 1950s. It would become an icon to Canada, British Columbia, and Princess Louisa Inlet. Today many smaller airlines in the Pacific Northwest use this aircraft, which has been tested by years of experience flying in this rugged land. Airlines using the Beaver have provided a much needed service by moving freight and people from one point on the coast to another, including Princess Louisa Inlet.

While many well-known British Columbia airlines and pilots have made a mark in Canadian and British Columbia aviation history, three companies have become known for their place at Princess Louisa Inlet: Kenmore Air Harbor, Tyee Airlines, and Pacific Wings Airlines.

Kenmore Air Harbor and the DeHavilland Beaver bush planes go hand in hand. DeHaviland Beavers have evolved since their first flight in 1947 and new additions to their design have helped keep it up-to-date with new safety, propulsion, and technological enhancements not foreseen in 1947. Some of the Beavers have been brought back to life by refurbishment of their airframes. The most notable company that performs this type of work is Kenmore Air Harbor of Seattle.

In the later 1940s, Robert 'Bob' Munro took over the business interests of flight service partners on the north shore of Lake Washington from two high school friends. Bob had attended the Boeing School of Aeronautics in Oakland, California and, after completion of his course, began work for Pan American at the Boeing Field maintenance base in Seattle during World War II. Initially he started a business called 'MCM Flight Service' with a couple of friends as partners, and the name was later changed to Kenmore Air Harbor. Air services began on March 21, 1946 with one aircraft, a restored Aeronca Model K seaplane that had been restored by Munro. The fleet was expanded with a Taylorcraft and a Aerona Champ. When Bob became the sole owner in the late 40s, he decided to integrate his experience of airframes and mechanics to give a different direction for the company. He was instrumental in the modifications to the popular Republic Seabee amphibious airplanes and created a vast parts department and service section, assisting the many owners of these aircraft. The Campbell's Seabee that flew Rayburn up to Malibu was maintained at this base in Seattle. Bob was able to obtain the first of many contracts with the US Government and the US Navy to fly personnel back and forth from bases in Puget Sound to Seattle. These contracts continue to this day. The 1950s were also the start of charter flights to many popular fishing and hunting spots throughout the Northwest, which included flights to and from Princess Louisa Inlet for an occasional yachter, and eventually for Young Life staff to Malibu.

In 1963, the introduction of the DeHavilland Beaver as part of their fleet changed the service significantly. Bob and another gifted individual, Bill Peters, began to rebuild and modify these fine aircraft for customers and airlines around the world. Thus far over 160 Beavers have been rebuilt and are known as 'Kenmore Beavers'. The modification to a DH Beaver included the addition of a three blade prop, which decreases the noise during take-off, reduces cowling wear due to vibration of the propeller, and gives greater water clearance due to reduction of wear on the propeller. The most visible changes were the addition of a rectangular window where the porthole used to be, and instead of flat glass for the trapezoidal shaped windows of both passenger doors, clear bubble-shaped windows were to aid in better visibility. Another change was the addition of endplate fins on the horizontal stabilizers, replacing the original float plane vertical fin which used to interfere with docks.

Taken by C.W. Hitz of One Eye Images & Sound

A Kenmore Beaver Unloading Passengers at Malibu (2001)

Today Kenmore provides and sells refurbished white DH Beavers with distinctive yellow and brown trim colors. It is considered THE sea-plane site west of the Mississippi River. The company owns two locations in the Seattle area. The main site is still at the north end of Lake Washington in Kenmore, Washington, with the other located at the south end of Lake Union near the heart of downtown Seattle. The two allow easy access to scheduled flights to popular stops in the Pacific Northwest, like Victoria BC and popular fishing resorts in

Desolation Sound. Kenmore also provides private charters throughout Western Washington, British Columbia, including the Jervis and Princess Louisa Inlets, and parts of Southern Alaska. Kenmore's main base also provides storage of individual float planes, plus a fully equipped FAA-approved facility and mechanics to provide service to customers or to the individual pilot flying in for gas and oil.

'Tyee for free' or 'for fee' was the term often heard during the author's years at Malibu in the early 1980s. It referred to leaving Malibu because one had done something unethical, unsafe or something really bad enough to have warranted a flight out by a Tyee Beaver. Tyee Airlines was based out of Sechelt, BC and flew several aircraft including Beavers and Cessnas on floats.

Tyee was started in the 1970s by owner Al Campbell, and operated in the area until 1992. It was the key airline which provided most of the deliveries to Malibu, logging camps, yachters, and Chatterbox Falls during those years. A person with a keen ear could distinguish the airline by the sound of the engine flying overhead. For example, Air BC used the Dash 8 dual turbo prop that made a high quiet whine when it flew overhead. But it would be the low vibration of the Beaver that was the trademark aircraft sound and was instantly recognizable.

If the weather was clear at Patrick Point, but foggy on up to Malibu, the pilot would often land and motor the airplane on floats up to Malibu like any boat. It would be surreal to hear a Pratt and Whitney radial engine come up from the Inlet but not see anything airborne, only to have the black shape of a floating DeHaviland Beaver break out of the gray mist. One the most famous pilots at Tyee, and a well-known BC aviator, was Jack 'Blackie' Apsouris. He had worked for Tyee as their chief pilot for over ten years and was particularly known for his departures from Princess Louisa Inlet as described at the beginning of this chapter. He would take off down the Inlet, turn around and be only a few feet 'off the deck' while gaining speed as he approached the entrance of Princess Louisa Inlet, only to pull up quickly once he reached the middle of the rapids. It was a fascinating spectacle to watch from the ground. It was amazing to see a Beaver go so fast, so low, and then go so high. Not to mention what the passengers experienced - the weird sensation of their stomachs moving into their throats from the G-force as the Beaver abruptly climbed. There was a rumor going around Malibu back in the 1980s that there was an ex-World War II German Luftwaffe pilot from Germany named Klaus working for Tyee and that he was wild on the stick. If asked, he would do some amazing stunts with a Beaver. While this rumor was never substantiated, possibly the pilot was Blackie. His name 'Blackie' came from one of the Tyee dispatchers who gave radio call signs to two pilots - Black Jack and Little Jack. In time Black Jack became Blackie. Blackie eventually started his own company, Coast Western Airlines, which serviced most of the BC coast and Malibu till 2002. Blackie also acquired a Beaver he affectionately called 'Blossom' and he flew it until his death in 1996. His ashes were scattered over Princess Louisa Inlet and the Malibu Rapids.

There are, however, bigger companies that have been and are currently flying in the area. The major two airlines are Air BC and Harbor Air each with their own type of aircraft. Unfortunately the demise of Blackie's Coast Western Airlines in

Taken by C.W. Hitz of One Eye Images & Sound

Grant Starrs of Pacific Wings (2003)

2002 left an air transportation gap in the area. But another airline, called Pacific Wings Airlines located in Sechelt BC has taken its place. It was started by the owner and pilot, Grant Starrs, who grew up in Sechelt BC, and is filling the role Blackie and Tyee had provided many years ago.

Kenmore Air, Tyee, and Pacific Wings have been and are companies truly labeled as 'icons of the Inlet'.

The beauty of the Inlet is evident from all vantage points - on the ground, in the air, and even in space. But it is most spectacular and awesome when seen firsthand. This book points out how many people have explored, lived, and worked in this area, and gives testament to the intoxicating pull this place seems to have on a person. It is a place, which is untouched, even while some have tried to promote and log the area. Today, many people make Princess Louisa Inlet a destination; whether they are young or old, famous or ordinary, rich or poor, it doesn't matter. For all it's the desire to experience or reconnect with this place. To see the Inlet first hand and, like the author, tap into a past generation and reconnect with family long gone through mutual appreciation of the unchanging land. It is hoped that many will come through the rapids to participate in a Young Life program, or to see the splendor the Inlet has to offer. It has a fascinating history to share.

A Pilot's View of Malibu (2003)

ENDNOTES

i   McCormick, *Cruise of the Calcite*. page 46 & 51.

ii Whitford & Craig, *Forests of British Columbia* pages 342-344. 1918.

iii *British Columbia Coast Howe Sound to Toba Inlet*, Bulletin #6, page 10. 1934.

iv Thirkell, *The Sisters Time Forgot* The Vancouver Province Newspaper. page A21 June 11, 1995.

v   *ibid.*

vi *Timber Buy Kills yachtsman's resort – US millionaire's dream ended by Princess Louisa Inlet deal*. Vancouver Sun, February 13, 1956.

Epilogue

There are ways to experience the Inlet, even if you don't own a private yacht or attend a camp at Malibu. Below are listed some contacts, and information about each, which will give an interested individual access to this amazing area of land and water.

The only way to get to Princess Louisa Inlet is by boat or seaplane. However, there are a number of ways to still experience this special and beautiful place even if you don't own a boat or a plane. The Sechelt Chamber of Commerce is an excellent place to start, for they will be able to provide the necessary businesses and tour group information in order to help you get to the Inlet.

SECHELT & DISTRICT
CHAMBER OF COMMERCE
PO Box 360
Trail Bay Mall
Sechelt BC V0N 3A0
Email: secheltchamber@dccnet.com

SECHELT & DISTRICT
VISITOR INFORMATION CENTER
Email: visitorinfo@dccnet.com
Phone: 604 885-0662
Fax: 604 885-0691
Toll Free: 1-877-633-2963
Web: www.thesunshinecoast.com

Taken by C.W. Hitz of One Eye Images & Sound

The Malibu Princess Underway (2003)

The reader can also use the web to get a complete list of available tours and guides by using any web search engine and by typing "Princess Louisa Inlet" or "Princess Louisa Inlet Tours". In particular, the Malibu Yacht Tours provides an excellent tour of the area with the use of their *Malibu Princess*. And they probably know the area better than anybody by this time! The Tours leave from Egmont, BC, and follow the Jervis Inlet up to Princess Louisa Inlet, with a stop at Chatterbox Falls for a afternoon of cruising and exploring this pristine area.

MALIBU YACHT TOURS
P.O. Box 49
Egmont BC/Canada
V0N 1N0
Phone: 604-883-2003
Fax: 604-883-2082
Web: www.malibuyachts.com/
Email: malibuyachts@uniserve.com

Aside from boats, one can always get a tour of the Inlet by air and there are a number of floatplane companies that provide this service from Seattle, Washington, Vancouver, BC and Sechelt, BC. Kenmore Air Harbor of Seattle Washington is perhaps the largest seaplane operation on the west side of the Mississippi River in the United States. It has a large fleet of DeHaviland Beavers and Otters, plus Cessna 185s capable of handling any charter or group to Princess Louisa Inlet and elsewhere around Washington's Puget Sound, San Juan Island chain, Gulf Island, and many of the fishing resorts of the BC area.

Taken by C.W. Hitz of One Eye Images & Sound

A Kenmore Beaver on Final (1982)

KENMORE AIR HARBOR
6321 NE 175th St., Kenmore, Washington.
Mailing address: P.O. Box 82064,
Kenmore, Washington. 98028-0064
General Phone: (425) 486-1257
Reservations Phone: (866) 435-9524
Web: http://www.kenmoreair.com
Email: reservations@kenmoreair.com

A flight from Kenmore is recommended if one is coming from Seattle. Another option is to fly out of Sechelt, BC near the entrance of the Jervis Inlet to allow for more time at the Inlet and falls. If this is desired, then Pacific Wings Airlines is recommended and provides scheduled daily flights, charters, and excellent sightseeing tours to Princess Louisa Inlet and Chatterbox Falls. Pacific Wings is owned and operated by Grant Starrs of Sechelt, BC. Grant and his pilots provide first-hand local knowledge with their sight seeing flights to Princess Louisa Inlet that makes the experience memorable to for anyone who has not visited the area before, at very reasonable rates.

Taken by C.W. Hitz of One Eye Images & Sound

A Pacific Wings Beaver at Princess Louisa Inlet (2003)

PACIFIC WINGS AIRLINES
5764 – Unit 3 Wharf Street
(next to Lighthouse Pub). Sechelt, BC.
Mailing address: P.O. Box 82064,.Sechelt, BC. V0N 3A0
General Phone: (604)885-2111
Toll Free Phone: (866) 885-2111
Web: http://www.pwairlines.com
Email: pwairlines@dccnet.com

Young Life's Malibu Club camp is still functioning as it has been for over 50 years, and continues to host over 300 high school kids a week during its peak summer season. The popularity of Malibu is increasing and the demand of campers each summer is at an all time high. Regrettably, a number of high schoolers are turned away each year because the facility just cannot accommodate them. The reason is because all of the buildings that Tom Hamilton had originally built were to accommodate only one or two guests a week. Currently, a single room houses over 12 to 15 teenagers and that is significantly more than the original plan was designed for. Young Life, however, has tried over the years to increase accommodations by renovating rooms, adding bunk beds and other buildings to help with this demand. Fundraising is essential to Young Life and the Malibu Club, and anyone wishing to contribute to this organization, or to Malibu itself, can do so by contacting:

YOUNG LIFE
P.O. Box 520
Colorado Springs, CO. 80901
Phone: 719-381-1800
Web: www.younglife.org

MALIBU CLUB IN CANADA
6545 Maple Road
Egmont, BC / Canada
V0N 1N0

Mailing address:
P.O.Box 49
Egmont BC/ Canada

Phone: 606-883-2582
Fax: 604-883-2082
Email: info@malibuclub.com
Web: www.malibuclub.com

The Princess Louisa International Society is a non-profit organization, chartered to preserve the Inlet from all commercial interests. It is currently running a fundraising campaign in order to raise money to buy the property of the inlet aside from what Young Life owns, with the help of the Nature Conservancy of Canada. Please contact the Society at the following:

PRINCESS LOUISA INTERNATIONAL SOCIETY

PO Box 17279
Seattle, WA, 98107, USA
or
Box 33918 – Station "D"
Vancouver, BC, V6J 4L8, Canada

Email: info@princesslouisa.bc.ca
Web: www.princesslouisa.bc.ca

Taken by C.W. Hitz of One Eye Images & Sound

The Buoy at the Entrance
of the Princess Louisa Inlet (2003)

APPENDIX

A

Queen Victoria Family Lineage

Alexandrina Victoria, at the age of 18, became Queen of Great Britain and Ireland (also Empress of India) through some very complicated royal successions ending with William IV's (The Duke of Kent) death in June 1837. Queen Victoria's reign began in 1837, and lasted until her death in 1901. The final reach of the Jervis Inlet is named after the Queen Victoria – Queen's Reach. In 1840, the Queen married her cousin, Prince Albert of Saxe-Coburg-Gotha (Mt. Albert is named in his honor), and they became inseparable. During their marriage, they had nine children, creating a large family.

HRH Victoria Adelaide Mary Louisa 'Vicky' was the first child and daughter born on November 21 1840 (died in 1890), to the royal couple. Vicky had the title of Princess Royal, of which the second arm of the Jervis Inlet was named– *Princess Royal Reach*. She would be the future wife of the German Emperor (Prince Friedrich Wilhelm, the heir to the German Prussian and German thrones. *Mt. Fredrick William* at the head of the Jervis Inlet is named for him) and the mother of Kaiser Wilhelm II, who abdicated from the German throne after Germany's surrender in World War I.

HRH Francis Albert Augustus Charles Emanuel, 'Bertie' was the second child, born on November 9, 1841 (died 1910), and the future king (became Edward VII from 1901 to 1910) of England, who also happens to be the Great Grandfather of the current Queen of England (Elizabeth II). The Prince was invested with the titles of Duke of Saxony, the Prince of Coburg and Gotha, and the *Prince of Wales,* of which the first arm of the Jervis Inlet is named for.

HRH Alice Maud Mary was the third child, born in 1843 and sadly, she would be the first of Victoria's children to die early, at the age of 35. The Princesses married 'Louis, Grad Duke of Hesse and by Rhine'. She was the Grandmother to Sir Louis Mountbatten and was the Great Grandmother to Prince Phillip (husband to the current Queen of England). *Mt. Alice* is named after her and is located at the head of Jervis Inlet.

HRH Alfred Edward 'Affie' was the fourth child, born in 1844 and given the title Duke of Edinburgh and of Saxe-Coburg. *Mt. Alfred* was named in his honor and is also located at the head of the Jervis Inlet.

HRH Princess Helena Augusta Victoria 'Lenchen' was the fifth child born to the family in1846 (died in 1923), and she married Christian of Schleswig-Holstein Augustenburg. *Mt Helena*, located behind Malibu and the entrance to Princess Louisa inlet, is named in her honor.

HRH Princess Louise Caroline Alberta The sixth child born to the royal couple arrived in 1848 (died in 1939) and married to John Campell, Marquess of Lorne, 9th Duke of Argyll. This is the Princess for whom the Inlet featured in this book was named after – *Princess Louise Inlet*. Note the variation of this name and that of Princess Louisa Inlet because the German articulation of Louise conflicted with the English pronunciation. In English, the "e" at the end a world is considered silent where in German it is not and would sound like a short "a". The spelling was changed in English to reflect the correct pronunciation of the Young Princess's name.

HRH Prince Arthur William Patrick was the seventh child, born in 1850 (died in 1942). He was later given the titles of Duke of Cannaught. *Patrick Point* is named after this Prince.

HRH Prince Leopold George Duncan was the eight child, born in 1853 and would later die in 1884. No known waterway or landmark was named after this Prince at the Jervis or Princess Louisa Inlet area

HRH Princess Beatrice Mary Victoria 'baby' was the ninth, and last, child born in 1857 (died 1944). She married Heinrich Henry of Batenberg and she is the Great Grandmother to Juan Carlos I of Spain. *Mt. Victoria* is named after the baby Princess.

APPENDIX

B

Geographic Locations at Princess Louisa Inlet
(Latitude and Longitude)

PURPOSE

This list describes the geographic locations and points throughout the Jervis and Princess Louisa Inlet area. The following table only gives the latitude and longitude of each specific point of location that might be helpful to the reader if searching for these points on a map, GPS device, or even satellite photos on the web. This table, however, is only for reference and general information and should not be used in precision navigation wither it be marine or aeronautical.

LOCATIONS

Head of the Jervis Inlet 123°59' W 50°12' N	**McDonald Island** 123°48' W 50°11' N
Malibu 123°51'W 50°9' N	**Patrick Point** 123°48' W 50°5' N
Chatterbox Falls 123°46'W 50°12' N	**Vancouver Bay** 123°52'W 49°55' N

APPENDIX

C

Tom Hamilton Ownership of Property at Princess Louisa Inlet
(1941-1953)

PURPOSE

This list describes the total amount of property held by Thomas F. Hamilton and the Hamiltair Corporation Ltd. This corporation ran the Malibu Club in Canada, Malibu SeAero, and Malibu Yacht Charters in the Princess Louisa Inlet, BC area and up the west coast of the United States from 1941 to 1952. This information does not include current owners of the property and others who may have been issued Crown Grants in the area before or after the 1941-1952 timeframe. This document only specifies the holdings of Mr. Hamilton and his many enterprises in the area.

DEFINITIONS

All the survey information of Princess Louis Inlet, BC and surrounding and at is located and cataloged in Group 1 of the New Westminster District in British Columbia, Canada.

ARCO OR TERM	DEFINITON
CG/Vol	Crown Grant / Vol – all priority
IR	Indian Reserve Land
FB/PH	Form Book & Pigeonhole – Terms used by surveyors to record and organize surveys.
1946 Data	Info From Real Estate Document dated 12/31/1946

THE PROPERTY

LOT: 3412
DATE: 2-20-41
NAME: T.F. Hamilton
ACRES: 640
PRICE: See Lot #3534
CG/VOL: 2582/696
NOTES: OinC#827 6-16-41
          Survey 20 Feb 1913
          FB 132/12 PH 25
          E. Shore Queens Reach – Jervis Inlet

LOT: 3513
DATE: 2-20-41
NAME: T.F. Hamilton
ACRES: 413
PRICE: See Lot #3534
CG/VOL: 2583/696
NOTES: Survey 6-12-41
          FB 172/41 PH 43
          Princess Louisa Inlet

LOT: 3514
DATE: 2-20-41
NAME: T.F. Hamilton
ACRES: 528
PRICE: See Lot #3534
CG/VOL: 2584/696
NOTES: Survey 6-12-41
FB 172/41 PH 43
Princess Louisa Inlet

LOT: 3515
DATE: 3-1941
NAME: T.F. Hamilton
ACRES: 528
PRICE: See Lot #3534
CG/VOL: Data 1941
NOTES: Survey 6-12-41
FB 172/41 PH 43
Princess Louisa Inlet

LOT: 3516
DATE: 3-1941
NAME: T.F. Hamilton
ACRES: 605
PRICE: See Lot #3534
CG/VOL: 2585/696
NOTES: Survey 6-12-41
FB 172/41 PH 43
Princess Louisa Inlet

LOT: 3517
DATE: 3-1941
NAME: T.F. Hamilton
ACRES: 607
PRICE: See Lot #3534
CG/VOL: 2586/696
NOTES: Survey 6-12-41
FB 172/41 PH 43
Princess Louisa Inlet

LOT: 3518
DATE: 3-1941
NAME: T.F. Hamilton
ACRES: 450
PRICE: See Lot #3534
CG/VOL: 2610/696
NOTES: Survey 6-12-41
           FB 172/41 PH 43
           Princess Louisa Inlet

LOT: 3519
DATE: 3-1941
NAME: T.F. Hamilton
ACRES: 571
PRICE: See Lot #3534
CG/VOL: 2587/696
NOTES: Survey 6-12-41
           FB 172/41 PH 43
           Princess Louisa Inlet

LOT: 3520
DATE: 3-1941
NAME: T.F. Hamilton
ACRES: 250
PRICE: See Lot #3534
CG/VOL: 2696/697
NOTES: Survey 6-12-41
           FB 172/41 PH 43
           Princess Louisa Inlet

LOT: 3521
DATE: 3-1941
NAME: T.F. Hamilton
ACRES: 469
PRICE: See Lot #3534
CG/VOL: 2588/696

NOTES: Survey 6-12-41
FB 172/41 PH 43
Princess Louisa Inlet

LOT: 3522
DATE: 3-1941
NAME: T.F. Hamilton
ACRES: 514
PRICE: See Lot #3534
CG/VOL: 2589/696
NOTES: Survey 6-12-41
FB 172/41 PH 43
Princess Louisa Inlet

LOT: 3523
DATE: 3-1941
NAME: T.F. Hamilton
ACRES: 427
PRICE: See Lot #3534
CG/VOL: 2590/696
NOTES: Survey 6-12-41
FB 172/41 PH 43
Princess Louisa Inlet

LOT: 3524
DATE: 3-1941
NAME: T.F. Hamilton
ACRES: 640
PRICE: See Lot #3534
CG/VOL: 2591/696
NOTES: Survey 6-12-41
FB 172/41 PH 43
Princess Louisa Inlet

LOT: 3525
DATE: 3-1941
NAME: T.F. Hamilton
ACRES: 640
PRICE: See Lot #3534

CG/VOL: 2592/696
NOTES: Survey 6-12-41
          FB 172/41 PH 43
          Princess Louisa Inlet

LOT: 3526
DATE: 3-1941
NAME: T.F. Hamilton
ACRES: 640
PRICE: See Lot #3534
CG/VOL: 2593/697
NOTES: Survey 6-12-41
          FB 172/41 PH 43
          Princess Louisa Inlet

LOT: 3527
DATE: 3-1941
NAME: T.F. Hamilton
ACRES: 418
PRICE: See Lot #3534
CG/VOL: 2593/696
NOTES: Survey 6-12-41
          FB 172/41 PH 43
          Princess Louisa Inlet

LOT: 3528
DATE: 3-1941
NAME: T.F. Hamilton
ACRES: 640
PRICE: See Lot #3534
CG/VOL: 2594/696
NOTES: Survey 6-12-41
          FB 172/41 PH 43
          Princess Louisa Inlet

LOT: 3529
DATE: 3-1941
NAME: T.F. Hamilton
ACRES: 640

PRICE: See Lot #3534
CG/VOL: 2595/696
NOTES: Survey 6-12-41
FB 172/41 PH 43
Princess Louisa Inlet

LOT: 3530
DATE: 3-1941
NAME: T.F. Hamilton
ACRES: .5
PRICE: See Lot #3534
CG/VOL: 2596/696
NOTES: Survey 6-12-41
FB 172/41 PH 43
Princess Louisa Inlet

LOT: 3533
DATE: 3-1941
NAME: T.F. Hamilton
ACRES: 43.3
PRICE: See Lot #3534
CG/VOL: 2596/696
NOTES: Survey 6-12-41
FB 172/41 PH 43
Princess Louisa Inlet

LOT: 3534
DATE: 3-1941
NAME: T.F. Hamilton
ACRES: .295
PRICE: $6,000
CG/VOL: 2596/696
NOTES: Survey 6-12-41
FB 172/41 PH 43
Princess Louisa Inlet

LOT: 3535
DATE: 3-1941
NAME: T.F. Hamilton

ACRES: ?
PRICE: $11,000
CG/VOL: 2596/696
NOTES: open

LOT: 4211
DATE: Dec. 1940
NAME: T.F. Hamilton
ACRES: 88.5
PRICE: $18,000
CG/VOL: Data 1946
NOTES: Bought from MacDonald (Island)

LOT: 4212
DATE: Apr. 1941
NAME: T.F. Hamilton
ACRES: 25
PRICE: $1,650
CG/VOL: Data 1946
NOTES: Bought from H.Parcel

LOT: 5567
DATE: Apr. 1941
NAME: T.F. Hamilton
ACRES: 26
PRICE: $1,000
CG/VOL: Data 1946
NOTES: Bought from J.Larnie

Total Cost (Buying Property at PLI)

$37,650*

* *Assume amounts in Canadian Dollars but no record to
substantiate claim.*

NOTES

- The Malibu Resort is located at the entrance of PLI and is on Lot 5567. This location was not in the historical record books under Hamilton and is currently being investigated.

- Malibu Isle or Forbidden Island at the mouth of PLI was listed under Indian Land (IR 12A)

- There is no record for the acquired number of # 0140291.

- Per OinC #827 – this land was purchased for $6,000.00 on 6-12-1941 with the desire to develop a pleasure resort, at the expense roughly of $75,000.00 (Malibu)

REFERENCES

- Ministry of Environment, Lands, and Parks (Province of British Columbia)

- Crown Land Registry Services.,3400 Davidson Ave. Victoria BC. Land Registers #4888-5285, New Westminster 1. Group 1. Pages 85, 119-126.

- Malibu Club Real Estate Totals and Property Purchases. December 31, 1946

Map of Property Held By Tom Hamilton at Princess Louisa Inlet
(1940-1953)

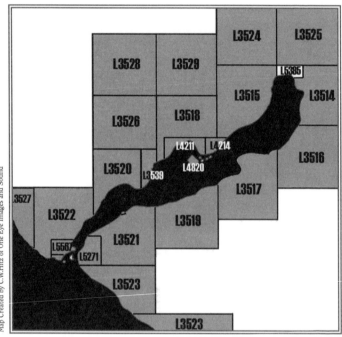

Map Created by C.W.Hitz of One Eye Images and Sound

Map of Malibu Facility Under Tom Hamilton's Ownership
(1940-1953)

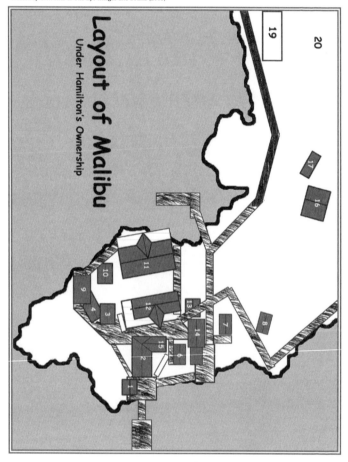

Layout of Malibu
Under Hamilton's Ownership

APPENDIX

F

Construction and Location of Malibu Buildings Under Tom Hamilton and Hamiltair Ltd.
(1940-1953)

This list describes the construction sequence and cost associated with building Malibu during the years of 1941 & 1945. The Map of Malibu from the following page has numbers associated with building which correspond to the building list below.

COSTS OF CONSTRUCTION

YEAR	LABOR	OVERHEAD	MATERIALS	TOTAL
1941	$28,124.10	$29,352.89	$37,714.87	$95,191.86
1945	65,185.78	59,440.12	55,000.00	179,625.90
Total				$274,817.76

BUILDING LIST

No.	Name	Build Date
1	Boathouse	1941
2	Boathouse Lounge & Game Room	1941
3	Trading Store	1941
4	Restaurant	1941
5	First Aid Cabin (Unknown Location)	1941
6	Sioux Lodge	1941
7	Siwash Lodge	1941
8	Sequoia Lodge	1941
9	Dining Room (Extension to Restaurant)	1945
10	Staff Mess Hall (Also known as Summer Kitchen)	1945
11	Navajo Lodge	1945
12	Aztec Lodge	1945
13	Power House	1945
14	Sitka Lodge	1945
15	Library	1941
16	Sechelt Cottage	1941
17	Malibu Bar	1945
18	Dock	1941/1945
19	Tennis Court	1945
20	Golf Course	1945

APPENDIX

G

Yachts and Vessels Owned by Tom Hamilton and Hamiltair Ltd.
(1941-1953)

This list describes the vessels owned by Thomas F. Hamilton and the Hamiltair Corporation Ltd while the corporation ran the Malibu Club in Canada, Malibu SeAero, and Malibu Yacht Charters in the Princess Louisa Inlet, BC area and up the west coast of the United States from 1941 to 1952. This is not a complete list and does not break out the vessels prior to or after World War II.

DEFINITIONS

ARCO OR TERM	DEFINITON
Reg #	Vessel registration Number
Name	Malibu's name of the vessel
Build Date	Date of when vessel was built and where.
Type	Type of boat (shipyard)
Notes	Info about the vessel

THE VESSEL LIST

The Fairmile was used for Malibu's yacht and charter operations. Names of these vessels are highlighted in bold case fonts.

REG.#:   Unknown
NAME: *Chief Malibu I*
BUILD DATE: 1940-Algonac, MI
TYPE: 40ft-Chris Craft
NOTES: Based in Newport Beach, CA.
              Unknown whereabouts

REG.#:   Unknown
NAME: *Henrietta H*
BUILD DATE: 1936-Algonac, MI
TYPE: 19ft-Chris Craft
NOTES: Unknown whereabouts

REG.#:   Unknown
NAME: *Malibu Chinook*
BUILD DATE: 1940-Algonac, MI
TYPE: 34ft-Chris Craft
NOTES: Based in Newport Beach, CA.
              Unknown whereabouts

REG.#:   Unknown
NAME: *Malibu Mala Bula*
BUILD DATE: 1938-Algonac, MI
TYPE: Chris Craft
NOTES: Sold and known as "Don Jon".

REG.#:   Unknown
NAME: *Malibu Sailfish*
BUILD DATE: 1942- Algonac, MI
TYPE: 34ft-Chris Craft
NOTES: Based in Newport Beach, CA.
              Unknown whereabouts

REG.#:	Unknown
NAME:	*Malibu Silver King*
BUILD DATE:	1940-Algonac, M
TYPE:	34ft-Chris Craft
NOTES:	Based in Newport Beach, CA. Unknown whereabouts

REG.#:	Unknown
NAME:	*Malibu Starfish*
BUILD DATE:	1942- Algonac, MI
TYPE:	30ft-Chris Craft
NOTES:	Based in Newport Beach, CA. Unknown whereabouts

REG.#:	Unknown
NAME:	*Malibu Tarpon*
BUILD DATE:	1942- Algonac, MI
TYPE:	32ft-Chris Craft
NOTES:	Based in Newport Beach, CA. Unknown whereabouts

REG.#:	Unknown
NAME:	*Malibu Tyee II*
BUILD DATE:	1940- Algonac, MI
TYPE:	34ft-Chris Craft
NOTES:	Based in Newport Beach, CA. Unknown whereabouts

REG.#:	Unknown
NAME:	*Princess Angeline*
BUILD DATE:	
TYPE:	50ft-Wheeler cruiser
NOTES:	Unknown whereabouts

REG.#:	Unknown
NAME:	*Princess Malibu*
BUILD DATE:	
TYPE:	48ft-Chris Craft
NOTES:	Unknown whereabouts

REG.#: Unknown
NAME: *Tara*
BUILD DATE:
TYPE: 120ft-twin screw diesel cruiser
NOTES: Built in the 1920s by Nevins.
Unknown whereabouts

REG.#: Unknown
NAME: *Vega*
BUILD DATE: 1930 - Germany
TYPE: 148ft - Steel hull sailing schooner
NOTES:

REG.#: 172213
NAME: *Malibu Arrow*
BUILD DATE: 1924 -New York NY
TYPE: 120ft-twin screw diesel cruiser
NOTES: Unknown
Sold and known as *"Eileen J."* and *"Bidgee"*.

REG.#: 173583
NAME: *Malibu Squaw*
BUILD DATE: 1941 Van BC
TYPE: Cruiser
NOTES: Unknown whereabouts

REG.#: 173610
NAME: *Malibu Papoose*
BUILD DATE: 1941-Van BC
TYPE: Cruiser
NOTES: Unknown whereabouts

REG.#: 175138
NAME: *Malibu Tepee*
BUILD DATE: 1940 Van BC
TYPE: 34ft-Chris Craft
NOTES: Sold and known as *"Jokar 1"*
Number V-377-A

REG.#:   75161
NAME: *Malibu Wahoo*
BUILD DATE: 1928 New York NY
TYPE: Cruiser
NOTES: Sold and known as *"Alaby Wahoo"*
                PT-Boat Prototype.

REG.#:   175695
NAME: *Malibu Tuna*
BUILD DATE: 1940-New Rochelle NY
TYPE: Cruiser
NOTES: Sold and known as *"Wannegin"*.

REG.#:   175707
NAME: *Malibu Wigwam*
BUILD DATE: 1943 New Rochelle NY
TYPE: 37ft-Chris Craft
NOTES: Unknown whereabouts

REG.#:   176231
NAME: *Malibu Inez*
BUILD DATE: 1943 Van BC
TYPE: Q129 Fairmile
NOTES: Ex-Q129 Sold and called the *"Huntress II"*.

REG.#:   176472
NAME: *Malibu Tyee*
BUILD DATE: 1943 Van BC
TYPE: Q122 Fairmile
NOTES: Ex-Q122, Re-named the *"Nancy H.
                Seymour"* and currently called
                "Sogno d'Oro".

REG.#:   176473
NAME: *Malibu Marlin*
BUILD DATE: 1943 Van BC
TYPE: Q123 Fairmile
NOTES: Ex-Q123, sold and called the *"Toluca"* .

REG.#:   176474
NAME: *Malibu Tilikum*
BUILD DATE: 1943 Van BC
TYPE: Q125 Fairmile
NOTES: Ex-Q125, sold called *"Gulfstream II"*

REG.#:   176483
NAME: *Chief Malibu*
BUILD DATE: 1941 Van BC
TYPE: Fairmile
NOTES: Ex-Q127, Sank at PLI (Total Lost).

REG.#:   176485
NAME: *Princess Louisa Inlet*
BUILD DATE: 1944 Van BC
TYPE: Q128 Fairmile
NOTES: Ex-Q128 Burned and sunk in
            Pendrell Sound BC. Dec 1955.

REG.#:   176486
NAME: *Malibu Princess*
BUILD DATE: 1943 New WM. BC
TYPE: Q126 Fairmile
NOTES: Ex-Q126

REG.#:   176486
NAME: *Malibu Tomahawk*
BUILD DATE: 1943 New WM. BC 1931-Marysville,MI
TYPE: 39ft- Gar Wood
NOTES: Unknown whereabouts

REG.#:   176492
NAME: *Malibu Malablitz*
BUILD DATE: 1936-Algonac, MI
TYPE: Chris Craft
NOTES: Unknown whereabouts

REG.#:   227599
NAME: *Malibu*
BUILD DATE: 1925 Seattle WA
TYPE: Cruiser
NOTES: Designed by Ted Geary
              TFH bought in 1938.

REG.#:   238650
NAME: *Malibu Dawn*
BUILD DATE: 1940-Algonac, MI
TYPE: 48ft-Chris Craft
NOTES: Based in Newport Beach, CA.
              Unknown whereabouts.

REFERENCE

List of Yachts of the United States and Canada (1948)

Image Gallery of the
Malibu Fairmile Yachts
(1945-1953)

From the Collection of C.W. Hitz

Princess Malibu Underway (1948)

Courtesy of Young Life – Used with Permission

The *Malibu Inez* tied up at Malibu (1946)

From the Collection of C.W. Hitz

The *Malibu Tilikum* (1949)

Courtesy of Young Life – Used with Permission

The Fairmile Fleet at Malibu (1948)
Princess Louisa Inlet (at end of dock), Malibu Tilikum
(at head of dock), & Malibu Chief (next to Tilikum)

APPENDIX

I

Malibu Club in Canada Brochures
(1945-1953)

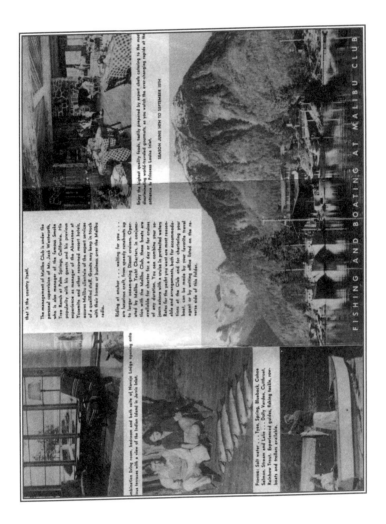

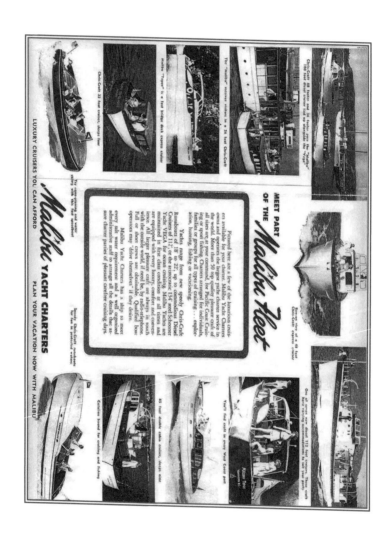

APPENDIX

J

Map of the Malibu Facility Under Young Life's Ownership

(1954-2003)

Created by C.W. Hitz of One Eye Images and Sound (2003)

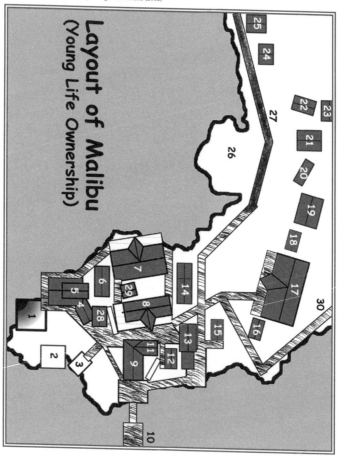

APPENDIX

K

Construction and Location of the Malibu Buildings Under Young Life's Ownership

(1954-2003)

This list shows the location and title of each building at Malibu under Young Life's tenure from 1954 & 2003. The layout of the Malibu facility from Appendix J has numbers which correspond to the Building List below.

BUILDING LIST

NO.	NAME	BUILD DATE
1	Swimming Pool	1959 & 1997
2	Volleyball Court	2001
3	Old Garbage Dock	1965
4	Dining Hall & Kitchen	Original Hamilton Add on in 1959
5	Sechelt	1960

No.	Name	Build Date
6	Capilano and food storage below	1968
7	Nootka – including Foc'sle, Nootka 1 1/2, & Boys' work crew dorm	Original Hamilton
8	Suivolet – including Lilloet, 2nd Lilloet, Girls' work crew dorm, and Main Street: Office, Medicine Man, and Totem Trader	Original Hamilton
9	Big Squawka – including Games Room and Café	Original Hamilton
10	Inner Dock	
11	Little Squawka	Original Hamilton
12	Sioux	Original Hamilton
13	Sitka – including the New Linen Nook (2003) & Laundry	Original Hamilton
14	Power House – including shops and Plumping Shack	1975 with additions in 1992 & 2003
15	Siwash	Original Hamilton
16	Sequoia	Original Hamilton
17	Gym – including Beyond radio room and Storage	2001
18	Chimo	1972
19	Tilikum	1989
20	Haida	Original Hamilton
21	Chilkoot	1970

No.	Name	Build Date
22	Minatch	1967
23	Golf Shack	1969
24	Kekuli	1992
25	Tree House	1965
26	Flag Point	Original Hamilton
27	Path to Hamburger Point, Malibu Beach, & the Outer Dock	Original Hamilton
28	Totem Inn	Original Hamilton
29	Work crew lounge	1984
30	Path to Gas Dock and Boat House	Various Years

APPENDIX
L

Young Life Property Managers at Malibu
(1954-2003)

This list describes the people who were involved in the leadership, maintained, and services at Malibu from 1954 to 2003.

MALIBU PROPERTY MANAGER LIST

YEAR: 1954-1958
NAME: Add Sewell
TITLE: Camp Manager

YEAR: 1955-1964
NAME: Ray & Marge Anderson
TITLE: Care Taker

YEAR: 1955-1964
NAME: Bob & Diane Hagstrom
TITLE: Superintendent

YEAR: 1959-1962
NAME: Frayne Gordon
TITLE: Property Manager

YEAR: 1965-1973
NAME: Vic & Nene Hookins
TITLE: Superintendent/ Care Taker

YEAR: 1963-1971
NAME: Ken Parker
TITLE: Property Manager

YEAR: 1972-1977
NAME: Mike Sheridan
TITLE: Property Manager

YEAR: 1973-1986
NAME: Gail Grimston
TITLE: Guest Service Coordinator/Operations Manger

YEAR: 1972-1977
NAME: Mike & Jacquelyn Lewis
TITLE: Mechanical Superintendent

YEAR: 1972-1979
NAME: Jack Lewis
TITLE: Property Superintendent

YEAR: 1978-1985
NAME: Tim French
TITLE: Property Manager (also Care Taker from 1975-77)

YEAR: 1980
NAME: Peter Talbot
TITLE: Superintendent/Care Taker

YEAR: 1981-1993
NAME: Frank Poirier
TITLE: Superintendent/Care Taker

YEAR: 1986-1993
NAME: Kathy Murphy
TITLE: Guest Services Coordinator

YEAR: 1986-1997
NAME: Don Prittie
TITLE: Property Manager

YEAR: 1993-1997
NAME: Jan Quiring
TITLE: Guest Services Coordinator

YEAR: 1994-1998
NAME: Paul Bailey
TITLE: Superintendent/Care Taker

YEAR: 1998
NAME: Steve Fisher
TITLE: Interim Property Manager

YEAR: 1999-
NAME: Mike Schroeder
TITLE: Care Taker/Construction

YEAR: 1999 -
NAME: Harold Richert
TITLE: Property Manager

YEAR: 1999-2003
NAME: Dane & Trudy Ruck
TITLE: Superintendent

YEAR: 2000-
NAME: Carolyn Mortensen
TITLE: Guest Services

YEAR: 2003-
NAME: Gill & Linda Fuller
TITLE: Superintendent

APPENDIX

M

Young Life Beyond Directors
(1970-2003)

This list describes the people who were involved as directors of the Malibu Beyond hiking ministry from 1970 to 2003.

MALIBU BEYOND DIRECTORS LIST

YEARS: 1970-1976
DIRECTOR: Barney Dobson

YEARS: 1977-1979
DIRECTOR: Gordy Anderson

YEARS: 1980-1982
DIRECTOR: Tom Buckley

YEARS: 1983-1987
DIRECTOR: Art Kopicky

YEARS: 1988-
DIRECTOR: Rob Dyker

APPENDIX
N

Image Gallery of Malibu Construction
(1954-2003)

Taken by B. Prichard – Used with Permission

Building Capilano (1969)

Taken by B. Prichard – Used with Permission

View of Capilano's Construction (1969)

Taken by B. Prichard – Used with Permission

Building the Golf Shack (1969)

Taken by B. Prichard – Used with Permission

Building the Original Basketball Court (1969)

Courtesy of Young Life – Used with Permission

Building the Power House (1975)

Taken by B. Prichard – Used with Permission

Installing the Septic Tank (1970)

Taken by C.W.Hitz of One Eye Images and Sound

The New Gym Under Construction (2001)

Bibliography

BOOKS

Barratt, Glynn. 1993. *Russian Shadows on the British Northwest Coast of North America 1810-1890*.

Blanchet, M. Wylie. 1993. *The Curve of Time,* Seal Press.

Bungey, Lloyd M & the Canadian Museum of Flight & Transportation. 1992. *Pioneering Aviation in the West.* Surrey BC: Hancock House.

Calhoun, Bruce. 1969. *Northwest Passages Part One.* San Francisco CA: Miller Freeman Publications.

———. 1972. *Northwest Passages Part Two.* San Francisco CA: Miller Freeman Publications.

———. 1976. *Mac and the Princess - The Story of Princess Louisa Inlet.* Seattle, WA: Richwalt Publishing Company.

Campbell, Elsie. 1984. *Young Life's Malibu.* Olympia, WA: Good News Book Store.

Cecil, Lamar. 1989. *Wilhelm II - Prince and Emperor, 1859-1900.* Chapel Hill, North Carolina: The University of North Carolina Press.

Cummings, Al & Jo Bailey. 1989. *Gunkholing in Desolation Sound and Princess Louisa Inlet.* Edmonds WA: Nor'westing Inc.

Dawson, L.S. 1885. *Memoirs of Hydrography - brief biographies of the Principal Officers who have served in H.M. Naval Surveying Service between the years 1750 and 1885.* Eastbourn, England: Henry W. Keay, the 'Imperial Library'.

Gough, Barry M. 1971. *The Royal Navy and Northwest Coast of Washington (1810-1914).* Vancouver, BC: UBC Press.

Gough, Barry M. 1984. *Gunboat Frontier: British Maritime Authority and Northwest Coast Indians (1846-1890).* Vancouver, BC: UBC Press.

Harris, Lorraine. 1984. *Gold along the Frasier*. Vancouver, BC: Hancock House Publishers LTD.

Harris, R. Cole, ed. 1987. *Historical Atlas of Canada*. 2 vols. Vol. I: University of Toronto Press.

Haslam, Rear-Admiral D.W. 1960. *The British Contribution to the Hydrography of Canada*.

Hill, Beth. 1985. *Upcoast Summers*. Ganges, BC. Horsdal & Schubart Publishers Ltd.

Johnson, Patricia M. 1958. *A Short History of Nanaimo BC (1858-1958)*. Victoria, B.C.: BC Centennial Committee.

Kendrick, John, ed. 1990. *The Voyage of Sutil and Mexicana 1792*, Northwest Historical Series XVI. Spokane, WA: The Arthur H. Clark Company.

Lambert, John. 1985. *The Fairmile 'D' Motor Torpedo Boat*: Conway Maritime Press.

Leslie, Betty C. Keller & Rosella M. 1996. *Bright Seas, Pioneer Spirits*. Victoria, B.C., Canada: Horsdal & Schubart Publishers Ltd.

Mayne, Richard Charles. 1861. *Four years in British Columbia and Vancouver Island - An account of their forests, rivers, coasts, gold fields, and resources for colonization*. London, England.

McCaffrey, Howard White and Margaret. 1977. *Raincoast Chronicles First Five*, edited by H. White: Harbor Publishing.

McCormick, John A. 1973. *Cruise of the Calcite*. Seattle, WA: B & E Enterprises.

Meany, Edmond S. 1915. *Vancouver's Discovery of Puget Sound*. London, England: The Macmillan Company.

Meredith, Char. 1978. *It's a Sin to Bore a Kid*. Colorado Springs, CO: Word, Inc.

Murry, Robert. 1858. *Rudimentary Treatise on the Marine Engine and on Steam Vessels and the Screws*. 3rd ed. London, England.

Norton, Sullivan Henry. 1896. *The Life and Letters of the late Admiral Sir Bartholomew James Sullivan*, k.c.b. London, England.

Parker, Peter Corley Smith & David. 1985. *Helicopters - The BC Story*. Victoria, BC: The BC Provincial Museum.

Peterson, Lester. 1990. *The Story of the Sechelt Nation*. Sechelt BC: Harbor Publishing.

Pinkerton, Katherine. 1991. *Three's a Crew*. Ganges BC: Horsdal & Schubart Publishers LTD.

Rayburn III, James. 1984. *Dance, Children, Dance*. Wheaton, IL: Tyndale House Publishers, Inc.

Richards, Captain George Henry. *1898. British Columbia Pilot*. 2nd ed. London, England.

Richardson, David. 1990. *Pig War Islands*. Eastsound, WA: Orcas Publishing Company.

Rossiter, Sean. 1999. *The Immortal Beaver*. Vancouver, BC: Douglas & McIntyre.

Schweizer, William H. 1989. *Beyond Understanding – the complete guide to Princess Louisa, Chatterbox Falls, and Jervis Inlet*. Seattle, WA: EOS Publishing.

Southern, Karen. 1987. *The Nelson Island Story*. Surrey, B.C.: Hancock House Publishers.

Vancouver, George. 1984. *The Voyage of George Vancouver 1791-1795*. Edited by W. K. Lamb. Vol. II: Victoria, BC:Hakluyt Society.

Walbran, Capt. John T. 1909. *British Columbia Coast Names (1592-1906) – their origins & history*. Ottawa Government Printing Bureau.

Warren, James R. 1993. *The Centennial History of the Seattle Yacht Club 1892-1992*. Seattle, WA.

Wilson, Eugene E. 1950. *Slipstream – The Autobiography of an Air Craftsman* New York, NY. McGraw-Hill Book Company.

Rosen, George & Anezis, Charles A. 1984. *Thrusting Forward*. Hamilton Standard Company. Hartford, CT.

PERIODICALS

Blueprint of Sport and Pleasure - "Sky Chief" First Air Unit in Vast Scheme Incorporating B.C.'s Famed Malibu Lodge. 1945. The Boeing Beam, page 4.

Cliff, Donna. 1997. *Generation to Generation*. Young Life Relationships, January, pages 4-5.

Ever-Popular Princess Louisa Inlet. 1946. Pacific Motor Boat, pages 50-51.

Gilbert, Evelyn. 1946. *Malibu Club*. BC Digest, August, pages 29-31.

Haig-Brown, Alan. 1993. *The Senior Captain*. The Westcoast Mariner, October, pages 16-17.

Haworth, Patricia. 1941. *A Yachtsman's haven at Princess Louisa*. Pacific Motor Boat Magazine, pages 5-7.

———. 1941. *An Indian Story of the Inlet*. Pacific Motor Boat, June, page 7.

Hendon, Rick. 1986. *Yacht Designer Ted Geary*. Marine Digest, May 31, pages 11-15.

Macdonald, Mac. 1941. *How it Happened*. Pacific Motor Boat, June, pages 7 & 38-39.

Malibu Club in Canada Invites Yachtsmen. 1946. Pacific Motor Boat, September, 31.

Moss, Herbert C. 1913. *A Cruise into the Yachtsman's Paradise*. The Argus, December 13, pages 28-32.

New 50-yacht charter Fleet for Pacific Coast. 1945. Pacific Motor Boat, July. pages 25-28.

Richard B. Waitt, Jr., and Robert M. Thorson, 1983, *The Cordilleran Ice Sheet in Washington, Idaho, and Montana: IN: H.E. Wright, Jr., (ed.), 1983,* Late-Quaternary Environments of the United States, Volume 1: The Late Pleistocene (Stephen C. Porter (ed.)): University of Minnesota Press, Chapter 3, p.53-70.

Rustic Lodge Design Approved for Princess Louisa Inlet. 1971. SEA & Pacific Motor Boat, August, 30-31.

Sandilands, R.W. 1979. *I am Become A Name...* CANOMA 5 (1):12-15.

NEWSPAPER ARTICLES

Apsouris, Jack Thompson (Blackie). 1997. *Obituary Column for the Vancouver Sun*, January 4. page A16

Baxter, Gill. *'Blackie' will be remembered as a flying legend*. Unknown source, January 1997.

Boeing Plant at Sea Island May be Sold – if new contracts unavailable. 1945, The Vancouver Province, September 10, page 1.

Connelly, Joel. 2001. *In the Northwest: Don't look now, but scientists think Big One is just about due*. Seattle Post-Intelligencer (PI), March 02.

Crooks, Royal. 1945. *Seattle Yachtsmen to British Columbia Coast*. The Seattle Times, September 2.

Disease Record Remarkable. 1948. Vancouver Sun, September 2, page 6.

Duin, Steve. 1994. *The Spirit of Malibu*. The Oregonian, July 10.

Fairmiles, $195,000 to Build, Sold Here for $3000 Each. 1945, Vancouver Province, October 12. page 27.

Farrow, Moira. 1975. *Students use Millionaire's Resort where Hollywood Stars once Played*. The Vancouver Sun Newspaper, June 23, page 25.

Funeral for Girl Student. 1948. Vancouver Sun, September 4, page 3.

Girl Sick Only 3 Days. 1948. Vancouver Sun, September 3, 4 page 4.

Halak, Brenda. 1978. *Scenic Splendor - only 150 km Away*. Vancouver Sun, October 17, page C8.

Howard, Frank. 1955. *A New Life for Malibu – teenagers learn of God in former millionaires' resort.* The Vancouver Sun Magazine Supplement. June 18. page 3.

Indian Motif Featured at Malibu Birthday Party. 1947. Vancouver Sun, August 5.

James F. Macdonald, 89. of Princess Louisa Inlet, dies. 1978. The Seattle Times, June 8.

Knight, Bill. 1969. *Spectacular Princess Louisa Inlet in Financial Trouble.* Seattle Post-Intelligencer, June 22, page 63.

Lane, Polly. 1989. *Malibu Charters inc – Cruise operators cater to lovers of luxurious life.* The Seattle Times, October 30, page F5.

Malibu Inez Survives Seas Off Mexico 1948. The Vancouver Sun. October 9. page 24

Malibu Resort Sold - Luxury Lodge to be Bible School. 1954. Vancouver Sun, January 9, page 46.

Mason, Don. 1941. *Millionaire Airplane Manufacturer Builds Great Resort On BC Coast - Princess Louisa Inlet Scene of Unique Holiday Village.* Vancouver Daily Province, July 5.

McDonald, Cathy. 2000. *British Columbia – History, scenery merge during cruise of inlets.* The Seattle Times. August 6. page K5.

Meek, Jack. 1941. *Jervis Inlet to Become Great BC Tourist Attraction – U.S. Aviation Magnate Building Unique Resort at Beauty Spot.* Vancouver Sun, July 5.

Montgomery, Christina. 1997. *30-year harbor Vet Departs – Age, dwindling space sends Princess Malibu to Egmont.* February 27. page A10.

Paulson, Tom. 2001. *Major quake could launch deadly tsunami.* Seattle PI, January 22.

———. 2001. *Tale of a whale in the river and the tide that never left.* Seattle PI, June 19, page 2.

———. 2001. *When Thunderbird battled Whale, the earth shook.* Seattle PI., March 2.

Press, Canadian. 1964. *Park given to Province.* Vancouver Province, 9-26, page 11.

Quarantine at Malibu Club. 1948. Vancouver Sun, September 2, page 18.

Schulz, Blaine. 1984. *Birdnest: Kenmore Air Harbor biggest around.* Seattle Times, August 29, page G4.

The Great Sea Serpent. 1849. Illustrated London News, April 10.

Thirkell, Keith. 1995. *The Sisters Time Forgot.* The Province, page A21.

Timber buy 'kills' yachtsman's resort. 1956. Vancouver Province, February 13. page 15.

Vancouver Girl Polio Victim. 1948. Vancouver Sun, September 20, page 2.

Yachtsmen's Paradise Given to Public Use. 1953. The Vancouver Sun, September21, page 19.

Youth dies in plunge off cliff. 1967. Vancouver Province, August 15, page 9.

Youth Group buys Malibu. 1954. Vancouver Sun, January 8, page 2.

OFFICIAL DOCUMENTS

BC Archives.1940. *Hamiltair Ltd.* In GR-1526, Reel # B-5506, file # BC-17230. Incorporation Documents: Microfilm.

————. 1945. *Malibu SeAero Service Ltd.* In GR-1526, Reel # B-5527, file # BC-19404, Incorporation Documents: Microfilm.

————. 1945. *The Malibu Club.* In GR-1526, Box 207, file # S-2987, edited by. Incorporation Documents: Paper.

————.1919. *Death of Ivan Johnstone.* #1919-09-248571, GR-2951, Micro# B13115, GSU# 1927143. Death Certificate: Microfilm

————.1948. *Death of Sydney Diane Harris.* #1948-09-008119, GR-2951, Micro# B13198, GSU# 2032482. Death Certificate: Microfilm.

————.1967. *Death of Edward Anastasio.* #1967-09-010630, GR-2951, Micro# B13285, GSU# 2033929. Death Certificate: Microfilm

————.1969. *Death of Herman Alwin Harry Casper.* #69-09-009097. Death Certificate: Microfilm.

Archives, British Columbia. 1954-1966. *Princess Louisa Inlet Park Information.* #GR 1614, Box 27.

Boeing Company Archives. 1946. *Boeing Aircraft of Canada - Malibu SeAero, refurbishment of the Grumman Goose,* Box 9. File 3561/24 Orders, letters, notes, & invoices: Paper.

Crown Land Registry Services. Land Registers #4888-5285, New Westminster 1. Group 1. Pages 85, 119-126.

From Leadline to Laser. 1983. Paper read at Centennial Conference of Canadian Hydrographic Service.

Hydrographic Office, Ministry of Defence, Taunton, Somerset, UK. Remarks & Minutes Book of the HMS Plumper (1846-1860).

Ministry of Environment, Lands, and Parks (Province of British Columbia)

National Air and Space Museum, Archives Division. 1965. Harold E. Morehouse Flying Pioneers Biographies Collection – *Thomas F. Hamilton "Early Plane builder-Aviator-Propeller Manufacture".* In Box 5, file #25, Accession No. XXXX-0450 Biography: Paper.

———. 1965. Early Birds of Aviation, Inc. Collection – *Thomas F. Hamilton*. In Box 30, file #27, Accession No. XXXX-0566. Biography: Paper.

National Archives of Canada, 1946. *War Assets Corporation – Second Annual Report*. In Box 77, Acc#1977-78/118, RG-101. Annual reports: Paper.

———. 1998. *Passenger List into Halifax* 8/14/1928 (H.Casper #26). In Vol 11, page 200, edited by T-14816. Immigration records: Microfilm.

Phillip F. Spaulding and Associates, 1965. *Design Specifications for the vessel – the Malibu Princess*: Drawings and legal documents.

Province of BC, Ministry of Lands, Parks and housing. 1980. *The Legend of Princess Louisa Inlet*. Brochure.

Public Records Office. Kew, London, UK. 1856-1861 *The Logs of the HMS Plumper* . #ADM 53/6851-6858

Puget, Lt. Peter. 1792. *Log Book of Discovery*: University of Washington. Original edition, Original Journal from the British Museum MSS17546, London.

Third Report of the Department of Health and Welfare. 1948. Fifty-Second Annual Report of Public Health Services:Z50-51.

United States Patent Office. Patent #2,032,254 – *Adjustable Pitch Propeller* issued to Frank W. Caldwell, Pittsburg PA. Application date of April 21. 1931 and patented on February 25, 1936.

WA State Department of Social and Health Services (Bureau of Vital Statistics). 1978. *Death of James F. MacDonlad*. #13020. Death Certificate: Official Document.

Whitford, H.N. & Craig, Roland. 1918. *Forests of British Columbia* Commission of Conservation Canada, Committee on Forests. Ottawa.

Young Life Real Estate Dept. *Malibu Legal and Miscellaneous Documents*. Colorado Springs. Various Files under Malibu Real Estate, Legal, and Gifts.

UNPUBLISHED DOCUMENTS

Brock, Rear-Admiral P.W. 1950. Dossier. *HMS Plumper (1848 - 1866)* .Maritime Museum of British Columbia Victoria, B.C.

Dustin de La Mothe, Ollie. 1997. Memoir. *Young Life of Canada – The Early Days*.

Garrison, James A. 1966. Letter. *Invitation to the Launch of the Malibu Princess*, March 9.

Hitz, Charles W. 2000. Thesis. *Moving from a 2D to 3D Environment in Computing Visualization*. School of Business and Economics, Seattle Pacific University. Seattle, WA..

Nobes, David Charles. 1984. Thesis. *The Magnetometric Off-Shore Electrical Sounding (MOSES) Method and its Application in a Survey of Upper Jervis Inlet, British Columbia*, School of Graduate Studies, University of Toronto, Toronto.

Young Life - Malibu Club. 1957. Report. *Malibu Short & Long Term Improvement Plan*. Seattle, WA.

ELECTRONIC SOURCES

Office of the Legislative Counsel, Nova Scotia House of Assembly, and 1998 Crown in right of Nova Scotia. *Company Act*. October 1, 1998. (http://www.gov.ns.ca/legi/legc/statutes/companie.htm).

Heli-logging in British Columbia 2003. [cited February 15 2003]. (http://www.heli-og.com/loggingaircraft.htm).

Office of the Legislative Counsel, Nova Scotia House of Assembly, and 1998 Crown in right of Nova Scotia. *Societies Act* . October 1, 1998. (http://www.gov.ns.ca/legi/legc/statutes/societie.htm).

Stucchi, Dario. 2002. *Long Term Trends in Deep Water Properties of BC Inlets*. Institute of Ocean Sciences/ Fisheries and Oceans Canada, Sidney, B.C./Canada 2001 [cited December 12 2002]. (http://www.pac.dfo-mpo.gc.ca/sci/osap/projects/bcinlets/Jervis_Inlet_e.htm).

Talbot, Peter. 2000. *Malibu Hydro our existing system* [cited November 12, 2002]. (http://rptelectronics.com/malibuhydro/existinghydro.htm).

Young Life Web Site. 2003. [cited January 3, 2002] (http://www.younglife.org).

INTERVIEWS

Anderson, Marge. 2002. *Young Life's Early Years at Malibu*. At Bothell, WA.

Burleigh, Doug. 2000. *Malibu Experiences and Memories*. At Wildhorse Canyon, OR, May 31.

Cook, Kathy. 2000. *Polio and the Malibu Club*. Phone Interview to Vancouver BC, November 11.

Hamilton, Larry. 1999. *Early Malibu History*. At Portland OR, August 19.

Kautz, John. 2002. *Construction, Facility, & Personal memories of Malibu*. At Tukwila, WA November 15.

Muncy, Frank. 1997. *The Purchase of Malibu by Young Life*. At Monetary, CA, August 26.

Prichard, Bob & Alda. 2003. *Malibu Building History in the 1960s*. At Shelton WA, Febuary 18.

Prittie, Don & Janice. 2002. *The Years at Malibu as Property Mangers (1986 to 1997)*. At Victoria BC, November 25.

Sunde, Elizabeth Hamilton (Betty). 2003. *Tom Hamilton's family, the Malibu Club, and his Life*. In Stanwood, WA, March 19.

PERSONAL COMMUNICATIONS

Fulton, Captain Robert. 2000. *Hamilton's Fairmile Yacht Fleet*. Vancouver Maritime Museum Library, April 5.

Garrison, James A. 1966. *Invitation to the launching of the Malibu Princess*. March 9.

Hamilton, Larry. 1998. *Tom Hamilton and the Malibu Club*, February 28.

———. 2001. *Tom Hamilton Questions*. Portland, WA, December 11.

McBride, Brent. 1999. *Information on Hamilton's enterprises at Princess Louisa Inlet*. Victoria BC, December 9.

Morin, Marc-Andre. 2001. *Details of the Hamilton Fairmiles*, December 18.

Muncy, Frank L. 1953. *Recommend transaction of money for purchase of Malibu from Hamilton*. Memphis TN, Dec 20.

Richter. 1998. *Birth records and family history of Herman Casper*, November 24.

Sewell, Add. 1992. *The Beginning of Malibu*. Seattle WA, March 16.

Williamson, George F. 1998. *Experiences as a Pilot flying for Malibu SeAero Ltd*. Victoria, BC, August 13.

OTHER REFERENCE SOURCES

Botham, Bill. 2002. Princess Louisa International Society Fall Newsletter.

Dustin de La Mothe, Ollie. 1992. Additional items of Malibu's History.

Dyker, Rob. 2002. *YL purchases property for Base Camp*. On Belay – The Young Life Beyond Malibu Newsletter, January 2002.

Information, Province of British Columbia Bureau of Provincial. 1934. *British Columbia Coast - Howe Sound to Toba Inlet*. In Land Series. Victoria BC.

Province of British Columbia Ministry of Lands, Parks, & Housing. 1983. Coastal Marine Parks of British Columbia Map. Victoria BC: BC Ministry of Lands, Parks, and Housing.

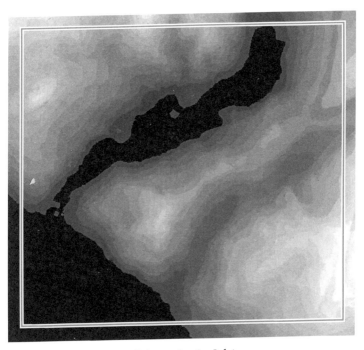

Princess Louisa Inlet

P.O. Box 2604
Kirkland, WA. 98034
1-888-346-4218
www.hitzcomm.tv

Quick Order Form

Web Orders: www.hitzcomm.tv
E-mail Orders: orders@hitzcomm.tv
Fax orders: 1-888-346-4218 (use this form)
Telephone Orders: 1-888-346-4218
(leave voice mail and an operator will call back for info).
Mail Orders – Send to:
Sitka 2 Publishing, c/o Orders. P.O. Box 2604
Kirkland, WA. 98083-2604

"Through the Rapids –
The History of Princess Louisa Inlet"

Name: _____

Address: _____

City: _____State/Prov: _____Zip: _____

Country: Telephone: (   )_____

E-mail Address: _____

PRICE PER BOOK	SHIPPING PER BOOK*
US. . . . . $19.95 CAN . . . . $28.95 Other . . . . Call	Standard (US). . . . . $3.95 Standard (CAN) . . . . $5.95 Standard (Other) . . . . Call Airmail or other . . . . Call

*Please allow 3 to 6 weeks for each order to be processed and shipped.

ORDER
Qty _____ of books multiplied by price of books . . . . . . $_____ Qty. of books multiplied by shipping costs . . . . $_____ Subtotal. . . . . $_____ Washington State Residents include 8.9% Sales Tax . . . $_____ Total Due. . . . . $_____

PAYMENT (THANK YOU!)
❑ Check or Money Order (send with form). Please do not send cash! ❑ VISA ❑ Mastercard ❑ Discover Card #_____ Name on Card:_____Exp. Date _____ Signature: _____ *If you have any questions, please call.*